THE
STRANGERS
ALL ARE GONE

BOOKS BY
ANTHONY POWELL

NOVELS
Afternoon Men
Venusberg
From a View to a Death
Agents and Patients
What's Become of Waring

A DANCE TO THE MUSIC OF TIME
A Question of Upbringing
A Buyer's Market
The Acceptance World
At Lady Molly's
Casanova's Chinese Restaurant
The Kindly Ones
The Valley of Bones
The Soldier's Art
The Military Philosophers
Books Do Furnish a Room
Temporary Kings
Hearing Secret Harmonies

BIOGRAPHIES
John Aubrey and his Friends

PLAYS
The Garden God and *The Rest I'll Whistle*

MEMOIRS:
To Keep the Ball Rolling
Vol. I. Infants of the Spring
Vol. II. Messengers of Day
Vol. III. Faces in My Time
Vol. IV. The Strangers All Are Gone

The Memoirs of
Anthony Powell

Volume IV

THE
STRANGERS
ALL ARE GONE

HOLT, RINEHART AND WINSTON

New York

First published in the United States in 1983 by
Holt, Rinehart and Winston, 383 Madison Avenue,
New York, New York 10017.
Published simultaneously in Canada by Holt, Rinehart and
Winston of Canada, Limited.

Library of Congress Cataloging in Publication Data
Powell, Anthony, 1905-
The strangers all are gone.
(To keep the ball rolling ; v. 4)
Includes index.
1. Powell, Anthony, 1905-   —Biography. 2. Authors,
English—20th century—Biography. I. Title. II. Series:
Powell, Anthony, 1905- . To keep the ball rolling
(New York, N.Y.) ; v. 4.
PR6031.074Z476 1983   823'.912 [B]   82-23363
ISBN: 0-03-063279-X

The Strangers All Are Gone is the fourth volume of an autobiographical
series by Anthony Powell entitled To Keep the Ball Rolling.

First American Edition
Printed in the United States of America
1 3 5 7 9 10 8 6 4 2

ISBN 0-03-063279-X

CONTENTS

LIST OF ILLUSTRATIONS

Between pages 22 and 23

Between pages 54 and 55

List of Illustrations

Between pages 86 and 87

THE
STRANGERS
ALL ARE GONE

I

Reflation; haunts of Ross and Brooke

The second war (as the first had done at an earlier age) drew a hard line across the story of one's days after which nothing was ever quite the same again. Those six years not only concentrated into a short span of time contacts and experiences that could not otherwise have come my way, but by drastically altering normal routines penetrated almost every area of existence.

Drastic changes are by no means essential to a novelist. They can hinder as well as help. It is sometimes naively thought that novelists need to taste every cup, but there is no absolute necessity to be, like Dostoevski, kept for several hours wearing only a shirt in temperature under freezing expecting to be executed. What matters is an individual appreciation of life's contingencies in those or more humdrum circumstances; capacity to apply the result of that understanding in a novel.

Certain writers continued to produce books throughout the war in spite of military or other employments. I found that impossible as much from disruption of inner machinery as from sheer lack of time. This total abstinence from writing undoubtedly had the consequence of storing away material, past and current, that might otherwise have been dissipated piecemeal. To that extent the war had a stimulating effect, something new jobs and changed scenes can never guarantee a writer.

Meanwhile an untidy scrawl of death and disjunction had been traced by Time across the pages of our address-book: a toll of names that showed no very marked sign of decreasing now that peace was restored. War casualties might have ceased, but on the upward grade were natural

3

causes, the occasional suicide, madness among the once relatively sane, not to mention mere passing into oblivion. Such wastage among friends and acquaintances is one of the liabilities of middle-age. At the same time new names were to some extent taking the place of these deletions, often those of a younger generation of writers and poets just released from the Services.

A Buyer's Market, second volume of *A Dance to the Music of Time*, came out in the spring of 1952, the moment when this fourth and last volume of memoirs might be said in principle to begin, though at times there will be some looking back to earlier periods. Recent American critics have conveniently abbreviated the title of the novel-sequence to *Dance*, a curtailment I shall use here; while the first three volumes of memoirs, *Infants of the Spring, Messengers of Day, Faces in My Time*, will be referred to as *Infants, Messengers*, and *Faces*.

Hitherto a comparatively sustained chronological narrative has been achieved, but the last twenty or thirty years are not always tractable to continuity of design. As one picks one's way between the trees of Dante's dark wood of middle life its configuration becomes ever less discernible. All one can say of the trees is that most are gnarled, some hollow, not a few struck by lightning. Books are published; professional schemes take shape or fade away; journeys are made; new persons met. All the time a perspective that once gave at least the illusion of order to the past diminishes. The outlines of individuals and events, perhaps clear enough in themselves, grow ever more blurred in relation to each other.

Alick Dru (*Faces*) used to complain that one of the least supportable things about later life was the fact that you began to see almost everyone else's point of view. I had to agree with him that tolerance becomes an increasing burden with age. A slowing up of former antagonisms perhaps accounts to some extent for lessening in the sense of pattern.

Then uncertainties invade the mind as never before regarding what is true, what worth writing about. Fallibilities of reportage become only too apparent after reaching an age when biographies begin to appear dealing with personal friends, or even individuals known slightly. I reflect on the extraordinary views and remarks attributed to myself from time to time by newspaper interviewers. Pilate certainly had a point.

In short how are these memoirs to be rounded off? I have chosen to make a kind of album of odds and ends in themselves at times trivial enough. In the course of my own reading I have often found the trivial to be more acceptable, even more instructive in the long run, than some attempts at being profound.

2

One of the strangest figures to surface after the war was Julian Maclaren-Ross. He was produced in the first instance by Bobby Roberts (*Messengers*) in 1946. Roberts, just returned from India as demobilized squadron-leader from the Public Relations branch of the Royal Air Force Volunteer Reserve, was himself soon to disappear from sight into an amorphous underworld of backstage provincial theatre undertakings. He may still have drawn a trickle of income from hiring out camp-stools to pit queues, but was probably existing for the most part on an RAF gratuity.

Roberts would sometimes turn up, rather self-consciously sober, at 1 Chester Gate (the Regent's Park house to which we had returned before the end of the war in spite of bomb damage) in order to gossip about friends in common; above all to ventilate the ever complex problems set in motion by his determination to get married again. At times he would bring with him for inspection one or other of the candidates docketed as potential bride. These were never insignificant.

Like Bagshaw in *Dance*, for whom (as for Fotheringham in *Afternoon Men*) Roberts was to some extent model (showing how a good one may be used more than once), he was a guest never unendurably to overstay his welcome, since an iron law of self-discipline ordained that every night of his life the words 'Last orders, please—time, gentlemen, time' had to ring in his ears. No matter where Roberts found himself, the day's intake of alcohol must categorically include at least one drink in a pub—no matter what pub—to hear the angelus of closing time.

If Roberts went out of his way to exhibit some individual, male or female (including wives designate) encountered on a devious and almost consistently intoxicated pilgrimage through life such persons—not necessarily types with whom one wanted to spend a great deal of time again—were nevertheless always of authentic interest in one direction or another. He possessed acute, if vagrant, perceptions as to human character.

5

Among *convives* warmly canvassed by Roberts (who was surprisingly strong-willed where his own whims were concerned) was a certain Maclaren-Ross, whom he propagated as a writer of excellent short stories, and—very acceptable recommendation after nearly eight years without publishing a book—a fan of my own pre-war novels. Roberts positively insisted on the introduction. Violet and I gave in, and agreed to meet this Roberts literary discovery at a pub in Great Portland Street, the name of which I have forgotten.

In due course I took some liberties with the theatrically projected personality of Maclaren-Ross—elaborating the scope a little—in constructing the character of X. Trapnel, who (like Bagshaw) appears in the later volumes of *Dance*. I was to continue to see Maclaren-Ross intermittently until within a few years of his death in 1964. 'I warn you,' said Roberts, when we arrived at the rendezvous. 'He's rather an egotist.'

This prefigurement turned out no less than the truth, even the first few minutes making plain the colossal ego that Maclaren-Ross wielded. At the same time one was immediately impressed by the unusual texture of this tall, dark, good-looking, faintly foreign figure (then about thirty-two), with an unstemmable flow of talk. That was about books (chiefly novels of the past twenty years but capable of extension backwards in time), and movies (chiefly gangster films though not exclusively), a running commentary delivered in a rasping authoritative stylized tone of voice that defied either class or professional identification.

Maclaren-Ross perorations were entertaining when not drawn out too long, but (since he did not share the Roberts compulsion to leave any private premises not later than a quarter to eleven at night) could grow more than a trifle repetitive. Nevertheless even his most afflicting ramblings were based on a really astonishing familiarity with novels and films of the past, on the subject of which he was more reliable than when recounting his own experiences, themselves often odd enough. I used sometimes to test him with obscure novels from the Duckworth list in my publishing days. He was rarely caught out.

During any evening's performance indication that the machine was creaking ominously, if not actually breaking down, was introduction of the name of Sidney Greenstreet. Greenstreet announced the need for eviction in as friendly a manner as possible of the protagonist (surely here legitimate use of that much abused figure of speech) as soon as Maclaren-Ross

6

gave pause in the imitation that always followed of the rotund middle-aged film-star (said himself to possess intellectual leanings), master in his own particular line of quietly villainous rôles. Greenstreet was Maclaren-Ross's unambiguous King Charles's Head.

An habitual *tenue* of semi-tropical suit, ancient suede shoes, teddy-bear overcoat (in winter), stick with silver (gold when in funds) knob, gave the air of a broken-down dandy, though just what brand of dandyism was not easy to define. There was something Mediterranean about the get-up, hints even of more distant climes, Conrad or Maugham islands, Gauguin in the South Seas, though the walking-stick seemed to denote *boulevardier* rather than beachcomber. The equally invariable dark green sun-spectacles (their lenses latterly of a kind to reflect the vis-à-vis) belonged to much the same geographical regions, at the same time hinting of security agent or possibly terrorist.

All this swagger did not entirely mask the hard-up literary man of the post-war London epoch. Maclaren-Ross personified that too, even quintessentially; perhaps as much by leaving his own mark on the times as the times leaving a mark on himself. He wrote as J. Maclaren-Ross, was addressed by friends as Julian, though indications (an old passport once produced) suggested that he had been christened James, the Apostate's name substituted or added as less commonplace. Never in the least insistent on religion in his writings or manner of life, Maclaren-Ross was in fact not himself apostate, remaining the Roman Catholic he had been born.

When we first met he had already published three collections of short stories (those about the army in general the best), also a novel. Another (fairly brief) novel had reached proof stage, then—becoming in some manner bedevilled—lay frozen in a publishing limbo from which the author was unable to summon up sufficient will or dexterity to extract this work. A third novel was due to appear the following year.

His origins, unusual ones, are touched on in a lighthearted piece called *My Father was born in Havana*, then rather more fully in a volume of memoirs *The Weeping and the Laughter*. The father in question was half-Scotch, half-Latin American; a grandfather (possibly great-grandfather), on one side or the other, came from the Southern States of North America.

Maclaren-Ross *père*, son of an engineer and shipowner, had fought as an officer of Imperial Yeomanry in the South African War, afterwards knocking about all over the world. He came to rest in the South of France where his family (two sons and a daughter) had been largely brought up. There were inevitable hints of a Secret Service connexion—irresistible in the circumstances—which seemed mainly based on a certain amount of translating books from French into English which took place in the home. Maclaren-Ross himself spoke fluent French.

Presumably on his father's death he had inherited a little money just before the second war. This was quickly run through, and he found himself uncompromisingly on the rocks. At one moment he had attempted to earn a living as door-to-door salesman of vacuum-cleaners, a vocation bitingly but good humouredly recalled in the then forthcoming novel *Of Love and Hunger* (1947). For a time he was in the army, where—rare for an intellectual—he served three weeks detention in the Glasshouse (not the celebrated Aldershot military lock-up but a slightly milder one) for Absent-Without-Leave.

Maclaren-Ross would often give spirited and unselfpitying accounts of this incarceration. Three minutes were allowed for performing natural functions in the morning, after which period of time a soldier-warder would thrust his face in that of the prisoner attempting to evacuate, shouting: 'Come on, man, come on! What do you think you are? A woman having a baby?' At the sound of the air-raid warning at night the whole prison would be roused for turn-out in battle order including wearing a gas-mask. It was no wonder that men returned to their unit from the Glasshouse immensely smartened up.

This improvement in military bearing does not seem to have taken place in the case of Maclaren-Ross, who was invalided out on psychiatric grounds fairly soon after the Glasshouse interlude; not unreasonably since he was highly neurotic. He passed the latter part of the war as member (with Dylan Thomas) of a documentary film unit.

When first encountered, Maclaren-Ross had been married and divorced at least once. Considering the world in which he lived he was not temperamentally promiscuous, tending to stick to whatever girl (usually an unequivocally pretty one) who made up his establishment, until she herself moved off. He liked to boast of deep drinking, together with super-human powers of remaining sober whatever the intake, and the strength of his head has been confirmed by one or two of those who knew him. In my

8

own experience Maclaren-Ross potations were never excessive. Indeed he always seemed moderation itself.

In decline he would refer to 'my pills' (Purple Hearts someone later suggested), and, whether on account of these or from lack of them, he did turn up once at a Chancery Lane pub where we had a rendezvous (when I was on *Punch*) in a less than coherent state. That was a unique default in the course of our meetings.

The Maclaren-Ross ménage tended to be accommodated in an hotel, preferably a large one in Russell Square—'Something I could never afford myself,' once commented Henry Yorke (*Infants*, *Messengers*). Maclaren-Ross greatly admired Yorke's novels (written as Henry Green), and at a much later date wrote an accomplished parody of them in a *Punch* series on contemporary novelists he undertook.

I brought Yorke and Maclaren-Ross together. This delighted Maclaren-Ross, who warmly expressed his opinion of the Henry Green books, but on Yorke's side the introduction was less of a success. Yorke had by then already become rather crotchety about new acquaintances, in any case did not care for too strong whiffs of bohemian life, indeed could scarcely tolerate such social levels at all. It had to be admitted that the barrage of Maclaren-Ross conversation was not to every taste. There was no enthusiastic follow-up, though I think the two writers did meet again by arrangement at least once.

Since hotel existence was perforce maintained in terms not much short of utter penury, crises such as laundry being held in hock until the bill was paid were not infrequent. At such junctures loans from friends would sometimes tide over an awkward week or two until an article or story was sold and paid for. During a very brief period some sort of a household was maintained in a decidedly seedy furnished flat in the Holland Park area, but even that comparative domesticity palled.

The caravan was soon back on the road, another hotel circuit littered with unpaid accounts and summonses for obtaining credit by methods more or less unsanctioned. Somehow the worst retributions were always sidestepped. Chronically on the brink of disaster, Maclaren-Ross never, I think, was so drastically reduced as in the pre-war years when nights had been spent on the Embankment.

In the end this nerve-racking routine, both precarious and demanding, took its revenge. Books produced never lost a certain degree of competence, but the standard fell off in quality as their author travelled steadily downhill. Nor did he ever fail to find a woman to love and look after him.

The battle Maclaren-Ross fought as a writer was an increasingly losing one to keep contact (certainly hard enough for any writer whatever the circumstances) with things worth writing about. At his best—the army stories, the vacuum-cleaner novel, the parodies—there is a touch that remains individual to this day. *Memoirs of the Forties* (1965), of which he himself had high hopes, remained uncompleted at his death in the year previous to its publication. The book contains several amusing close-ups of fellow-writers (Cyril Connolly, Graham Greene), together with a certain amount of less interesting material. Nonetheless, had time allowed, jotted notes suggest that further memoirs might have been worth reading.

3

The Maclaren-Ross ménage used sometimes to dine with us at Chester Gate, and once—a publisher's advance denoting that life must be lived *en prince* for at least twenty-four hours—he insisted that we should be his guests for dinner at the Café Royal.

The occasion was marked by John Heygate (*Messengers*) and his most recent girl-friend joining our table later in the evening. Heygate, like his old crony Bobby Roberts, had spent most of the war in India, the former as bombardier in the Royal Artillery.

Heygate had gone to Ceylon for one of his leaves, where inevitably he ran into Roberts. Harold Acton (*Infants*), like Roberts in the RAFVR, also turned out to be in Ceylon, and for some reason Heygate had to apply to Acton (an Eton and Oxford contemporary) to arrange for being put up at the Services Club in Colombo. Acton, telling the story years later, said that all would have been well had not an impediment arisen in the shape of Heygate's diminutive Indian mistress, for whom he had paid a lump sum. Coming from one of the more primitive races of the Subcontinent, she was something under four foot high, always insisted on walking behind Heygate, and utterly refused to eat with him. How this delicate social problem was adjusted I do not know.

By the time Heygate arrived back from India, the war now drawing to a close, he was in very poor shape. On the way home he had celebrated the coming of peace unrestrainedly, was physically ill, and in a highly nervous condition. He must, however, have made some sort of temporary recovery that night at the Café Royal, because he seemed to have regained much of his old capacity for enjoyment.

When I first knew Heygate I had been rather shocked to find he wore braces in Old Etonian colours (black with a thin light blue line). On my enquiring about this habit, outré, at best Wodehousian, he explained that a year or two before he had shared a cabin or wagon-lit with an American. When the American was turning in for the night it was revealed that he was wearing OE braces (in America 'suspenders') which he had purchased from a shop-window in Piccadilly because he liked the colour. On learning of the solecism committed, the American—on the Aladdin principle of New Lamps for Old—insisted on handing over the braces to Heygate; receiving in exchange whatever battered equipment had hitherto been holding up Heygate's trousers.

In a somewhat similar fashion Heygate had mesmerized the authorities of UNRRA (United Nations Relief and Rehabilitation Administration) to take him on as an officer. He was sporting the UNRRA uniform in the Café Royal. A certain irony attached to the organization's resounding name and all-embracing duties embroidered on Heygate's shoulder, as the phrases only too well described what only a short time before he had been in need of himself at the receiving end, and was very soon desperately to need again.

Heygate's girl, who was in a flirtatious mood, kept sending him little notes under the table. Maclaren-Ross, who possessed that peculiar skill some have of being able to read handwriting upside down, deciphered one of these affectionate missives—evidently referring to himself—as commenting: *He is too esoteric.*

The occasion may have been an infelicitous one to record that judgment, but its truth was undeniable. Maclaren-Ross was too esoteric; certainly too esoteric to find life easy. For a few years he walked his own unique tight-rope above the byways of Charlotte Street and Soho, his gifts as a writer never quite allowing the headlong descent for ever threatened by his behaviour as a man.

At times, though rarely, he showed signs of grasping that a great deal of the chaos that surrounded him could have been avoided by even a little more restraint on his own part. Such glimpses of self-criticism never lasted long enough for substantial improvement to take place. In the end balance on the tight-rope was not adequately maintained. A life which with all its absurdities had been in many ways courageous and productive came to an abrupt termination.

4

Alan Ross, then working for the British Council, was a friend met at this period, who was later to marry Jennifer Fry, niece of Evelyn Gardner (*Messengers*), and edit *The London Magazine*. He had just been demobilized as a naval officer (having had some lively war experiences), and already possessed a name as a poet. He used occasionally to review books for the *Times Literary Supplement*, introduced there by the new editor Alan Pryce-Jones.

He had also been an Oxford cricket 'blue', and wrote very elegantly about the game. In spite of the attraction cricket exercises over many contemporary writers (Amis, Fuller, Larkin, Pinter, to name only a few) —something all but unknown at anything but a middlebrow level formerly its mystique holds no spell for me, nevertheless I read Alan Ross on the subject if I come across his articles because, analytical and romantic, they give meaning to the players.

Alan Ross composed one of the most penetrating obituary notices of Maclaren-Ross in which he spoke of that quirkiness that prevented the earning of a standard of living that should have been a right: 'The hidalgo, the author, the man on National Assistance, all spoke with the same resonant voice' well summarized his subject. Maclaren-Ross was certainly familiar with the Labour Exchange, but I believe never in fact drew the dole; probably his personal administration in any case was not sufficiently in order for him to do so.

The obituary went on to say that in spite of deep rooted inability to adapt himself to other people's ways Maclaren-Ross was always the first to draw attention to books by his own contemporaries which he thought undervalued. On the whole a reliable critic (as early as 1957 he wrote that Roy Fuller was that rarity, a good poet who also wrote good novels), he had a true passion for the art of writing, always preferring to recommend rather than be dismissive or malicious. Certainly he could display violent dislikes—these quite unaffected by current fashion—but in the literary world, surrounded by lesser talents that were achieving far more commercial success than his own, Maclaren-Ross was one of the least envious of men.

Among other posthumous memoranda left in relation to *Memoirs of the Forties* was a note: *Anthony Powell plays Happy Families.* This refers to an afternoon when Maclaren-Ross turned up at Chester Gate, probably to discuss some article or book to review for the *TLS*. After that was settled we had tea, followed by the card game Happy Families (Mr Bones the Butcher, etc), played with our elder son Tristram, then about six years old.

I regret the piece about myself was never written as it would undoubtedly have been funny, and told me things about my own behaviour of which I was quite unaware. Maclaren-Ross must have recalled that game in the year of his own death, because Tristram, by then a television producer, mounted a programme in 1964, *Writers during the War*, with contributions by John Betjeman, Cyril Connolly, Alan Ross, Julian Maclaren-Ross himself. It was one of those unforeseen turns of the wheel. This programme of Tristram's was introduced by another friend, Jocelyn Brooke, of whom now a word.

5

Jocelyn Brooke really belongs to the period after our move from London, but I first heard of him about the time of which I have been speaking as author of *The Military Orchid* (1948), a book which received very approving notices. I did not read it, partly because I was busy with Aubrey (the Selection coming on top of the biography), partly because (being in that respect like Wyndham Lewis's Tarr, for whom 'the spring was anonymous') I thought a book which seemed largely concerned with botany would be out of my line.

Quite fortuitously I reviewed Brooke's next book *A Mine of Serpents* (1949) for the *TLS*, treating it more or less as a novel. There was some excuse for that as certain ostensibly fictional characters seemed intended

13

for future development, a note at the beginning saying this work was 'complementary' to *The Military Orchid*, rather than a sequel.

I did not grasp that here was the second volume of a loosely constructed autobiographical trilogy. The review now strikes me as rather pompous, but I recognized Brooke's talent at once, and remarked (at that moment about to come to grips with *Dance*) that the epigraph used by Brooke from Sir Thomas Browne's *Christian Morals*—'Some Truths seem almost Falsehoods and Some Falsehoods almost Truths'—contains 'in a sense the justification of all novel writing.'

I knew nothing of Jocelyn Brooke himself except what was to be gathered from *A Mine of Serpents*. He was in fact then about forty, and had recently emerged from the ranks of the Royal Army Medical Corps, in which he had re-enlisted two years after the end of the second war. A collection of his poems had appeared in 1946, but *The Military Orchid* was his first published prose work.

By the time I reviewed Brooke's Kafka-like novel *The Image of a Drawn Sword* in the spring of 1950 I must have read *The Military Orchid*, and by that autumn, when *The Goose Cathedral*, third volume of the trilogy, came out, I had marked Brooke down as one of the notable writers to have surfaced after the war. I wrote an Introduction to these three books when they appeared in one volume as *The Orchid Trilogy* in 1981.

In those days reviewing in the *TLS* was unsigned so there was no question of Brooke having known of my liking for his work when, in 1953, a laudatory article by him appeared in one of the weeklies on the subject of my first novel *Afternoon Men*, published more than twenty years earlier. *Afternoon Men* had, as it happened, been reprinted in a new edition about a year before, but when I sent a letter to Brooke expressing appreciation of this unexpected bouquet he turned out to be unaware of the republication. He had merely reread his own 1931 copy, on impulse rung up a literary editor and asked if he might write a piece on the subject.

In due course we lunched together, met from time to time afterwards (though never often), and continued to correspond fitfully until Brooke's death in 1966.

All writers, one way or another, depend ultimately on their own lives for the material of their books, but the manner in which each employs that personal experience, interior or exterior, is very different. Jocelyn Brooke used both elements with a minimum of dilution, though much imagination. However far afield he went physically—which included the Middle East and Italy—he remained morally from birth to death in his own part of Kent, the childhood days which for him never lost their fascination. He was by nature keenly interested in himself (as suggested earlier in these memoirs, apropos of Cyril Connolly, a comparatively rare preoccupation in its truest sense), though (unlike some aspects of Maclaren-Ross) without vanity or the smallest suggestion of exhibitionism.

Brooke had been born in 1908 and came on both sides of his family from wine merchants, the paternal business at Folkestone, with a residence at Sandgate. His parents also possessed an inland holiday cottage at Bishopsbourne in the Elham Valley, a favourite setting for imaginary adventures. Brooke's nanny (from some early mispronunciation always known as Ninny) was a preponderant figure in Brooke myth. Latterly—a circuitous but effective reconstruction of childhood—Ivy Cottage, Bishopsbourne, was shared with his mother and Ninny, until their deaths took place only a few years before Brooke's own demise.

The passion for botany seems to have begun by the age of four years old, the taste for fireworks soon developing with almost equal strength; the name of a firework providing the title for *A Mine of Serpents*.

After running away twice in the first fortnight of his first term at King's School, Canterbury (alma mater of Marlowe, Pater, Somerset Maugham, Hugh Walpole, Patrick Leigh Fermor), Brooke was sent to Bedales, of which he has left an amusing account, where he decided he was a disillusioned Aldous Huxley character. At Bedales sex was decried as 'silly'—the novelist Julia Strachey told me that one girl there with her was so 'silly' she had a baby—which did not solve all Brooke's problems, though he was reasonably contented. Of Worcester College, Oxford, he afterwards retained only dim memories, and seems to have been a fairly typical Proust-Joyce-Firbank-reading undergraduate. *The Isis*, then edited by Peter Fleming, accepted an article called *Oxford Decadence*, but regrettably Fleming and Brooke never met, which might have given one or both an anecdote.

On coming down there were the endemic employment difficulties. For a time work was found in a bookshop. This must have been about the same moment as George Orwell's bookshop assistant period in Hampstead, of which Orwell left a picture in *Keep the Aspidistra Flying* (1936) and elsewhere in his writings. Incidentally a correspondent who remembered

15

the Orwell shop told me it was a gloomy cave of a place which sold all sorts of other odds and ends as well as books. The Brooke bookshop in the City was at rather a higher professional level, one imagines. It was followed by a spell in the family wine business, and attempt to grow a moustache, neither a success. Then Brooke suffered some sort of breakdown.

When the second war came he at once joined the RAMC. The army recurs throughout most of his works, providing some of their best material. Though much of Brooke's service must have been far from comfortable he felt after a time that his life was too easy, and volunteered for the branch treating venereal disease. He again served in the VD branch—in army parlance the Pox-Wallahs—when he rejoined the Corps again after the war. By that time the Brooke family had moved to Blackheath, and he managed to get a posting conveniently near them at Woolwich Military Hospital.

Brooke always seemed to me to have resolved pretty well his homosexuality in life. In supposing this, I may be mistaken, because David Cecil, who saw something of him soon after *The Military Orchid*'s publication, had the impression that Brooke was going through painful experiences on that account. In his 'straight' novels he never appears wholly at ease with the subject, which is usually treated satirically. This is perhaps to say no more than that Brooke was more skilful in his own particular art, one not altogether definable, than in the give-and-take of traditional novel form.

The hint of mutual homosexual attraction, faint but perceptible, is better handled in *The Image of a Drawn Sword*, unquestionably to be categorized as a novel, though set in Brooke's familiar Kentish landscape. There is a touch of Kipling as well as Kafka in this haunting book, though Brooke was not on the whole well disposed towards Kipling, and told me he had not read Kafka at the time of writing it. *The Military Orchid* contains the phrase 'a curious paranoid quality, like a story by Kafka', so that either *The Image* was written before *The Orchid*, or—more probably—Brooke, like many others, invoked Kafka's name before he read him.

Perhaps Brooke's best book is *The Dog at Clambercrown* (1955), its title the odd name of a Kentish pub and village, a work that contains all the essential Brooke myth. In it the author reflects on his feelings about the army:

'Anyone'd think you *liked* the Army.'

'As it happened, Pte Hoskins' unlikely hypothesis was perfectly correct: I did like the Army—though 'like' is hardly an adequate word to describe my feelings about it. 'Love' would perhaps be nearer the mark, though here again the word required qualification, for my liaison with the armed forces (and I use the word in its erotic rather than military sense) was by no means a starry-eyed, spontaneous affair the word love suggests. It resembled, rather, the kind of relationship described by Proust, in which love is apprehended, so to speak, only in its negative aspects—the pain of loss, the absence or infidelity of the loved one, the perverse satisfaction of possessing (like Swann) some woman who isn't one's type, whom one doesn't even like, but with whom one has become so fatally obsessed that life without her is unendurable.'

A good deal of acute criticism is scattered through the pages of *The Dog at Clambercrown*. Of *Ulysses*: 'It is, I suppose, the most fascinating and the most devastatingly boring novel ever written.' Of *The Rainbow*: 'A genius for evoking landscape, a sense of character, a marvellous apprehension of human relationships. Yet after a further chapter or two I was finally bogged down . . . Lawrence's secret—if one can call it that—was, I suppose, that he was profoundly homosexual.' Lawrence, however, like Shakespeare and Proust, comes well out of Brooke's investigation of the capabilities of writers invoking botanical images.

As already remarked, I cannot claim to have known Brooke well, but we quite often corresponded, and he was one of those people to whom I always wrote with a sense of ease. He speaks more than once of his own liking for the sort of relationship which did not make him feel hemmed in. In his books are several incidents in which the narrator, from his own awareness of being 'different', refuses an invitation from someone with whom he has been getting on pretty well.

It came therefore as no very great surprise, after we had lunched together several times, and Brooke had stayed with us for the weekend, when he politely excused himself from another visit on grounds of work. That may also have been true enough. 'Writing time' is a kind of Old Man of the Sea for ever exerting a strangling grip. Nonetheless one suspected an unwillingness to cope too often with face-to-face cordialities that might be acceptable in letters. David Cecil told me later that he himself had a very similar experience in Brooke dealings.

Brooke liked a fair amount to drink, and after luncheon was inclined to say: 'Shall we be *beasts*, and go to *my* club now, and have another glass of port.'

In 1964, when Violet and I were staying with Harry and Rosie Goldsmid at Somerhill (*Faces*) we drove over to Bishopsbourne to see Brooke in his own realm. By that time his mother and Ninny were no longer alive, and he himself had only a couple of years more. Writing somewhere of the Beatrix Potter books he had remarked that as a child 'the world of *Mr Todd* and *Jemima Puddleduck* seemed indistinguishable from our village.' Brooke was absolutely right. Ivy Cottage, however snugly furnished and full of books, was uncannily like Mr Jeremy Fisher's 'little damp house', and in wet weather the resemblance must have been even closer.

The three of us lunched at the Metropole in Folkestone, only slightly less hallowed ground than Bishopsbourne itself in the Brooke Legend.

In appearance Jocelyn Brooke was tall, pale, not bad looking, with an air of desperate melancholy that would suddenly lift when he laughed. Photographs, especially those he used for his books, are apt to give him a haggard stare, as of one mesmerized or mesmerizing, an expression perhaps assumed before the camera for fun and hardly doing him justice. He often reminded me of Orwell, not so much in feature as by a kind of hesitancy of manner, as if thinking for a second about the true meaning of what had been said before committing himself, but he was altogether without Orwell's burning desire to set the world right, and Brooke's laughter was quite unOrwellian.

In spite of having died comparatively young Jocelyn Brooke realized himself as a writer, I think. He said what he had to say in the form he wished. No doubt his critical views would always have been of interest, but he had already achieved his own particular method of self-expression; an art not like that of any other writer known to me in its manner of marking out a region, both actual and imagined, a magical personal kingdom.

Brooke quite often invokes A. E. Housman in his books, half-respectfully, half-deprecatingly, recognizing the poetic mastery, the shared rural images, the homosexuality in common, yet at the same time keenly aware of a certain over-lushness in Housman directed towards both fields. Nonetheless one feels a suitable epitaph might be provided by only the smallest adaptation of Housman's much quoted lines:

Reflation; haunts of Ross and Brooke

Far in a Kentish Brookeland
That bred me long ago
The orchids bloom and whisper
By woods I used to know.

II

Rustication; chantries and war memorials

Once I should have looked on existence anywhere but in London as exile, a preference shared by Violet, who had at the same time always contemplated a country retreat. After six years of war one felt differently about London as about much else. The place was at its most uncomfortable and dejected. Work was for ever interrupted by the telephone. There were a lot of stairs at Chester Gate, a fact that looking after children or bouts of flu increasingly brought home.

My mother's younger sister Aunt Vi (*Infants*) had died ten years earlier, leaving a life interest in what she possessed to a long estranged soldier husband whom I barely knew. In 1950 he too deceased, and the resources such as they were came to me. A house in the country was now a possibility. We began to look for somewhere not much more than a hundred miles from London, where a day or two each week would still have to be spent.

I should have liked country associated with at least some family origins, but the Welsh Marches and Lincolnshire were too far, the Borders even more remote, Norfolk cold in winter and not easy for weekly travel. Violet had two sisters living in Wiltshire: Pansy married to Henry Lamb (*Messengers*), Julia to Robin Mount (*Faces*). I knew Wiltshire to some extent myself, having lived at Salisbury as a boy; a more theoretical acquaintance with that county coming from 17th-century research into Aubrey's life there. Wiltshire seemed the answer.

We aimed first for the Hampshire side, but (in terms of those days) prices were high. After inspecting properties all over the place, dozens of them, the photograph of one called The Chantry, a few miles into Somerset, seemed to hold out hope. It was only twenty miles from where Julia Mount lived in a village 'under the Plain', so she was asked to make a preliminary report.

Pretty, goldenhaired, plump, Julia was a mixture of energy and lethargy, withdrawn shyness and neatly ironic phrase. For a report on a house for sale she was unlikely to be stampeded into ill-judged enthusiasm as she did not go in much for enthusiasms. Her reserve, a kind of weapon in her hands, is well illustrated by an incident before her own marriage, when the Lambs had taken her over to luncheon with the Augustus Johns at Fordingbridge.

Mutual hospitalities between Coombe Bissett and Fryern Court, always a little delicate in the light of Henry Lamb's former close association with Dorelia John, were nevertheless regularly exchanged. Lamb died in 1960; John in 1961. At some moment between these dates John said to me: 'I saw you at that very enjoyable funeral the other day . . . who was it? . . . I can't remember . . .' It had in fact been Lamb's, attended by both the Johns. John had braced himself for Lamb's obsequies with a few drinks, his deep voice echoing on and off throughout the service. At John's own funeral the clergyman caused an audible intake of breath among the congregation by reminding them in his address that in the Next World 'at His Right Hand are pleasures for ever more.'

At the Johns' it was apt to be assumed that everyone present knew everyone else; indeed might easily know them pretty well. John himself in his latter days found habitual difficulty in remembering, particularly among the younger persons present, who were his children, who his grandchildren, who his current girl-friends, who his sons' current girl-friends, who guests brought to the house for the first time.

On this particular occasion, before the assembled party entered the dining-room, a little man unknown to Julia Pakenham (as she then was) showed signs of feeling that he was insufficiently appreciated. That may easily have been true as guests at the Johns' were expected to look after themselves. When the meal was announced, and Julia passed through the door beside him, it became apparent that (very unwontedly) name-cards had been set out in each place. The little man remarked:

'I wonder whether they have put Shaw on my card.'

'Why do you wonder that?' asked Julia.

21

'Because I have several names.'

'Oh, have you?' said Julia.

There the matter rested, as she saw no reason to pursue this somewhat self-regarding opening.

On leaving the Johns' house Henry Lamb (who must often have met their fellow luncheon guest, and felt no great affection for him) remarked on the presence of T. E. Lawrence, probably then approaching the close of his RAF period. Lawrence's had been the ego Julia refused to propitiate.

2

Julia Mount gave a restrained but favourable report on The Chantry. We ourselves paid a couple of visits. I made an offer. Another bidder put up a larger sum. The property passed out of our field of vision, and the search for somewhere to live began again.

Some months after this The Chantry's owner, Wing Commander (later Air Chief Marshal Sir John) Barraclough, got into touch and said he would like a talk. On coming to Chester Gate he explained that the other potential buyer became too exigent about minor matters. Negotiations had been broken off. For a very small increase of the original offer I could have the house. The hand of fate seemed at work. A deal was made.

Since *Dance* to some extent celebrates the chance connexions that often pass unnoticed in life one of these should be mentioned. Violet, while supervising our younger son John in the sandpit of Park Square, used to read the typescript of *A Buyer's Market* before that book was published just before we left London. Among other small children playing in the sandpit was one pert and redhaired called Jane Asher. Miss Asher had then no idea that she would play the part of Jean Templer (who starts to take a prominent rôle in *A Buyer's Market*), when the BBC began the radio adaptation of *Dance* in 1979.

Our cat of that moment, Albert, tabby with white shirtfront, had been given us as a kitten by the traffic policeman who had found the body of a briefly owned Russian Blue, victim of an accident in the Outer Circle of Regent's Park. Albert (complaining loudly all the way in a crowded railway compartment) accompanied me as advance party for the first night at The

4. The Chantry

5. Albert

. Julian Maclaren-Ross, 1964
(Tristram Powell programme
– copyright BBC)

2. Cyril Connolly at The Chantry, 1963

3. Jocelyn Brooke, 1964 (Tristram Powell
programme – copyright BBC)

6. AP and Flixey Fum

7. Tristram and AP bottling wine
at The Chantry

8. Violet on the terrace, 1968

9. Virginia with Fum, 1968

Chantry, while Violet remained a last night in Chester Gate to enact final rites. She had hardly any sleep because, Albert having been a very popular member of the local cat community, feline wailings at his departure were kept up all night.

Albert was also on exceptionally good terms with dogs, one Alsatian barking for him to appear if Albert were not sleeping on the area steps. On first seeing country fields from the windows of the house Albert refused to go out of doors for three days; afterwards greatly enjoying himself jumping high over small tufts of grass. He settled down rather self-consciously as a country cat, and became greatly attached to a small terrier bitch living nearby, being disturbed when she was on heat and neighbouring dogs tended to congregate. Albert was a compulsive eater and succumbed from this indulgence in his thirteenth year.

To complete here the history of our cat dynasty, Albert was followed by Kingsplay Flixey Fum, a dark brown Burmese whose name indicated high descent, and was in fact brother of the Burmese Champion. Fum, though he liked being photographed on social occasions, was unambitious in the professional field. Something of an intellectual, a strong character with a warm nature, he was universally loved and respected. He died full of years and honour at the venerable age of nineteen-and-a-half.

Flixey Fum was succeeded by Trelawney, a Cornish Rex also of aristocratic origins. He was given his name partly as a characteristically Cornish surname, partly because one of his ancestors was called Marina Mystic, thereby recalling Dr Trelawney in *Dance*. Light grey, almost lilac in some lights, Trelawney's coat curls in a series of neat semi-circular ripples of fur, which can be stroked in either direction without objection from himself.

Coming from an ancient breed of cats living on remote Cornish farms, though one only recently recognized in cat shows, Trelawney's pale blue eyes register an absolute innocence and pathos. He is indeed one of the most affectionate cats I have ever met, and one of the most intelligent, though less intellectual than Fum. On the other hand, when it comes to breaking into elaborately fastened cupboards, he is not over scrupulous; at times recalling Dumas the Elder's description of his own cat as a 'hardened criminal and hypocrite.'

3

The Chantry, a Regency structure in the classical style of the Italianate villas of Bath (about sixteen miles away), indeed probably designed by a Bath architect, had been completed in 1826. Although not in the direst decay the house, surrounded by undergrowth hardly short of jungle, was far from spick and span. The interior still recalled use during the second war as a refuge for the bombed-out, a school (an establishment apparently attended by no pupils), and briefly a chocolate factory.

Passers-by along the road beyond the field enclosed by a wall in front had been known to deny existence of any place of residence within the heavy burgeonings of laurel, bramble, elder, uncut grasses. Only a little time before we took over, all domestic water was pumped up by a giant wheel from the reservoir made by an artificially created pond or lake two fields away to the south. Electric light had been even more recently installed. I have seen a bill of sale for The Chantry in the 1890s which did not overstate the case in saying the property would be a nice one if it had been kept up. Sixty years later that estimate remained no less true.

The Chantry had been built for the Fussells (a name widespread in the West Country), this branch being ironmasters, more specifically welders of agricultural implements, who towards the end of the 18th century established several Fussell houses in the neighbourhood. The Fussells of The Chantry turned from industry to the Church and the Bar, while the commercial side of the family, finding the West unsuited to the development of their business, moved to the North Midlands, where scythes and sickles are still manufactured bearing their name.

The sheet of water to the south of the house had been contrived in a hollow of the land that was formerly an orchard. Beyond this lake the country rises again, a steeply wooded slope, then more gently ascending fields with hills in the distance. The unsightly outlines of two limestone quarries to the south-west are at times obscured by mist; their effluents intermittently immolate fish in the lake.

Though rather late in the day for Romantick fancies, the Fussells also brought into being two grottoes (possibly designed to give labour in the Hungry Forties), one of these cavernlike follies marking the entrance to a small secret garden, ingress to which was so hidden by laurel when we came to the house that it was discovered only after three weeks. One evening a cow found its way into this small enclosed grotto, and the cow's owner felt too uneasy about the presence of ghosts there to extract his beast until the light of morning.

The further grotto, more grandiose in conception, was made round a channel feeding the lake from a much lesser pond on higher ground. The surface of water, once eight and a half acres, had through some defect in the flow sunk at about the turn of the century to less than half that extent: bringing into being a Lost World of trees and shrubs rising from a marshland of reeds, now a nature reserve of tangled thickets and stagnant pools, where brontosaurus and pterodactyl might be expected to roam.

4

Even in recent times the village had been known as Little Elm as well as Chantry. A chantry is an endowment attached to an ecclesiastical foundation for singing masses for the souls of the dead; sometimes a separate chapel, more often only a gift of land producing rent. It looked as if the name came from some such local fields.

In Whatley church a mile away lies the recumbent figure of a knight in 14th century armour, the head of a stag (*cerf*) on his shield indicating a member of the now apparently extinct but once powerful de Servington family. After research I found that the income from an unnamed chantry in Whatley church had fallen so low in 1452 that the chaplain had been excused from its obligations.

It looked as if this chantry had been dedicated to Sir Oliver de Servington, knight of the tomb, probably owner of the small manor house nearby, though another chantry at Whatley seems also to have been raised to St Edmund the Archbishop (of Canterbury), a 13th-century cleric associated with these parts. Whatley Manor is now a modest farm, its fine archway said to mark the boundary of Selwood Forest, formerly a royal hunting ground.

One concludes, therefore, that long memories continued to call certain fields at Little Elm 'the chantry lands', and the local name, hinting at antiquity of tenure, appealed to the newly rich Fussells. Perhaps the house was actually built on those fields, as no dwelling was there before. The front door leads into what is in fact the first floor—or *piano nobile*—of the house. The basement below opens on to a grass lawn on the far side where I planted a vine and fig tree. This architectural form is often to be seen in the Lowlands of Scotland, and, when in Northern Ireland during the second war, I used to find myself during an army exercise occupying houses built on those lines. I am familiar with no other in England, though doubtless they exist.

5

The Fussell-endowed church at Chantry (1845) is said to be the first built by Gilbert Scott, who certainly signed the plans for this choice example of Victorian neo-gothic, the original interior impaired only by a 20th century incumbent's transference of the massive rood screen to the north wall of the nave.

Another Fussell benefaction was a school over the road from their house, which (in the manner of similar institutions of that date) included in the same range of buildings an Industrial School, the National School, an Infant School, and a Boarding School for training teachers and governesses.

One of the pupils at the last of these was Helen Mathers (1853-1920), a novelist whose bestseller *Comin' Thro' the Rye*—a title of genius—is probably not much remembered, but whose photograph finds a place in the National Portrait Gallery. The novel gives a glimpse of life at The Chantry in the 1860s. We discovered this fact only some little time after living in the house, but as it happened I had seen one of the two (possibly three) silent films made from the book.

Comin' Thro' the Rye (1875) seems to have been the first novel, of which there were to be so many later examples, dealing with a large family dominated by a domestic tyrant of a father. Some of the story was so Mitfordish that I asked Nancy Mitford if she had been brought up on Helen Mathers, but the name was unknown to her.

An undated edition of *Comin' Thro' the Rye*, which probably belongs to the 1930s, claims one hundred and fifty impressions. Its illustrations appear to be 'stills' from one of the movies. Helen Mathers (also author of *Side-Shows*, *Ban Wildfire*, *Dimple*, *Griff of Griffinscourt*, *The Lovely Malincourt*, no doubt lots more) writes with a good deal of attack. Her humour is unforced and she clearly possessed a creditable background of general reading. The narrative is a bit confused, the author also regrettably addicted to the historic present.

The NPG photograph, taken when Helen Mathers must have been about forty, depicts a figure from a Du Maurier drawing, every inch a lady novelist, robust, coquettish, amused. She is already a shade plump to be squeezed into the wasp waist of her evening dress, wears coloured gloves (doubtful chic at the period), and clutches to her bosom a bunch of lilies of the valley.

Nell, heroine of *Comin' Thro' the Rye*, is packed off to Charteris (Chantry) School by her irate father for some trifling misdemeanour; no doubt a necessary loophole to explain why a girl moving later in the high society demanded by novelistic convention of that date has to be sent to train as a governess.

Unlike a Brontë heroine, Nell thoroughly enjoys school, especially when she develops a pash for Mr Russell (Mr Fussell) of The Charteris (The Chantry), a clergyman (like his model), who sportingly arranges for the girls to discard their crinolines, and, wearing only their bloomers, play cricket at the back of his (now our) house. Nell just misses a boundary, but can congratulate herself on knocking about the opposing team's bowling with sufficient vigour to break the spectacles of the German mistress, who had been unwillingly co-opted to field. Even Alan Ross could scarcely have done justice to such a match.

Unfortunately the story moves away from The Chantry after two or three chapters. The rest of the book chronicles one of those characteristic Victorian narrations of frustrated love in the course of which Nell's sweetheart marries the wrong girl; then, rather inexplicably, becomes involved on the French side in the Franco-Prussian War. He is killed at Sedan, his dying message sent to his old love: 'Comin' Thro' the Rye—God's rye, Nell.'

6

The dialogue used by Helen Mathers to describe her heroine's large family and dictatorial father could hardly be in stronger contrast with Ivy Compton-Burnett's novels, also teeming with brothers, sisters, domestic tyrants of both sexes, but the same sort of family is nevertheless being described, probably in both cases from a comparatively limited field of observation. I now regret that I never asked Miss Compton-Burnett (as one instinctively thinks of her) whether she had dipped into the works of this pioneer in her own genre. She would certainly have given her attention.

Some years before I met Ivy Compton-Burnett I spoke of her books to Roger Hinks, putting the accent on the last syllable of the hyphenated surname. Hinks, an accomplished mimic, remarked: 'Búrnett, we call it.' The icy coldness of his tone, one of quiet reduction to powder, made evident that he reproduced the voice of Miss Compton-Burnett herself. Before saying more of her, a word about Hinks.

He was son of A. D. Hinks, from the nature of his job at the Royal Geographical Society popularly known as the Geographer Royal, a distinguished and rather crusty old gentleman, who was my fellow member at The Travellers. He once observed to me of the club secretary (who did not in fact stay very long): 'I don't like the new secretary—he is so rude.' I answered that I had not yet spoken with the new secretary. 'Neither have I,' said old Hinks, 'but he *looks* so rude.' This no doubt true of certain countenances, a categorization not without all validity.

Roger Hinks, remembered chiefly—if unjustly—for his too rigorous spring-cleaning of the Elgin Marbles when employed in the British Museum, was one of the accomplished talkers belonging to Ivy Compton-Burnett's little court. Some of Hinks's best anecdotes referred to Sir Edgar Bonham-Carter (with whom he had, I think, an official contact), an *haut fonctionnaire* noted for his vagueness.

At some social gathering Sir Edgar had once said to Hinks (who temperamentally preferred his own sex): 'Will you give this cup of tea to your wife—I mean *my* wife.' His words were even odder once at a moment during the second war when Hinks, off on a wartime assignment, had called to take leave. He found Sir Edgar lying on a sofa in the drawing-room with his eyes closed.

'I've come to say goodbye,' said Hinks.

'Goodbye,' said Sir Edgar without opening his eyes.

Hinks was about to depart when Sir Edgar raised the lids of his eyes. 'Have some rubber,' he said. 'I mean butter.'

But to return to Miss Compton-Burnett, I first heard of her as a writer —I. Compton-Burnett—perhaps as early as my Oxford period. I could not be sure about that, but certainly Henry Yorke introduced her name to me as 'the only young novelist Bloomsbury thinks any good. She's about twenty-eight, and lies on a sofa all day long scribbling her novels in an exercise book.'

Whenever that remark was made—possibly after Yorke and I had both come to work in London—Ivy Compton-Burnett (b. 1884, though accustomed to advance that date a few years) must in fact have been considerably older than twenty-eight. Although he invoked the title of no book at the time, possibly did not himself know any of them, Yorke's comment probably had reference to *Pastors and Masters* (1925). I read that novel some years after publication, finding it obscure, but the absolutely individual manner impressed me.

That was more or less where I settled in relation to the Compton-Burnett books, which (like those of P. G. Wodehouse in a very different context) I admire for their wit and *aperçus*, though never found easy to read. Nonetheless I regard Compton-Burnett as one of the most gifted novelists of her generation; a writer of much deeper understanding than, say, Virginia Woolf.

Hilary Spurling (to whom I must be ever grateful for her *Handbook* to *Dance*, 1977) has treated admirably of Compton-Burnett's life biographically (which has much bearing on her books), and Violet's *A Compton-Burnett Compendium* (1973) provides a series of clear outlines of what are usually complex narratives. This summarizing is of enormous help in relieving the reader from too much concentration on the bearing of conversation on plot, thereby by allowing unobstructed enjoyment of the brilliantly stylized dialogue.

The Compton-Burnett convention for dialogue is entirely her own, highly formalized, infinitely skilful in bringing home the point the novelist wants to make in illustrating the speaker's character. Humbug is ruthlessly revealed under pretension of fine sentiments, while of no writer is it more true to say that her 'dialogue is action'.

The scene of all Compton-Burnett stories is laid towards the end of the 19th century, a large upper-middle class family, moderately rich, living in a country house. These persons, all at odds with each other, lacking contact with any world but their own (either those above or those below, except perhaps their butler), exist in a state of almost hysterical inward-looking intensity. Notwithstanding the deliberate stylization, the domestic dramas that take place are in themselves wholly convincing, even if motives are sometimes improbable.

There are peculiarities in this Compton-Burnett world, not on the whole insurmountable from the naturalistic angle, but at times stretching reality. Sport is never mentioned (nor the army or navy, professions to be expected within the social circumstances described), but 'varsity men' and their women folk—one uses both terms advisedly in the picture presented —abound.

In any exact resemblance Compton-Burnett life has all but disappeared in England. One suspects that pockets of resistance are still to be found, anyway so far as conversation and certain social attitudes are in question. These elements are likely to percolate no longer from spacious country houses (the Compton-Burnett sort of residence, large though not a 'stately home', having probably taken institutional shape), rather from characters based no longer in the countryside but in dormitory suburbs or seaside towns.

My reason for supposing the Compton-Burnett world not wholly extinct rests both on the vitality of the novels themselves (if there were ever people so credible as that, such people will always exist), also because from time to time one's ears are assailed—in railway carriages or public rooms of hotels—by sudden bursts of pure Compton-Burnett dialogue.

7

There was a certain appropriateness in first setting eyes on Miss Compton-Burnett, some time before we left London, at a party given for the Oxford and Cambridge Boat Race. Although, as remarked, sport has no place in her novels, this event belongs so profoundly to Victorian myth (still retaining a touch of those days) that it could be inserted without doing her plots damage.

Margaret Jourdain, Ivy Compton-Burnett's lifelong friend and sharer of their South Kensington flat, was by that time dead. No doubt Miss Jourdain's expert knowledge of Regency furniture (a subject upon which she had written authoritatively) explained connexion with the host on this occasion, who was Ralph Edwards, head of the Woodwork Department at the Victoria and Albert Museum.

Ralph and Marjorie Edwards had a riverside house in Chiswick Mall. Ralph Edwards was a polemical Welshman always prepared to give his opinions—usually worth hearing—on all matters in a voice calculated to penetrate the furthest corner of any room; more especially if he had something to say of an outrageously indiscreet nature. Edwards was himself by no means inconceivable as a Compton-Burnett character, though the directness of his spoken views would have become more involuted in manner to tone down their brisk delivery without losing any of the biting content.

An Edwards idiosyncrasy was completely to disregard his own previously expressed judgments. He was a recognised authority on the 18th century painter Joseph Francis Nollekens (father of the better known Joseph Nollekens, sculptor), and when Edwards was staying with us I once referred to 'our Nollekens'.

'Who told you it was a Nollekens?'

'You did.'

'When?'

'Two or three years ago.'

'Show me.'

Edwards this time scarcely bothered to do more than throw a glance at the canvas:

'Not a Nollekens at all.'

The picture (bought by my maternal grandfather) had, I later discovered, evidently been painted from an engraving (accordingly reversed) of a *fête champêtre* by Watteau. I have since been told by competent critics that Nollekens did at times copy pictures of the French School from engravings. The legs of the figures certainly show a stiffness of drawing Nollekens imparts. Whatever the truth, that was the Edwards way. When he took us round the collections at Ham House (which he had

31

himself assembled and arranged there) the tour included a blistering commentary on the contemporary world of art as illustrated by galleries and sale-rooms, a denunciation not to be missed by any art-lover.

Ralph Edwards's healthy contempt for mealy-mouthed discretion where his own job or indeed anything else was concerned linked him with that hearty masculine 19th century society that the Boat Race still peculiarly invokes at all social levels; a firm leathery approach which Ivy Compton-Burnett possessed too in her own way. I did not meet her on this particular occasion, but marked the severe expression and black tricorn hat.

I think it would be true to say that she was severe. She saw life in the relentless terms of Greek Tragedy: its cruelties, hypocrisies, injustices, ironies—above all its passions—played out against a background of triviality and ennui. Seduction, adultery, bastardy, incest, homosexuality (male and female), not to mention embezzlement and murder, haunt her pages. Such things are deeply discussed by her characters, though never explicitly, always within the muted terms of the period; indeed precisely as they would have been discussed in, say, my own grandparents' house (*Infants*), a thoroughly Compton-Burnett ménage playing a game that all the players understood.

Miss Compton-Burnett and Miss Jourdain always declared themselves very fond of eating, their sensuality, as sometimes happens, perhaps sublimated in this pleasure. According to Ralph Edwards they decided to expend a sizable proportion of their capital in undergoing a certain medical treatment which would allegedly make possible for them to eat as much as they liked without ever growing fatter. Whether or not this Edwards story was to be believed, it was generally admitted that the treatment, had it indeed taken place, was in outward effects less than successful in the case of Miss Jourdain.

Ivy Compton-Burnett had expressed a liking for my books (though she could not read the war trilogy within *Dance*, finding any reference to war unbearable after the death in action of a much beloved brother), and after exchange of letters we met several times. I liked her, while always feeling some of the constraint experienced by a child talking with an elder person, a grown-up who, though sympathetic, will never fully apprehend the complexities of one's own childish problems. That was absurd because she and I shared many unexpected likes and dislikes where books were concerned. For instance, she too felt lukewarm about *Wuthering Heights*, writing to me (29 November 1963): 'Posterity has paid its debt to her [Emily Brontë] too generously, and with too little understanding.'

I think now that my sense of unease was due neither to more nor less than what has already been indicated, that Ivy Compton-Burnett embodied in herself a perfectly unmodified pre-1914 point of view, one allied to a powerful intelligence. I was in truth meeting the prototype of severe well-read unmarried ladies of uncertain age who would have been alarming to have encountered in childhood. Remembrance of such past sensations belongs to the instincts that produce writers, and she brought back grown-ups at their most unyielding and embarrassing who robbed one of ability to know what to say next.

Ivy Compton-Burnett's uniqueness was in preserving this bearing through the upheavals that have taken place in the world since her own younger days, while at the same time losing none of that subtlety, intensity, even impishness if such an epithet could be applied to her, which made her so completely of her books, and her books of herself.

8

Compton-Burnett novels, placed comfortably short of the first war, may once in a way hint at social and intellectual changes taking place, but never suggest the overwhelming forces in the arts which reached their fullest expression just before that war, to be reshaped and deflected by the confusion of hostilities, then emerge as what is often spoken of as typical of the Twenties.

A character in a Compton-Burnett book might write a poem or a novel, but the essentially different flavours of Edwardian life, Georgian life, wartime life, are never differentiated, in spite of the author having lived through them all. These 20th century historical nuances will be referred to again in a later chapter, when I speak of Rupert Hart-Davis, whose story straddles those epochs.

The country neighbourhood in which we found ourselves after moving to Somerset from London illustrated several aspects of these closely allied but diverging periods too; among other things causing one to wonder, as so often, whether, when the 'modern movement' came, a different sort of person 'seized power', or whether the same exponents of the arts merely adapted their terms.

Close to where we now lived was Mells, its Manor House owned for four centuries by the Horners, the first of them by tradition steward to the Abbot of Glastonbury at the time of the Dissolution, when the lands were acquired by the family. Like many of the rather loosely termed 'new men' of that time the Horners in question appear already to have been fairly well-to-do locally. When the Fussells built The Chantry, they, as a later form of 'new men', had many tussles with the Horners as neighbours.

In 1917 the heir to Mells, Edward Horner, died in action unmarried. His sister Katharine was by then wife of Raymond Asquith, son of Herbert Henry Asquith the Prime Minister, created 1st Earl of Oxford and Asquith in 1925. Raymond Asquith was also killed in the first war. Mells accordingly passed in due course to Katharine Asquith's son, Julian Asquith, 2nd Lord Oxford and Asquith (succeeding his grandfather), who, after coming out of the army at the end of the second war, held a succession of appointments abroad under the Colonial Office.

Accordingly Mrs Raymond Asquith (who had refused the accession of rank available to her on the death of her father-in-law) lived at Mells with her unmarried daughter. After the death of her husband, Katharine Asquith had been converted to Roman Catholicism, and since 1947 the Mells household had also included Monsignor Ronald Knox as chaplain.

Considering the comparatively long residence of four centuries at Mells of the Horners as lords of the manor the family had raised surprisingly few monuments in the church, a large one, and, so far as earlier centuries are concerned, these few are of no special interest. On the other hand three memorials, one belonging to the late 19th century, two to the first war, are not only exceptional in themselves, but convey, so it seems to me, a haunting sense of their time, making Mells church in its way a unique sanctuary of the world leading up to the first war and that war itself. In all three memorials I know none elsewhere which imparts quite the same feeling.

Although true that changes in art and letters conveniently styled the Modern Movement are set well back in the 19th century, the Eighties and Nineties (if not the Fifties) heralding the explosion, the earlier assumptions were still operating vigorously while the modernists were gathering force.

The one was not displacing the other, Latin quotations running parallel with Free Verse. A somewhat far-fetched comparison might be drawn between these Edwardian, Georgian, Great War cultures, and the early years of the (inappropriately styled) Dark Ages, when classically named high civil servants of the disintegrating Roman Empire governed side by side with chieftains of Barbarian nomenclature.

Mells church provides striking examples of the early 20th century cultural mélange; both of the civilization in retreat, and hints of changes soon to come. The three memorials that catch the attention are those to Laura Lyttelton, Raymond Asquith, Edward Horner; while for good measure Siegfried Sassoon lies under a tombstone in the churchyard. The Lyttelton and Asquith memorials face each other at the west end of the church under the belfry tower; the Horner memorial in a small chapel at the east end.

The mural tablet to Laura Lyttelton, eight or nine foot high, is a bas relief in gesso on wood, executed in 1886 by none other than Edward Burne-Jones. The design, an effective one, represents a peacock, emblem of resurrection. The bird's ornate tail trails down towards the base of the tablet, beside its length a Latin inscription to the effect that she there commemorated lies in the North, yet her friends in the South love and remember her.

Laura Lyttelton (née Tennant), married only a year, had died in childbirth in her early twenties. She had been one of that group of young people, rather self-consciously gifted with beauty and wit, called in derision The Souls. The designation did not altogether fit those to whom it was applied, suggesting the current Aesthetic Movement rather than the ambitious young politicians and far from unworldly ladies who tended to be recruited to The Souls.

The Souls might affect to sit on cushions placed on the floor of their drawing-rooms, and show devotion to parlour games, they were not soulful in any unpractical sense. All the same Burne-Jones's peacock does suggest an inner melancholy, not only a search for less material things, but also an inexplicable yet pervasive fear for the future.

This last response in the beholder is no doubt largely induced by the memorial's association with that on the opposite wall, one so peculiarly expressive of what was to be visited on the next generation; a record of mortality that was to fall with especial grimness on the sort of people The

35

Souls had been; indeed directly on some who have been termed 'second generation Souls'. Here again is an overpowering sadness, though sadness of a very different mood from that of the peacock.

The memorial on the opposite wall is Raymond Asquith's. A notable figure of the group to which he belonged, he had learnt aristocratic arrogance in a single generation, but learnt the aristocratic virtues too. His published *Letters* provide an absorbing example of that parting of the ways between the new things and the old; a scholar treating the classicists with irony, while at the same time himself hesitating as to which way to move forward.

Below a wreath of laurel cast in greenish bronze hang (or rather hung) the sword in leather scabbard and steel helmet that were Raymond Asquith's actual army equipment. On this memorial too the inscription, quite a lengthy one, is in Latin. The tall capital letters are carved on the wall of the church itself with avoidance of too much appearance of ornamental finish, almost with roughness, the concavities picked out in now faded dark blue and dark red.

I find hard to define the powerful effect of this memorial. It seems to me, remembering the period as a child, perfectly to express the emotions of that moment in history, the manner anyway the intellectuals wanted those emotions recorded. Something about the whole conception of the memorial—which would have been different a few years earlier or a few years later, one could almost say a few months in each case—bringing back with a force comparable to no other monument I can think of an overwhelming sense of the first war, its idealisms, its agonies, its tragedies.

The Latin inscription still appeals to a classical past, yet sensibilities at once more dramatic and more down to earth strain forward to some modern form of expression, though perhaps dimly understood. There is the same fretting towards a less traditional aesthetic that thirty years before applies to the Laura Lyttelton tablet.

No such hint of uneasy stirrings, indeed the very reverse, belongs to the equestrian statue of Edward Horner in the small chapel at the other end of the church. This memorial is by (Sir) Alfred Munnings, better known for pictures of horses and race-course scenes than as a sculptor, later President of the Royal Academy and blusteringly antagonistic towards 'modern art'.

The dimensions of the statue itself, naturalistic within its idealized terms, firmly academic in technique, are not happy. Although less than life-size (perhaps three-quarters) the magnitude still seems too great for the chapel's interior. There is a suggestion of crampedness in addition to the sculptor's less than sensitive viewpoint.

The bareheaded saintly young horseman, an Arthurian knight from the pages of Tennyson, rides out on his charger. Here is no reminder, as in Raymond Asquith's memorial, of the brutal realities of war. Even Edward Horner's cavalry gauntlets that lie beneath on the plinth recall the parade ground rather than the barrage. This is quite another approach to honouring the fallen in battle.

Yet the equestrian figure, the Burne-Jones peacock, the Roman capitals incised on the stone of the church wall, together complete the picture of a span of years given over to mixed and changing symbols.

9

After the Edward Horner gauntlets were stolen from their place in Mells church further despoliation was intercepted by removal of Raymond Asquith's helmet and sword. In short the ensemble described is no more to be seen in its most effective form. All the same much remains to ponder, and, even if robbing tombs stretches back to the earliest antiquity, the fact that such measures have been found necessary emphasizes changes in the English countryside.

It would be a pity if such pilfering made the churches of England difficult of access. Their idiosyncrasies of furnishing possess an individuality and charm to be found nowhere else in Europe. Wyndham Ketton-Cremer (*Infants*) was always full of stories about the churches and clergy of his native country of Norfolk, where a tradition of eccentricity had long and obstinately flourished.

Ketton-Cremer's own incumbent, about to take a service in a neighbouring parish where the parson was ill or absent, moved a candlestick on the altar of the dark and untidy church and caught his finger in a mousetrap. His experience was less disturbing than that of another clergyman friend of Ketton-Cremer's, also officiating for a congregation not his own.

This Norfolk parson, not knowing the church, had arrived early for a funeral in order to have a short time to look round. In an embrasure over a tomb he saw a mediaeval or renaissance helmet. Helmets, even whole suits of armour, were dedicated to churches in the past, but I believe those to be seen in country churches have not always been worn in war or even for tilting, but come to rest in their surroundings after being used, like hatchments, merely to display at his funeral the coat-of-arms of a local nobleman or squire.

Whichever type, Ketton-Cremer's parson friend lifted the helmet down, and as there remained time to kill before the service, tried it on. Assuming this iron head-dress was easy enough, but when the moment came to replace the helmet the clergyman was unable to extract himself. All efforts failed. When the mourners, followed by the undertakers and coffin, arrived at the church they were surprised to be received by a cleric wearing a knight's bascinet. Presumably he had contrived to lift the vizor, though of that Ketton-Cremer was uncertain. All he knew was that the burial service had to be pronounced by a priest thus accoutred.

The village of Stiffkey, at one time famous owing to the goings-on of its vicar (*Messengers*), was comparatively near Felbrigg, Ketton-Cremer's house, and he was a friend of one of the churchwardens of its combined parishes. Ketton-Cremer used to call this versatile and somewhat choleric figure (who united the status of country gentleman with that of dealer in secondhand furniture) 'the old pirate', a type our host undoubtedly resembled when we dined at his house.

The Old Pirate, together with the rest of the neighbourhood, had long been exasperated by the behaviour of their vicar, who had some ecclesiastical commitment with the Stage and was always in London. Once or twice a year the vicar of Stiffkey would arrive on a motor-bicycle, preach a hurried sermon while eating a sandwich in the pulpit, then deal as best he could with the administrative needs of the parish in the time left for getting back to London from the northern parts of East Anglia.

Ketton-Cremer was one day lunching with the Pirate, who had been complaining that it was impossible to be baptized, married, or buried locally on account of the irregularities of the vicar, when a dramatic incident took place. Ketton-Cremer's seat at the luncheon table was facing the window and the drive of the house. A very ramshackle car drove up to the door in which sat a clergyman, and a personage who looked like a bookmaker, wearing a bowler hat and exceptionally loud check suit. The clergyman stepped out of the car, disappearing from sight as he walked towards the front-door. The bell rang. The Pirate's face went crimson.

'Continue with luncheon,' he said. 'I'll deal with this.'

Ketton-Cremer did as he was told. He heard some altercation in the hall. A moment later—as in a slapstick comedy—the clergyman staggered past the window again, this time clutching the seat of his trousers where he had evidently just received a hearty kick. He managed to reach the car, and drove off with the man in the check suit and bowler hat. The Pirate returned to the dining-room.

'I settled that,' he said.

Luncheon continued with conversation about other rural matters.

Inevitably there was a row later, which received a fair amount of publicity. The Pirate was fined, in consequence having to resign from the Bench as a magistrate. Cheques and postal-orders poured in to pay his fine, a Yorkshire miner sending a pair of clogs with the recommendation that they be worn on the next occasion when the Vicar had to be admonished. The Vicar himself, as is well known, was in due course unfrocked for relations with prostitutes, earned a living by appearing at fairs in a coffin being consumed by the fires of Hell, and finally succumbed to a circus lion.

10

After moving to the country we used for many years to bottle some of the wine we drank. A hogshead would be ordered from a shipper in Bordeaux, a bill of lading arriving from Bristol about twenty-five miles away, whence the wine would be delivered at the house. In early days we would share the hogshead (about two hundred and eighty bottles) with the Drus, once with the Mells household, but in the end organized the operation on our own, easier to undertake as our sons grew older and could be used in Dickensian child labour.

On the occasion when the wine was divided between ourselves and Mells, that is to say Katharine Asquith and Ronnie Knox, we had hoped Knox might assume for the ceremonial broaching of the hogshead the elegant monsignor's cassock with purple piping and sash which he wore in the evening; thereby recreating those 19th-century pictures of cardinals

39

carousing. That was not to be, though, when after the bottling we bathed in Mells swimming-pool, his bathing pants were of a light and decidedly ecclesiastical green.

In appearance Knox—called Ronnie by most of those who knew him, Ronald by Katharine Asquith and a few close friends—had a long thin face, longish nose, and was usually smoking a pipe. He looked very straight at you when he talked. Evelyn Waugh, who wrote Knox's biography, greatly revered him. Waugh's book gives a good impression of the circle associated with Mells in which Knox's wit and intellectual brilliance had brought him; a Youth if golden, also aggressive in its self-confidence, represented by those two commemorated in the church, the Grenfells, Patrick Shaw-Stewart, Charles Lister, several others, most of them killed in the war, of whom much has been written.

'Evelyn looks on Ronnie as Bossuet', Alick Dru used to say.' I myself don't go as far as that. I think he's just a nice intelligent man.'

Although in general two more different personalities could scarcely be conceived, there was something in Knox's early career that resembled Cyril Connolly's emergence from obscurity at Eton to become, through similar powers of wit and intelligence, a popular figure among a crowd of hearty ambitious school contemporaries. College at Eton had been a launching-pad for both. Connolly's worldly schoolboy friends can claim none of the dazzling legend (though perhaps some also dignified by death in battle) of Knox's group, and Connolly himself turned to literature rather than religion, but the early promise, the attraction towards dashing types, the humour tinged with disappointment, find some parallel.

Katharine Asquith, in her day a beauty, had been one of those to be called 'second generation Souls'. When young she had moved much in the beau monde, but for many years now lived in comparative retirement. From existence under the same roof she and Knox had both developed some of those mild mutual asperities with one another to be associated with a couple long and happily married.

I never saw much of Ronnie Knox, but always found him a man of delightful humour. Waugh had written that he could be chilly if surroundings were in the least unsympathetic. I said I had never noticed that. 'You were at Eton and Balliol,' Waugh replied. Knox's disappointment—sometimes voiced in so many words—was that 'They won't make me a bishop'.

Violet once asked whether, when Katharine Asquith was a débutante, gentlemen paying a formal call had still brought top-hat and walking stick with them into the drawing-room. This was a fashion just beginning to change when my father was a young man, and he used to recall one of the social tortures of his younger days being whether or not to leave hat and stick in the hall. I don't remember Katharine Asquith's answer on this grave point, but she must have mentioned the question to Knox (who for some reason had not as usual accompanied her), because he telephoned to Violet later in the evening to add a footnote.

Knox said: 'A French priest wrote a book to try and make English priests more chic and less middle-class. He was very insistent that one of the most important rules of behaviour to bear in mind was that when a priest visited the sick he must above all not lay his hat and umbrella on the bed.'

Ronnie Knox was fond of telling stories to illustrate the vicissitudes of clerical life (the background of his own family), one of which described how he had been booked to preach in an outer London suburb. On approaching the neighbourhood of the church he lost his way. No one was about on Sunday morning. He was in despair when suddenly he saw a man advancing quickly towards him. The man was in fact running at breakneck speed down the hill in front. Knox thought twice about delaying anyone in such a hurry, but there seemed no alternative to stopping the runner and asking the way.

'I'm so sorry to trouble you, but can you by any chance direct me to the Catholic church?'

The man took a second or two to recover his breath.

'Straight up the hill,' he said. 'At the top on the right—but if you come with me we've just time to reach the other Catholic church quite near here *where there's no sermon this Sunday.*'

II

Although Knox has become one of the legendary figures of the pre-1914 generation, in one sense typical of that vintage, he was quite unlike Ivy Compton-Burnett in making me feel that he belonged to a period made utterly remote from my own. In that respect he also differed from Siegfried Sassoon, although the ages of the three of them were enclosed by about four or five years, and Knox in fact enjoyed talking of former ways of life. Siegfried Sassoon is buried at Mells, beside Knox who about ten years before his death had played some part in Sassoon's conversion to the Roman Church.

I had been no more than introduced to Siegfried Sassoon by Osbert Sitwell years before, but never came across him again until the early 1960s, although he lived now only about fifteen miles away at Heytesbury House. This was quite near Robin and Julia Mount at Chitterne, who used often to speak of Sassoon. Then he became a member of the dining-club to which I belonged occasionally referred to again in the memoirs.

Sassoon's *Diary* (1981) of the 1920s contains many references to 'Burton'; that is to say Nellie Burton, who let rooms to 'single gentlemen' at 40 Half Moon Street, Piccadilly. It was customary to drop in on her for tea, and Osbert Sitwell once took me to see Burton, who deserves to be recorded as a figure who must have played a part not wholly unlike that of Rosa Lewis, proprietress of The Cavendish.

Perhaps a dozen years younger than Rosa Lewis, a very different type within those terms of reference, Burton had a touch of the same suggestion that something a shade *louche* was taking place in the background of her premises; though compared with The Cavendish that was faint and diluted. Burton herself, respectful, chatty, infinitely understanding, had the air of a nanny or ladysmaid (more the latter, perhaps explaining the chic use of only her surname), retired after long service in a very 'good' family.

Wilde's friend Robert Ross had spent his declining years in Burton's rooms, where among others Lord Berners lodged, already renowned for his *diableries*; also (Sir) Roderick Meiklejohn, utterly unlike Gerald Berners, but eccentric too for a distinguished civil servant (Private Secretary with the art patron Eddie Marsh to Asquith). Meiklejohn had a curious manner of mumbling and gesturing that was often imitated by the young men who attracted him.

When reviewing Sassoon's *Diary* I mentioned that Burton catered only for single gentlemen, in consequence of which an anonymous correspondent wrote saying that his (or her) mother, then a young Canadian VAD, had stayed in an attic at 40 Half Moon Street during the first war, when Burton had been very kind to her. One of Burton's then frequent comments was that things must be 'shushed up'; no doubt wise.

I was surprised at this account of a woman having been accommodated in Burton's rooms, because Osbert Sitwell told me that some years before someone had attempted to introduce a female element, which had greatly annoyed Burton, who had shouted: 'I won't have any Tondelayos here'; Tondelayo being a dusky seductress in *White Cargo*, a play about young men going to pieces in a remote African trading station, which had made rather a hit.

One of Sassoon's habits was to take midnight rides in the darkness through the woods of his quite extensive property at Heytesbury. He must on those occasions have given the appearance of a spectral figure like Herne the Hunter. No doubt a shared interest in horses had connected Sassoon and Robin Mount in the first instance, and the pair of them would sometimes go out hacking together on the Wiltshire downs.

It is of note that both Siegfried Sassoon and Robert Graves served as officers of the Royal Welch Fusiliers during the first war, a regiment that also produced from its 'other ranks' Frank Richards, who wrote an excellent book of war reminiscences *Old Soldiers Never Die* (1933), and the poet/painter David Jones, whose novel (perhaps rather prose poem) *In Parenthesis* (1937) was called by T. S. Eliot a work of genius. The book certainly is a remarkable vision of trench warfare merging with Arthurian Romano-Celtic poetry and history. The RWF's Medical Officer also wrote a war book said to be of merit *The War the Infantry Knew*, by J. C. Dunn.

I just met David Jones in the 1930s, an agreeable reclusive figure about whom, in 1967, Tristram produced a television programme; after which Jones and I exchanged letters about our common interest in the Romano-Celtic Arthurian Age.

As an autobiography I prefer Graves's *Goodbye to All That* (1930) to Sassoon's *Memoirs of a Foxhunting Man* (1928) and *Memoirs of an Infantry Officer* (1930), especially the former's account of wartime soldiering. In this last respect *In Parenthesis* stands alone for its own particular qualities. Sassoon's war verse seems to me more effective as anti-war propaganda than as poetry, but he is a writer of undoubted idealism and honesty, whose moral and physical bravery make him one of the outstanding figures of the first war. In life he seems to have been not incapable of a joke (when I was at Duckworth's the firm published an anonymous

43

squib by him parodying the poems of Humbert Wolfe), but his memoirs are unlighted by a ray of humour, also his *Diaries, 1920–22* (1981).

In contrast with the literary record of the Royal Welch Fusiliers, The Welch Regiment (now incorporated with the South Wales Borderers as the Royal Regiment of Wales, 24th/41st Foot) seems to have produced only two novelists from its temporary officers, Ford Madox Ford (*Messengers*) and myself. When I met Ford he told me that his Commanding Officer had written on some report for which Ford had been responsible, the note: 'If the illiterate subaltern with the illegible handwriting will etc., etc.'

The Welch Regiment regular battalions can however claim an interesting writer, a figure who should not be forgotten, A. J. B. Wavell, a contemporary of my father's as subaltern in the South African War. Wavell left the army in 1906, and, disguised as a Zanzibari, made the pilgrimage to Mecca, giving an account of the experience in *A Modern Pilgrimage to Mecca* (1912), a good book in its genre. He settled near Mombasa. When the first war came he raised a force locally known as Wavell's Own, a private army of Arabic-speaking water-carriers (as it were a battalion of Gunga Dins), which held up a superior German force trying to cut off the road to Mombasa. Wavell was decorated, then shortly afterwards killed.

Siegfried Sassoon talked very much the army idiom of my father's generation, but with a gentle, remote, almost embarrassed air. He was only a few years from eighty when I met him, and looked like a ghost haunting the fields of Passchendaele or Bapaume. Unusually tall, gauntly thin, an apparent frailty made him seem almost transparent, though even in later life I suspect this outward unsubstantiality concealed a powerful will.

When Sassoon heard where we lived he suggested that Violet and I should visit him, come to tea. That was in the autumn of 1963.

'Ring up one day,' he said. 'I'm always there.'

I did so about a week later. By that time Sassoon seemed a shade nervous, worried at his own recklessness in having issued such an invitation. The *Diaries* show him even in early days to have felt such uncertainties.

'It's just you and your missus?' he asked apprehensively.

'Just us—but only if that's all right?'

'Yes, come along, of course, of course.'

All the same he sounded a little disturbed; disturbed rather than inhospitable.

'You know where it is—there's a long stone wall. Just before you get to that hutted army camp.'

Heytesbury House is said to occupy the site of a palace used by the Empress Matilda, mother of King Henry II. Several centuries after her time one of the Lords Hungerford began to build a house there in the reign of Henry VIII, a project brought to a close when Hungerford, attainted for sodomy, forcing his own daughter, and invoking devils by black magic, was executed for these alleged irregularities.

The present house, mainly of late 18th century or early 19th century architecture, was completed by the Wiltshire family of à Court, MPs for the former 'rotten borough' of Heytesbury, one of whom was raised to the peerage as Baron Heytesbury shortly before the First Reform Bill. Sassoon had bought the place in the 1930s on making a marriage that had later come adrift.

On that crisp luminous autumn afternoon the grey façade of Heytesbury House, dignified and massive, like its owner looked also a little sombre and ghostly. The gardens and background of woods with rolling downs beyond were absolutely still. These were evidently the grounds of an enchanted castle. We drove round to the entrance which was at the back of the building.

Nobody answered the front-door bell. Hammering at the knocker had no effect either. We strolled round to the front of the house, completing this circle a couple of times. A long sash-window had been left half-open. Stepping through we found ourselves in a large drawing-room. Croquet mallets leant against sofas, books lay open on tables. Life seemed to have stopped perhaps half a century before. If the outside of the house had suggested enchantment the interior seemed to confirm some such scene as the Sleeping Beauty's palace; the Sleeping Beauty's rather than that of the Empress Matilda, who was probably always on the look out for an un-friendly visit from King Stephen.

Then Sassoon suddenly appeared from nowhere. He showed no surprise at finding us in his drawing-room. We made some apology for forcing an entrance. He seemed to walk in a dream through a dream world.

'How beautiful this place looks on an autumn afternoon.'

'Tennysonian?'

He murmured the question.

'Yes.'

45

'That's what I always think. Tennysonian. Absolutely Tennysonian. I say, let's have some tea.'

Sassoon had now lost all earlier anxieties about the visit. He chattered away about Mells, the Mounts, local nuns he sometimes went to see. An electric kettle was attached to a plug in the skirting of the wall. Sassoon, evidently too stiff to bend from the waist, leant forward towards the kettle at an ominously acute angle. It seemed impossible that he would be able to maintain his balance, then straighten himself, but he brought about that manoeuvre successfully, and made the tea.

As I have said, like Ivy Compton-Burnett, though not like Ronnie Knox, Siegfried Sassoon belonged to another era, another civilization than one's own. He was less brisk than either of those, perhaps just more tired. So far as mannerisms were concerned Miss Compton-Burnett was as if the first war had never taken place; Monsignor Knox, perhaps by an act of will, seemed to be living in the present; for Captain Sassoon, though no longer himself involved in it, the first war was still in progress.

III

The London Charivari

Not long after moving to the country I lunched at the Authors' Club with Malcolm Muggeridge (*Faces*), then Deputy Editor of *The Daily Telegraph*. The job seemed to suit him pretty well, his heart being in 'news' journalism, while the particular gradation of rank—so to speak third in command—represented a reasonably powerful sphere of influence not oppressively incommoded by too much responsibility.

During the course of luncheon Muggeridge told me that he had been offered the editorship of *Punch*. Foreseeing amusing possibilities he had decided to accept, notwithstanding the satisfactory nature of his position at the *DT* and its good prospects. He suggested that I might follow him to Bouverie Street as Literary Editor. We talked this over at the time, and after further discussions about detail it was settled that I should begin work on *Punch* in the spring of 1953.

When my parents were living in St John's Wood (*Infants*) my father had acquired in a saleroom a bound set of *Punch* running from the paper's début in 1841 to the end of the century; so that from the age of about twelve or thirteen I used to spend a good many hours of what seemed on the whole rather uneventful holidays brooding over these volumes.

Back-number *Punch* reading at an early age now appears to have been a drug shared with more of my contemporaries than I ever guessed at the time: a powerful narcotic inducing reveries that shifted about among heavy swells, blue china aesthetes, lion-hunting hostesses, patriotic Rifle Volunteers, and—something that bound all classes together in an egalitarian haze—the ubiquitous Victorian drunk.

None of these elements would have come to life so vividly in print.

47

Punch letterpress, except for a few stray odds and ends, chiefly verse, was on the whole far less entertaining than the pictures, then in the hands of a dynasty of 'comic artists' later never equalled. Even as a boy I was conscious of the sharp change of gear when—with burlesqued Beardsley drawings and parodies of Ibsen's plays—the Nineties arrived bringing portent of the old order's briskly accelerated demise.

By the time Muggeridge suggested my taking over the literary editorship I had scarcely opened *Punch*—among highbrows a byword for philistinism and stuffy conformity—for years, while retaining a certain affection for the 19th-century volumes that had once been such a solace. In short I was well informed about past *Punch*, wholly ignorant as to the current paper. I liked the idea of working with Muggeridge, the job would not be badly paid, some days in the week would remain free for my own writing.

While the second war was still in progress the problem for all periodicals had been to obtain paper itself, rather than persuading the public to read whatever was thereon printed. The public would do that pretty well regardless of subject matter, reading material being in such short supply. In wartime and immediately after, *Punch* circulation (I speak from memory) was said to have reached a hundred and eleven or a hundred and twelve thousand. Since then an increasingly rapid descent had begun, the circulation (again I speak from memory) by now at the middle to lower end of the ninety-thousands, and steadily decreasing. About thirty thousand of these copies (something the management preferred to keep quiet) went to America.

The rise and fall in circulation of weekly papers is a complicated affair, apparently depending almost as much on how many of such periodicals are available on the market at a given moment as on the quality of what any particular weekly magazine can offer. Nonetheless, even if a determined stayer may automatically increase sales with the disappearance of even roughly similar rivals, obviously the contents must have at least some effect on the paper's standing with the public.

At this period *Punch*, still owned by Bradbury, Agnew & Co, was more or less a family concern. The offices were housed in a dignified and relatively historic building, 10 Bouverie Street, which runs south from Fleet Street. Its proprietors, hoping for some magical formula which would halt this steep decline, had now taken the hitherto unprecedented step of recruiting an editor—in short Malcolm Muggeridge—from outside the *Punch* staff, rather than make the traditional promotion from within.

This innovation was naturally looked on without much enthusiasm on the part of anyone on the spot who saw himself as a potential editor; being almost equally disesteemed by members of the staff not aspiring to such heights.

Of what the *Punch* staff actually consisted I had at that time little or no idea. I did not know personally by any means all the people responsible for *Night and Day*—designed in 1936 to put *Punch* out of business—a very mixed gang (*Faces*), but when it came to producing a comic paper I could make a goodish guess where most of the *Night and Day* crowd stood. The same awareness was even reasonably true, anyway on the literary side, of those employed on the 'serious' weeklies. *Punch*, on the other hand, represented an entirely unknown quantity, something altogether unexplored.

Before going there as Literary Editor I think the only *Punch* figure I had ever come across in the flesh, that only once or twice, was A. P. Herbert. Then in his sixties, Alan Herbert, though his name appeared from time to time in the paper's pages, could no longer be called a very active contributor. To have met only him among the *Punch* group was no mere chance. Herbert, author, publicist, MP, with connexions at the Bar, in the Theatre, even with certain forms of academic life, moved through a wide orbit very different from the restricted beat of his contemporary *Punch* colleagues; yet more from the generation (one tending to be in their early forties) succeeding those. Few of these younger people—so I found—cared to mix with anyone except other members of the *Punch* staff.

The younger *Punch* journalists were inclined (not wholly without cause) to find Herbert's general demeanour at Bouverie Street something of an embarrassment; especially on such supposedly festive occasions as the *Punch* Christmas Dinner, when without the least provocation Herbert would rise from his seat at the port-and-brandy stage to sing a lengthy old-time comic song. Indeed after one such Yuletide reunion the *Punch* Christmas Dinner was abolished out of hand by Muggeridge, to whom in any case all traditional or collective merrymaking of whatever nature was utterly abhorrent.

Herbert's fullblooded unconventional toryism was also inimical to these younger *Punch* colleagues, most of whom (B. A. Young one of the few exceptions), so far as politics played any part in their lives, being mildly

Leftish. They had never questioned the virtues of such institutions as the United Nations or the British Commonwealth, far less satirized their humbug. Muggeridge's anarcho-anti-Left-anti-Churchill-anti-intellectual-nihilistic-sex is fun/sex is sinful-diatribes against everything and everybody, expressed in a copious flow of political paradox, and four-letter-word imagery, naturally caused some astonishment, even dismay, at first onset.

In short so far from hearty Falstaffian mirth setting the tone at Bouverie Street the immediate impression given by the *Punch* ambience was one of lowish vitality sustained by a fairly dogged and longstanding complacency. That at least was my own first judgment; not an altogether fair one, because without much direction from above a coherent magazine was at least coming out every week, something that in itself required a certain degree of energy. Besides, the sitting tenants might understandably feel sulky as to criticism or innovation on the part of Muggeridge (no less his henchmen), more especially as one of their own number had now been passed over for the editorship a second time.

Nevertheless others as well as myself were struck by the peculiarly muted atmosphere of the *Punch* office, the apparent physical enervation, the inward-looking personal exchanges; a surrounding despondency alleviated only by an unusually charming team of girl secretaries. John Raymond, for instance (whose taste for the bottle and early death prevented him from fulfilling his promise as a literary journalist), observed that when he entered the *Punch* office he had the impression of arriving in a convalescent ward; no one seriously ill or crippled, indeed all likely to be out and about fairly soon, but still none of them quite A.1 at the moment.

It was, however, the health of the paper itself rather than its staff—some of whom were hale and hearty even to the point of actual athleticism—that needed urgent attention before its state reached palsied infirmity. What the cure should be was by no means obvious.

In one form or another most journalism depends on 'news', even a comic paper partaking to some extent of that need if its life is to be sustained. News may suffer thin periods, but, where 'serious' periodicals are concerned, never dries up entirely. A comic weekly, on the other hand, carries the additional weighty burden to that of merely reporting or commenting on the events of the day: it is expected to stimulate humour; be funny; make people laugh.

One might compare a paper like *Punch* with a human body subject to a recurrent weekly deficiency in certain essential cell-tissues, organisms only to be nourished by an inoculation of jokes: preferably good ones, but even indifferent or actively bad ones better than none at all. The more powerful the restorative, the better the patient feels in any given week, but, from the nature of the disease, even the utmost stringency of tonic injection can be calculated to last no more than seven days; when once again the ghastly symptoms of inanition begin to make themselves plain.

This incurable malady persists as long as the body's circulation shows a flicker of movement. The strain on practitioners called in to remedy the case can be severe. The different forms of treatment prescribed at earlier periods over more than a century are well set out in R. G. G. Price's *A History of Punch* (1957), which takes the story as far as the early impact of Muggeridge as editor.

The essence of the matter, as remarked, is that every week someone or other must fill the pages of a comic paper with at least relatively comic material: prose: verse: drawings. If an editor judges these slaves of the Lamp of Humour wanting in their duties they can be sacked, but—by an inexorable law if the paper is to continue—another chain-gang must be engaged to take up the hebdomadal burden of being funny.

The new brooms, especially if untried, may prove to possess less staying power than their predecessors, however much open to criticism, even crack beneath the strain. That must always be borne in mind. This particular problem, the regular weekly stint, is perhaps the main conundrum with which an intruding editor is faced.

Except for a few minor changes among out-of-office contributors in specialized fields Muggeridge retained the staff that had been producing *Punch* under the previous editorship. At the same time he introduced—a fairly mixed blessing—the practice of using a sprinkling of comparatively wellknown extraneous writers to sharpen up the tone of the paper. So far as new blood in the actual office was transfused, apart from myself as Literary Editor, the only addition was Leslie Marsh, an old colleague of Muggeridge's on *The Evening Standard*, a veteran journalist brought in to collate and administer *Punch* 'copy'.

The cartoonists—using the term loosely to denote all *Punch* draughts-men rather than limiting it to those who executed the weekly cartoon—did not present quite the same potential for making drastic change as the various forms of writer.

There are of necessity fewer capable comic artists from whom to choose. A high proportion of the best of these are bound to be under contract to daily newspapers, organs in a position to pay much higher rates than any weekly magazine. Although the individual cartoonist can undoubtedly be galvanized by the attention of an acute Editor (over and above what may be had from the Art Editor) editorial problems in relation to cartoonists are not altogether comparable with those affecting the letterpress.

The *Punch* 'Table' (an inner circle of the staff, promotion to which was often achieved only after long years of hard service) met at Bouverie Street for luncheon once a week. At this meal (ample to eat and drink) the political cartoon was discussed. Formerly the paper had sustained two such illustrated weekly comments, the more weighty termed 'the big cut'. By then only one survived, and at the moment of writing has been abolished.

The Agnews, father and son, partook of this weekly luncheon. Although not precisely skeletons at the feast—that would be going too far in speaking of a repast that was fairly lugubrious anyway—they inevitably constituted a faintly alien element among professional journalists who were their employees. The Agnews themselves never joined the debate to any noticeable extent, far less attempted to influence politically or otherwise the way things were going. I was on appointment to my job created a member of the Table.

2

Literary criticism, journalistic no less than academic, is by its nature bound to consist in some considerable degree of persons who can't write laying down the law to those who can. Literary Editors, whatever their own qualifications, are in a position to do no more than attempt to neutralize this perennial current (if not well disposed to its flow themselves) by eliminating so far as possible ungifted reviewers. That process is less easy than might be supposed, but just as Dr Arnold (I think) said the first, second, and third duty of a headmaster was to get rid of unsuitable boys, unsuitable reviewers are to be dispensed with just as expeditiously, as they do equal harm to a paper.

The literary editorship of *Punch*—anyway in my eyes—carried with it no obligation to be 'funny', although at first I had to resist certain pressures, internal and external, from those who assumed the book pages of the paper were principally dedicated by prescriptive right to humour. My view was —and is—that very little doubt exists each week as to which books ought to be noticed. Naturally length and manner of treatment must vary a good deal from paper to paper, but (except in specialized periodicals) not the books themselves.

So far as space allowed, the books I myself thought deserved attention would in future be reviewed in *Punch*. This meant imposing a relatively highbrow standard on a magazine with a long and obstinate tradition of active philistinism. Such a tradition, anyway so far as book notices went, was now to undergo a change.

In fact *Punch* book reviews, short and few in number, had been for many years on the whole tolerably if unadventurously written. The book pages—rather archly captioned *Booking Office*, a heading which perhaps too pious a regard for ancient usage prevented me from altering—almost universally a poor relation of the main body of any periodical, now gained a little status by the institution of a full-page weekly review. I usually wrote that myself, though from time to time Muggeridge would want to deal with a volume of political memoirs or something of that sort, while R. G. G. Price—a great standby for his accomplished short notices— might suggest some book he preferred to discuss at greater length. A few others also appeared on this opening page of the literary section.

Short notices were normally constricted to one hundred and eighty words. That just gave room to say what the book was about, express a coherent opinion as to worth, and—ideally—make some sparkling comment. Such notices were accommodated in a manner to convenience the printer (rather than the Literary Editor) when the paper was 'made up'.

I would send the book out for review, the reviewer would then return the 'copy' (not always punctually), but when the proof had been checked by the reviewer and returned once more, the notice itself (except in some special case) would be inserted only when just the right amount of space was available at the back of the paper. For book notices the extent varied. They had to take their chance. Thus a book could be reviewed in its week of publication, or (especially if the reviewer had gone a short way beyond the bounds of one hundred and eighty words) might wait for weeks before seeing light.

No book's reception by the public can ever be predicted with certainty (the main reason why people can always be found prepared to gamble on the publishing business), but all connected with the writing of books will have their own ideas on this aspect. Let me give an example of a literary editor's hazards in this field.

After glancing through the pages of the review copy of L. P. Hartley's novel *A Perfect Woman* (1955) I decided the theme would not attract very sympathetic notices. Accordingly (conforming to the worst suspicions of those who denounce all literary criticism as a racket) I sent this friend's book to another friend (of mine not Hartley's) Jocelyn Brooke, who would, I supposed, feel well disposed towards Hartley as a writer; and let down an indifferent novel fairly lightly.

My judgment proved wholly at fault. *A Perfect Woman* received rapturous notices on all sides. Jocelyn Brooke, unusual in him, did not send his review within a week or ten days. On the contrary he delayed so long that I was about to dispatch a reminder, when it arrived with a covering letter. The note enclosed said that Brooke was sorry to be late with his 'copy', had thought Hartley's novel ridiculously over-praised, and done his best to redress the balance by pointing out some of the faults. In short *Punch* was practically the only paper to give *A Perfect Woman* a shabby welcome.

Two years later when Hartley's *The Hireling* (1957) appeared I thought the sinister undercurrents of the story (a hire-car driver makes advances to a rich young widow who employs him) might appeal to Maclaren-Ross as showing a more robust development; Maclaren-Ross allowing Hartley's abilities but demurring at the mildness of the plots.

That also turned out a misjudgment. Apart from differences in style, Brooke's review of *A Perfect Woman* was repeated in a slightly varied form by Maclaren-Ross's treatment of *The Hireling*. Such can be the consequences (and a good thing too some will mutter) of attempting to accommodate one's friends in the literary world.

Maclaren-Ross himself raised yet another problem. His daily life was in general designed in a manner to dodge a voracious pack of creditors, whose legal representatives in the form of bailiffs were for ever on his

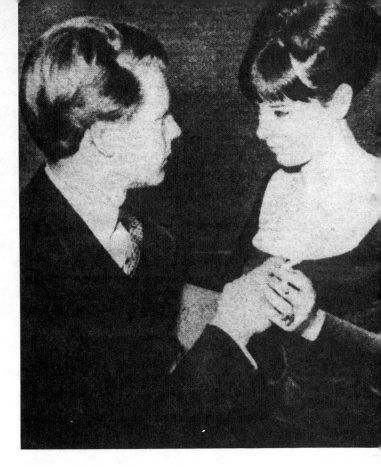

10. James Fox and Georgina Ward in *Afternoon Men* (copyright Lewis Morley – *Daily Telegraph*)

11. AP in front of John and Jean Mecks' house, Hanover, NH, 1961

12. Violet and John, Cornell, 1965

13. Arthur Mizener at The Chantry, 1963

14. Alison Lurie at The Chantry, 1967

15. Fuji from the aircraft

16. Alan Pryce-Jones in Bangkok, 1964

track. When the comparatively regular visits of Maclaren-Ross to Bouverie Street to collect review copies became known, a covey of bailiffs came into being outside, where they hung about ominously on the steps of the *Punch* office.

At last Agnew *fils*, with some justification as he had found physical difficulty in pushing his way through the mob of debt-collectors at, so to speak, his own front-door, came to me to complain. He asked if Maclaren-Ross could be dispensed with as a reviewer so that free egress might once more be established.

My answer was that I perfectly saw his point. As part of the proprietorship he was clearly in a position to lay down that Maclaren-Ross was no longer *persona grata* at Bouverie Street owing to the inconvenience his intermittent presence brought about. If Agnew *fils* stated that as an instruction from above, I was prepared to bow to the ruling without raising objection. But it must be an order. I was not going to abandon a good reviewer on my own initiative. There the matter rested.

3

'St Agnew's Eve—Ah, bitter chill it was!' Leslie Marsh used often to lament on the day of the Table luncheon, but if the Agnews did not enfold the assembled company conversationally in a blaze of wit, they did their best to be co-operative, and were patient about voicing disquiets that must from time to time have afflicted their minds during the birth-pangs of Muggeridgian *Punch*. It was indeed nearly five years before the Agnews became visibly restive, heralding Muggeridge's own resignation.

I liked Marsh, with whom I shared a large room, but if the Beadsman's fingers were numb, his breath frosted from the chilly atmosphere of the office, that was just as likely to have resulted from contact with Marsh's own cosmic despair as any frost-bound demeanour imputed by Marsh to St Agnew. On his more genial side Marsh was a connoisseur of beer, could give useful information about pubs not only in London but all over Great Britain, especially the Welsh Marches which he knew well, also possessing an encyclopaedic knowledge of Victorian and Edwardian music-hall 'artistes' and their songs.

Severely conventional in outward appearance, Marsh was not without his own inner fads. Like not a few journalists he nourished within him a passionate hatred of Fleet Street, every cranny of which was long familiar to him. I have been told (though cannot confirm the truth of the story) that—showing more enterprise than most romanticizers of rural life—Marsh had actually abandoned journalism for a time in favour of working in the fresh air as a hedger-and-ditcher or some such category of bucolic employment.

This rustic calling, whatever its nature, turned out less attractive in practice than to muse upon in Fleet Street, and, having naturally lost professional headway by the experiment, Marsh returned to journalism an embittered man. On that account there were those at *Punch* who found him hard to get on with. Personally I thoroughly enjoyed his harsh response to his surroundings.

Marsh's gloomy humours were not decreased by his job, the truly Herculean labour of bringing a modicum of order to the administrative chaos which had hitherto prevailed in an office where, for instance, some of the old hands had been accustomed to despatch their 'copy' direct to the printer without its passing under any editorial supervision whatsoever. In this area—or rather preAdamite formless void—Marsh did a great deal to pull *Punch* together. As an all-purposes journalist he would occasionally contribute a piece himself from the extensive medley of odds and ends at the back of his mind.

What Marsh did not cover in the way of administration was mostly dealt with by Peter Dickinson, a young man who also had his being in our room. A poet and Old Etonian he too sometimes contributed to the paper, usually verse. Later Dickinson escaped to earn an independent living as a successful writer of detective stories. Years afterwards he told me that, as one might have nightmares that one were back at school, he sometimes dreamt that he was still in Bouverie Street trying to straighten things out.

The *Punch* office had indeed something of school about it—perhaps a common-room from which some of the more disgruntled masters ran a typewritten magazine—the scholastic atmosphere enhanced by bookshelves filled with rows of bound records of past sporting and athletic events; useful for checking up on the sometimes dubious claims to athletic distinction, 'blues' and the like, claimed by acquaintances.

Among the ablest of the *Punch* staff was B. A. Young. He had remained in the army after the war, completing some ten years service in all, three years of which had been in different parts of Africa. Young possessed a capacity to write readably and knowledgeably about almost every subject required by journalism: politics, painting, music, books, sport, economics, naval and military matters. He was at home at a NATO exercise as at Prokoviev concert or an exhibition of Braque.

A similar journalistic universality is attributed to Bagshaw in *Dance*, but no other resemblance in the smallest degree exists to Young, who was made caretaker editor when Muggeridge left some months before his contract was up. Young would indeed have made a talented—for once unphilistine —editor of the paper, but the management took another choice. Later Young went to *The Financial Times* to edit the arts pages, where possibly he was more at home than at *Punch*. Freddie Young, incidentally, provided some useful hints in defining the music likely to be played by General Conyers on his 'cello.

Another adroit *Punch* writer to help with specialized information for *Dance* was Basil Boothroyd, who, having worked in a Lincolnshire bank in his early days, could supply just that smattering of professional jargon necessary for indicating the civil life employment of Territorial officers nearly all of whom came from banks. For a novelist to obtain such arcane trimmings, anyway in just the form needed, can be unbelievably difficult. Although there may be many bank clerks (or any other particular group) by no means every professional can provide from a given background the instances that carry conviction.

Boothroyd himself always retained a touch of the *Three Men in a Boat* trio, escaped from their London bank for a weekend, having a high old time on the upper reaches of the Thames. One could well imagine him in the straw boater and high straight collar of the period. It was a book for which we both had an affection, with its extraordinary mélange of knock-about farce combined with Walter Pater's most Pateresque prose. Like Freddie Young, Basil Boothroyd possessed musical aptitudes; once humming for me Vinteuil's 'little phrase', which, isolated and interpreted in such an individual rendering, deserved at least a few thousand additional words of Proustian analysis.

On the book pages Richard Price was an auxiliary with an unusually sure touch in undertaking the fairly thankless task of writing short notices; managing to convey what a novel was about (an essential sometimes disregarded by seasoned novel reviewers), make a joke, convey a word of warning to the potential reader without egregiously insulting the author; an action only rarely required.

I once discussed newspaper interviewers with Price, remarking on the sameness of their questions whatever writer was being interviewed, particularly the invariable enquiries about routine: 'Do you write with a pen or a typewriter, do you sit down at 9 o'clock every morning, etc?' Price replied: 'All people have a fantasy they could write a novel if only they knew the trick. They think that cunning interrogation might take a novelist off guard—cause revelation of the secret—a particular sort of pen, brand of typewriter, format of paper. Once that is accidentally divulged, the interviewer, all shrewd readers of the article, will themselves be able to become novelists.'

On this matter of interviews a military parallel strikes me. In the army it is not uncommon for a soldier to keep certain items of kit purely for the eye of the inspecting officer. Small odds and ends that are a trouble to clean or to assemble are stowed away for daily use, an unsullied example presented. That is rather like what writers usually hand out at interviews.

4

Muggeridge was always rightly determined that the weekly spread of pictures should not be reduced in number, an excellent principle to check what is for some reason always a tendency. He acquired Michael Cummings, a cartoonist with a keen political grasp, to draw for the Parliamentary pages. That was not easy owing to Cummings's other commitments. The next Editor on taking over sacked this very capable commentator.

Increased space was also given to the work of another excellent cartoonist, Ronald Searle, whose line had a real originality. Nonetheless—so it seemed to me—not enough was done to reorganize the 'art' side of the paper in the manner *Punch* required. Muggeridge was by temperament not sufficiently interested in drawing, as such, but even in pictures too the Muggeridge years provide at least some meat between the pretty dry crusts of bread that make the sandwich enclosing them.

The main political cartoonist was Leslie Illingworth, who had worked for *Punch* for many years and was then in his fifties. An efficient draughtsman in the John Tenniel/Bernard Partridge tradition, Illingworth brought something of his own to a dying convention of cartooning that could have become hopelessly wooden, and was at best oldfashioned enough. Although of Yorkshire extraction Illingworth had been brought up in South Wales, thereby having become a complete South Welshman in appearance, manner, sentiment, humour, and passionate attachment to the Vale of Glamorgan.

Wholly apolitical in outlook himself, Illingworth was in a chronic state of having to illustrate political contingencies of every kind both for *Punch* and *The Daily Mail*, which also employed him as main cartoonist. *The Daily Mail* by no means necessarily propagated the same political gospels as Muggeridgian *Punch*, indeed often took a precisely antithetical standpoint.

Illingworth, who liked to be instructed down to the smallest detail as to what he should draw (directions that he would follow with consummate attention, always adding a certain development of his own) used to laugh about this appearance of double-facedness. He would ask people if they thought it mattered advocating one policy in one paper, its converse in another, but I don't think the problem ever kept him awake at night.

There was something very sympathetic about Illingworth's gnomelike features, body, and demeanour. I used often to sit next to him at Table luncheons. He was not a great talker, but his opinions were always worth hearing, at moments unexpectedly phrased. On one occasion he said he had seen John Osborne's play *Look Back in Anger*.

'How did you like it?'

'Oh, I liked it very well, but some of the time I had to stuff my handkerchief into my mouth so as not to laugh.'

Illingworth once remarked to me: 'You can take it from a comic artist that, if any artist turns to comic drawing, something has *always* gone wrong in his life.'

I have often wondered what Illingworth blamed in his own case.

If the proprietors of *Punch* did not attempt to interfere on the editorial side of the paper, the same could not be said for some of the heads of department other than editorial. These, making up a convocation of perhaps a dozen souls, sat down together once a month at the same table where the weekly editorial luncheons were held, this time to discuss 'business' matters. At first, as Literary Editor, I was required to attend these joyless gatherings, but in due course Muggeridge decided that the Literary Editor's presence was not needed—something only too clear—and I was thankfully released.

Nonetheless I am glad to have witnessed the pressures to which an editor is subjected from some undercover elements within his own organization; something of which no notion can be grasped by merely working among these responsible for writing letterpress and drawing pictures; as opposed to printing, marketing, advertizing, space-selling, and the rest. Those concerned with such departments of *Punch*, no doubt quite properly from their own points of view, regarded their individual branch as of paramount importance in producing the paper each week. Accordingly not one of them hesitated to pontificate on how *Punch* ought to be run at the editorial end.

Members of the editorial staff, indeed all writers and cartoonists contributing to any periodical, may—almost certainly will—disagree to a greater or lesser extent with some of the decisions of their editor. Where Punch was in question, especially, an Editor could veer in individual policy between building up the relatively 'comic' and relatively 'serious' tone. At the same time Editor and editorial staff are likely to find some common basis from which to debate disagreements if these are voiced. In any case both parties are (or should be) all the time in touch with each other about the material making up each weekly issue.

Such common ground was often patently lacking during these 'business' talks round the *Punch* dining-table, where certain of those present appeared wholly unaware (some readers might have urged justifiably) that the magazine was at least intended to make people laugh. I remember, for example, one head of department firmly putting forward the opinion that a stimulating effect on sales would be achieved by a series of articles (practical rather than humorous) on such subjects as *How to Build a Boat*.

Similar textures of thought—though admittedly here 'comic' effect was to some extent taken into consideration—were given expression by discussions preceding the abandonment of the celebrated *Punch* cover, executed by Richard Doyle more than a century before, and continuously used since that period.

Arguments against Doyle's long established cover, however unappealing such might be to persons with any sense of continuity or appreciation of versatile design, were by no means out of reach; the most cogent being that a contemporary public for a comic paper had grown insensitive to the potency of Doyle's phantasmagoria (surprisingly erotic when closely examined), notwithstanding its long and popular reign. That such obtuseness could exist was made painfully clear by the comments of those sitting round the table.

Public indifference, however, was not urged as primary motive for supplanting Doyle's picture. Indeed sheer lack of interest one way or the other might have been advanced as a reason for retention. Muggeridge himself—in whom nostalgia for tradition would have been hard to detect with even the most delicate instrument—felt, I think, without *parti pris* in the matter; neither anxious for a new cover nor objecting to the old.

The proposition put forward by the adherents of change was a far more extraordinary one than allegation of public torpidity. On the contrary it was insisted that the Doyle cover was 'not popular' with bookstall assistants, because, being uncoloured, the magazine 'could not be seen' alongside other periodicals lying on the counter.

This—if, which seems highly unlikely, based on any form of enquiry over and above the hungovered daydreams and fevered nocturnal reveries of ad-men, running counter as it did to the simplest and most basic principles of camouflage—was extremely hard to swallow.

At that particular moment, doubtless in response to the ad-man doctrine being currently preached, multicoloured covers for weekly illustrated papers had become almost universal, *Punch* perhaps alone in sticking to its black-and-white (occasionally lightly tinted) cover. At the same time the *Punch* cover, a century or more old, was quite a different matter.

If those at Bouverie Street in favour of jettisoning Doyle had said: 'We cannot hold up our heads among our fellows because our illustrated weekly does not look exactly like every other illustrated weekly', they would at least have been nearer the truth. As it was, the argument put forward was manifestly absurd. Among piles of scarcely distinguishable covers in bright colours Punch and his Dog Toby in black-and-white engraving could not fail to stand out. In any case the Doyle design could easily have been topped up in bright colours had colour been everything. The fact was that Doyle was too good and had to be got rid of.

The postscript was that some *Punch* writer—possibly Richard Price—undertook a rough survey among bookstall assistants in his own neighbourhood some months after the change was made. He found none of them in the least aware that an alteration in *Punch*'s outward appearance had taken place.

6

Muggeridge showed himself perfectly capable of dealing with snipers from behind his own lines. He had knocked about the world much more than most *Punch* editors, and possessed not only wider experience but sharper wits and not a little guile. If an unacceptable suggestion was pressed by Production, Advertising, any other business branch, Muggeridge usually had at hand a serviceable technique for shelving unwanted projects in a manner calculated not to give undue offence to those who had begotten them.

Indeed, with his ingrained political instinct for bypassing an awkward problem, Muggeridge was possibly more at ease in such extraneous spheres than in editing proper, when editing came to tedious weekly routines. In any case every Editor has his own foibles (a previous incumbent at *Punch* had objected to advertisements for alcoholic drink appearing in the paper), and at best 'humour' must be largely subjective. Muggeridge had a far keener sense of what was 'funny' than his predecessor or successor, indeed stratospherically outdistancing either, but bees buzzed with increasing fury in his bonnet; public affairs and political personalities tending more and more to cause insensate rage than satirical laughter.

Although he never ceased to inveigh against the Press and the 'Media', Muggeridge believed devoutly (to use one of his own favourite adverbs) that everyone truly thought and acted as Press and Media represented them to think and act. The notion of an individual wholly uninterested in politics was inconceivable to him, and—although he might have denied this—he would be irritated by the view that such sources of information were themselves often wildly misinformed and conspicuously wrong in judgment about what the public thought.

I remember Muggeridge being quite incensed by George Orwell saying that the depressing thing about political canvassing was not that people wanted the opposite party to be elected, but that they did not know that an election was taking place, what an election was, nor what happened in the House of Commons when you got there.

This complete confidence in the existence of a universal passion for politics, expressed by reading the newspapers and devouring the Media, seemed to me at times too great; the Editor's personal fascination with such things leading to jokes in the paper unintelligible to people whose minds and bodies were not confined to Fleet Street.

Meanwhile an exterior element loomed. This was the moment when television was developing at headlong pace, calling into being as it did so a new genus of popular figure, the 'TV personality,' something now as familiar as—though much more powerful than—what used to be called a matinée idol.

The role of television personality—one judges merely by a row of striking examples—seems to impose an intense strain on its virtuosos. Perhaps (to adapt Lord Acton) all publicity is disturbing to the nervous system of the individual, total publicity totally disturbing. The peculiar characteristic of the television personality is freedom from responsibility, that apparently providing its own peculiar and acute pressures.

The actor is governed by the disciplines of art, the politician by the exigencies of political survival. The television personality is positively encouraged by the condition of existence to be answerable to no one but self, under no sort of restraint other than remaining a recognised 'personality'. The impression often given is that prolonged expenditure in that manner of the personality (as the Victorians used to suppose of masturbation) is cruelly hard on mind and body.

As television bounded into popularity Muggeridge, a born commentator in that medium, found himself more and more in demand. To invoke the image of Hercules—a potential television personality if ever there was one—the serpents so easily strangled in TV infancy finally gave place to a Hydra-headed monster, which, with its ferocious and multiple attacks on time and energy, might be said to have got the best of the battle so far as Muggeridge's (no less than Herculean) labours at *Punch* were concerned.

Interludes when the Editor could be pinned down in his room gradually became ever more fleeting. In my early *Punch* days some of the morning would almost always be spent talking of this and that in Muggeridge's office, a fusion of business and gossip that quite often produced features for the paper. Snap decisions, once characteristic of getting the week's number under way, were no longer on tap, while a pile of typescripts on the editorial desk grew ever more mountainous.

In short a rather different Muggeridge was now coming into being, a metamorphosis finally resulting in a parting of the ways with the proprietors; the *casus belli* being an old Muggeridgian stumbling-block, the deeply ingrained inability to grasp that *toute la verité n'est pas bonne à dire*.

Muggeridge was one of the most agreeable of men to work with; easygoing; quick on the uptake; aware of the absurdities of human life and human beings, most of all when concerned with journalism. Perhaps this latter perception became a little blurred as time went on, anyway if journalism be held to include television.

Muggeridge's nature had formerly seemed to me dual, indeed not much more complicated than the comparatively common dichotomy in many individuals between the frivolous and the serious. Now it appeared visibly (or rather televisibly) more nearly to approach triune form: the three persons making up the Muggeridgian Trinity each pulling violently in a different direction from the other as they took on an increasingly separate state.

In the beginning (such my own experience of the demiurge) was the sceptical wit mocking all, and the wit was with Muggeridge and the wit was Muggeridge. This First Muggeridge—never wholly exorcised but undergoing long terms of banishment from the Celestial City of the personality—would sometimes support, sometimes obstruct, what then seemed his sole fellow, Second Muggeridge.

Second Muggeridge, serious, ambitious, domestic (in fits and starts and when not led away by First Muggeridge's insatiable leaning towards licence), with a strain of Lawrentian mysticism (albeit D. H. Lawrence himself always coming in for Muggeridgian obloquy), had a spell-weaving strain and violent political or moral animosities (animosity rather than allegiance being essential expression of Second Muggeridge's teachings), both forms of vituperation in the main aimed at winning a proponderant influence in public affairs.

Third Muggeridge—doubtless always present in the spirit even when in the past invisible (at best faultily transmitted) to the eye of sinful man—was effectively made flesh during the later *Punch* period; a time when Second Muggeridge had initially seemed to be gaining in stature at the expense of First Muggeridge.

In due course, more than ever after *Punch* had been left behind, Third Muggeridge became manifest at full strength, hot-gospelling, near-messianic, promulgating an ineluctible choice between Salvation and Perdition. He who was not with Third Muggeridge was against him, including First and Second Muggeridge.

In this conflict without quarter First Muggeridge, who treated life as a jest—now so to speak a thief crucified between two Christs—came off worst (anyway for the moment, alternative avatars always possible), ending as a mere shadow of his former self.

The inner tensions of this trio of Muggeridgian personalities coursed like electricity through the *Punch* office during the last days of the Muggeridge reign at Bouverie Street. Indeed latterly I could sense an immediate buzzing in my own nerves on crossing the threshold of the Editor's door, so galvanic were they.

I stayed on a year after Muggeridge abdicated, being sacked at the end of 1959; release from a routine that was becoming increasingly unsympathetic, indeed decidedly irksome.

IV

Fit for Eros

The actor-director Erich von Stroheim had long interested me, and while I was on *Punch* Stroheim came to London in 1954 to launch a showing of his own pictures at the National Film Theatre. A party for the Press was held at The Savoy to which I went as *Punch* representative, not an ideal manner of being brought face to face, even then only for a short moment, but better than nothing.

Erich von Stroheim (1885–1957) was then nearly seventy. To this day much of his early life remains obscure in spite of many books about him. He was certainly Jewish, his father, owner of a straw-hat factory, could have been rich enough to buy a 'von' and put his son into the Imperial and Royal cavalry. One would have thought that Austrian army-lists making the last clear one way or the other must be in existence. If so, no one seems to have consulted them.

It has also been suggested as within the bounds of possibility that Stroheim was educated at Weisskirchen, that socially smart, otherwise somewhat gruesome military school, so hated by Rilke, vividly written of by Musil in *Die Verwirrungen des Zöglings Törless* (1906: tr. *Young Törless*, 1955). Weisskirchen would suitably complete the Portrait of the Artist as a Junker.

There seems no reason to disbelieve the accepted story that Stroheim left the Austrian army under a cloud, although the date he arrived in America (traditionally 1909, but placed by some as early as 1906 or late as 1913) is in dispute. Early methods of earning a living in the US included dish-washing, selling fly-papers, being a riding-master, the last consistent with the military background. After a few years he found his way to Hollywood, where he seems to have impressed his personality on the film world almost from the start.

Stroheim's art is a striking offshoot on the far side of the Atlantic of Vienna's *belle époque*, which lasted until 1914: the Secession painters; the Viennese school of architecture; the coming of age of psychoanalysis. The Œdipus complex was after all as much Vienna's gift to the world as Strauss waltzes or *Sachertorte*.

In Stroheim's version of *The Merry Widow* (operetta, 1905: movie, 1925) both elements are combined, so to speak, in the elderly millionaire who has a stroke on his wedding night (thereby leaving the heroine a *lustige Witwe*), and is a shoe-fetishist. Stroheim may be titillating the public, he is also expressing a new attitude towards sex in the arts. *Foolish Wives* (1921), which was intended to run for some three and a half hours, introduces this new approach with a cascade of shocks.

Stroheim himself plays the White Russian adventurer posing as a Count, who is living on his wits at Monte Carlo a few months after the Armistice in 1918. The Count, inhabiting a villa higher up the coast with his two mistresses, seduces the housemaid, plain and no longer young, accepting her meagre savings with the words (which have passed into my own family life): 'It is not much for a man who has given all for his country.' The Count blackmails an American lady (originally the US Ambassadress, perforce reduced in status to avoid offence), and there is a macabre incident when a cloaked American naval officer, insulted by Stroheim because he fails to pick up a book the lady drops, is revealed later as having lost both his arms.

The seduced housemaid attempts to take her revenge on the Count by setting fire to the hotel where he is attempting another seduction. He escapes, thrusting his intended mistress aside in anxiety to save his own life. Later he rapes a beautiful imbecile girl whose father, a professional forger, finally murders the Count, disposing of the body down the main drain; whence the corpse slowly floats out on the waters of the dolorous inland sea.

These incidents (many more) are in their way unforgettable. They are typical of Stroheim's method, which has about it something of Toulouse-Lautrec's power to impart, by wit, flourish, a sense of design, beauty and universality to themes in themselves sinister and tawdry.

Lautrec had in fact been an acknowledged influence on the Viennese Secessionist painters, notably Egon Schiele.

Another Secessionist artist, the proto-Surrealist Gustav Klimt, in his designs for the ceiling of Vienna University (the picture called *Jurisprudence*) represents an octopus about to swallow a bound and naked prisoner, a figure physically not at all unlike Stroheim himself in one of his sadomasochistic rôles. These frescoes, burnt by the German authorities in 1945, can now be seen only in reproduction.

Stroheim's gifts as an actor make one wish he had tried his hand in those Shakespearian parts (Macbeth, Othello, Antony) which give scope for that mixture of dominating brutality combined with inner weakness at which he excels. He would also be interesting as a director of classical drama.

The colossal sums Stroheim spent on production finally brought about banishment from Hollywood, and withdrawal to France, where he continued to make some excellent pictures. In the American movie world Irving Thalberg, sentimentalized by Scott Fitzgerald in *The Last Tycoon*, was one of Stroheim's bitterest adversaries; a group whose wanton malice destroyed the residue of Stroheim's unshown film art after he had withdrawn from Hollywood.

Not long before I left Duckworth's* the American edition of Stroheim's novel *Paprika* (1935) came in on offer. The novel was essentially not his medium. I could not recommend its publication, though I believe the book, much bowdlerized, did eventually appear in England. So far as I can remember the seventeen-year-old heroine was raped at least six times in as many opening pages describing her journey from Budapest to Vienna to seek her fortune.

Just as there are many roles one would have liked to see Stroheim play, there are certain novels (*Les Liaisons Dangereuses*, *A Hero of Our Time*, *Ulysses*, for instance) which he ought to have adapted for the screen. Two books by fellow Austrians come to mind: Robert Musil's great panorama

---

* On the subject of my publishing days I must correct a statement in *Messengers*, where I say the illustration depicting Covent Garden in Hogarth's *Morning* shows the house in Henrietta Street that was to become Duckworth's office. The plate, taken from an engraving of the original painting (like the supposed Nollekens after Watteau, p. 48), was reversed, accordingly showing King Street; familiar enough ground to me in those days, but not my office.

on the eve of the first war *The Man Without Qualities* (more correctly the man without *parti pris*), and a writer less wellknown in this country, Alexander Lernet-Holenia (1897–1976), poet and playwright as well as novelist.

The first of Lernet-Holenia's novels to be rendered into English (both admirably translated by Alan Harris) was published by Duckworth's, Lernet-Holenia and I exchanged letters at that time. After reading *Venusberg*, he said he thought we wrote in rather the same manner. I think, in fact, *A Young Gentleman in Poland* (1933) is perhaps more like early Evelyn Waugh; light-hearted, savage, approaching fantasy.

This novel of Lernet-Holenia's describes how a young (not yet shaving) German hussar officer gets left behind the enemy lines in Poland after a cavalry charge. To avoid capture he dresses as a dairy-maid, while retaining his black top-boots, which everyone tries to acquire from him. The transvestism naturally leads to incidents in which fairly broad comedy is mixed with touches of grimness much in the Waugh manner.

The Standard (1936) is quite different, a genre of novel of which I can think of no precise equivalent in British writing: romantic; realistic; satirical; moving. Beginning in Belgrade not long before the forces of the Dual Monarchy began to crack in 1918, a young officer of Austrian dragoons becomes involved with the lady-in-waiting of an Arch-Duchess visiting troops on their way to the front.

Mutiny breaks out. The hero–narrator finds himself entrusted with the Regimental Standard, which must neither fall into the hands of the enemy, nor those of the newly emergent national states coming into being at the break up of the Empire.

The girl he loves (eventually marries) accompanies the narrator on his hazardous journey to Vienna, the underlying theme being the manner in which preservation of the Standard finally obsesses him to the exclusion of love. The essential romanticism of the story in no way mitigates its realism, the confusion and horror implicit in the disintegration of an army. There is a terrible incident in which one Imperial and Royal regiment is called upon to fire on another that has refused to cross a bridge in the direction of the advancing enemy. Stroheim would have known how to treat such a scene, or that of the flight through the rat-infested catacombs under the Castle of Belgrade.

2

I have discoursed too long on Stroheimian possibilities, to which our brief meeting can be only an anticlimax. As ever with film stars he was smaller than expected, additionally dwarfed by a statuesque blonde lady standing beside him. Acting as hostess to the mob of journalists, she introduced them one by one as they moved forward in a queue.

Stroheim had not looked particularly young in a photograph I had seen of him in the uniform of a military cadet; now, trim, unsmiling, even sad, he did not look particularly old. I muttered my name and the paper I represented.

'From *Punch*,' said the blonde, after speaking the name.

Stroheim looked worried. *Punch* evidently did not strike a chord. The blonde offered a helpful word or two as to the magazine being a comic one well known in England.

'What will you drink, Mr Powell?'

The voice was deep, guttural, profoundly melancholy.

'A glass of dry sherry, please.'

Dry sherry seemed no more reassuring than *Punch*. Stroheim, this time almost in despair, glanced again at the blonde for help. Once more she elaborated, and dry sherry was brought. This failure in communication was becoming disconcerting. I took the initiative.

'At the close of the Monteblancan manoeuvres in *The Merry Widow* I was much impressed by your very individual touch in showing a group of foreign military attachés talking together. They gave absolute authenticity to the scene.'

I chose *The Merry Widow* on impulse, though Stroheim himself was said to be not at all proud of his version of Lehar's operetta, which, a box-office success, had been as usual savagely cut. This time he nodded vigorously. The observation had got home. I told him that I had myself served as liaison officer with the Allied military attachés during the second war. He took the point at once. The confrontation was saved.

'In those sequences,' said Stroheim. 'I also arranged for two military chaplains to appear, Roman Catholic and Greek Orthodox, because both religions were officially recognized in the Montenegrin army. I was considered quite crazy on account of those two chaplains.'

Montenegro—model for Monteblanco in *The Merry Widow* libretto—
had been the Balkan country in which the story was placed. We talked for
a minute or two about disregard shown by most film directors for correct-
ness in detail, especially military detail.

'For them it is just Horse Opera,' Stroheim said.

I tried to explain how long I had admired his art, both as director and
actor. Regarding the last he sighed.

'I no longer look like the *Oberleutnant* I once was.'

He was infinitely sad. I remembered how much that individual melancholy had struck me in a comparatively early photograph showing Stroheim
standing among a row of other Hollywood notables. I should have liked to
hear more of his views, spoken of Musil and Lernet-Holenia, but circumstances were not favourable to an extended talk. In the queue behind the
waiting journalists were getting restive for a drink. The blonde began to
cast glances towards us hinting that others too must have a chance. I saw
I must take my leave. Nevertheless the impact of the former *Oberleutnant*
with a genius for the art of the cinema had been worth experiencing.

3

In certain areas Stroheim might be said to have struck a blow for uninhibited treatment of sex in art, a subject now scudding in on a sharp
breeze which found public expression in the 'Chatterley Trial' at the Old
Bailey in the later months of 1960.

When the publisher of D. H. Lawrence's novel *Lady Chatterley's Lover*
was prosecuted I was one of those asked to appear if required as witness
for the Defence. I agreed, being in principle firmly against censorship, but
remained uncalled. Potential witnesses were given access to the Court so
that I found myself spectator of some of the scenes in this singular extra-
vaganza, something between a morality play and a pantomime.

It was no doubt just as well that my evidence was dispensed with. I
should certainly have found anything like enthusiastic support of the novel
on purely literary grounds far from easy; while merely to express conviction of the author's honesty of purpose, which I was quite prepared to
underwrite, carried no weight in law.

My feelings about Lawrence are that he is a good poet, talented short story writer, author of some first-rate fragments of autobiography (notably his Introduction to Maurice Magnus's memoir of the Foreign Legion), and a brilliant writer of letters. So far as his novels are concerned my reservations are much those quoted earlier made by Jocelyn Brooke.

Even the keenest Lawrence fans at the Trial inclined to begin their evidence by stating that they did not consider *Lady Chatterley's Lover* by any means the author's best work. One would heartily agree. Just to define the category of the book is not easy. In spite of an ostensible naturalism the story, a kind of allegory intended to express Lawrentian teachings on sex in the blunt language he said purified the subject, is often implausible; at times even illogical on what appear to be Lawrence's own premises.

The plot is well known: Constance Chatterley, daughter of a Royal Academician (a most unconvincing figure) is married to Sir Clifford Chatterley, a baronet of literary tastes who has been rendered sexually impotent by a wound sustained in the first war. Sir Clifford, who owns a country house set among the coalfields of Lawrence's own childhood, indicates to his wife that he would not be averse from her producing an heir by another man.

Lady Chatterley has an affair with Michaelis (a writer faintly modelled in Lawrence's habitually malicious manner on Michael Arlen), which is not a success. She then finds physical realization with Oliver Mellors, gamekeeper (ex-wartime officer) on the Chatterley estate. The essence of the novel is its detailed description of the sexual act in various forms between Lady Chatterley and Mellors, the story ending with their planned marriage.

The character who refuses to come to life is a flaw no novelist, even those in the top class, can ever wholly guard against; conversely, a single credible figure occasionally becomes incarnate in an otherwise indifferent novel. It might be argued that in 'real life' too the all but unbelievable individual is not unknown, but that does not excuse the novelist, who has to carry the reader into anyway momentary belief. The miracle must take place; the spirit descend; the blood of St Januarius liquefy.

The blood of Mellors does not liquefy. Although the personification of Marie Lloyd's song: 'Everything he does is so artistic', Mellors remains an author's ideal self-identification never galvanized into life: Lawrence, a few labels added or subtracted, as he would like to have been. Indeed the miniature (painter unknown) reproduced in the *Collected Letters*, Vol 1

(1979), immediately suggests the lineaments envisaged by his creator for the Chatterleys' gamekeeper.

The surname Chatterley (like Mellors apparently a fairly common one in Lawrence's neighbourhood) is in itself not without interest, occurring in Surtees, a novelist whose books would almost undoubtedly have been covered in Lawrence's wide and receptive reading; although also true that Chatterley is a Staffordshire place-name, and has a row of entries in the London Telephone Book, no doubt locally in the Lawrence county too. Nonetheless it seems to me possible that Lawrence returned to Surtees after deciding on a gamekeeper hero.

Among the comparatively rare occasions when Surtees writes of shooting rather than hunting he speaks of gamekeepers wearing the 'green velveteens' attributed to Mellors by Lawrence, while the following comparison is worth noting:

> He [Facey Rumford] returned the keeper's semi-military salute with a how are you?'
>
> *Facey Rumford's Hounds* (1865).

> The man Mellors faced lightly round, and saluted with a little gesture, a soldier's.
>
> *Lady Chatterley's Lover.*

Moreover Chatterley occurs as the name of a 'county family' in *Plain or Ringlets* (1860), when the Duke of Tergiversation is discussing with his steward Mr Cucumber the routine ducal party given from time to time for the neighbours:

> 'Well what are the Chatterleys queried for?' asked the Duke.
>
> 'The Chatterleys are queried, your Grace, because you struck them off before the last fête. Mr Chatterley voted the wrong way.'
>
> 'Then if they were struck off before, what occasion is there to put them back on the list?' asked the Duke,
>
> 'They have been presented at Court since then, replied Mr Cucumber.'

The Surtees Chatterleys may well have been ancestors of the Lawrence Chatterleys, either inheriting a baronetcy from a distant cousin, or perhaps being raised to the baronetage a generation or two later in consequence of the political adherence disapproved by the Duke of Tergiversation: their line ending with the dilettante Sir Clifford.

4

The proceedings taken by the Director of Public Prosecutions against the publisher were regarded as by no means inevitable. They followed close on the passing of the Obscene Publications Act (1959), intended by its sponsors to guard against that very contingency in the case of a 'serious' book. In addition, Lawrence's novel had not long before been ruled as free for publication in the US. Nevertheless after the book had been sent to the DPP to be 'cleared' proceedings were instituted.

The indictment took place at the Old Bailey in October 1960. Making my way there on a bus I overheard a conversation which has no bearing on the Chatterley Trial, but I record for its sheer oddness. Two men sitting behind me were talking English, plainly their natural language, but with a peculiar accent I could not place. They were evidently on a visit to London and seeing the sights. When we passed the Law Courts at the east end of The Strand one of them said:

'What is that building? Is it a church?'

'No, it's not a church,' his companion replied. 'I went in and had a look round yesterday. I rather think it's a sort of hotel.'

If the Law Courts gave the air of an hotel the Old Bailey when I arrived there was like a theatrical First Night with all sorts of literary figures wandering about its corridors. Based—like much of the best comedy—on material not in itself intended to be comic, the Trial was played by a cast of character-actors almost without exception accomplished in their individual roles.

In this aspect a high standard was set by leading counsel on each side: Gerald Gardiner QC for the Defence: Mervyn Griffith-Jones for the Prosecution; a couple who could not have been more aptly chosen.

Gerald Gardiner (Harrow, Magdalen College Oxford, later Lord Chancellor in a Labour Government, Garrick Club) spoke quietly and persuasively, without the smallest touch of bombast, indeed scarcely raising his voice. Tall, goodlooking, distinguished, Gardiner was just sixty.

Gardiner belonged to the Oxford post-first-war undergraduate generation just before my own. He had left something of a legend as President of the Union, President of the OUDS, and suchlike. There had been an

74

afterglow of rather showy brilliance. For the moment anyway all showiness had been eliminated.

Gardiner had also been moving spirit in founding the New Reform Club in Oxford, dedicated at its inception to Lloyd George Liberalism, and deriving very acceptable financial benefits from funds the former Prime Minister controlled. By my own day the New Reform had been infiltrated by members of the Hypocrites Club (*Infants*), of which it had become almost an annex. The original high Liberal intentions had been diverted to subsidizing the best half-a-crown luncheon in the University. Scenes of carousal used to take place there involving, for instance, Evelyn Waugh, Alfred Duggan, Robert Byron, *et al.* The Liberal Party finally decided that their funds could be better spent than on sustaining so wide a spectrum of political opinion, in consequence of which the New Reform had to close down.

Mervyn Griffith-Jones (Eton, Trinity Hall Cambridge, later a judge, White's Club) also possessed a good appearance. In contrast to Gardiner's air of sweetness and light Griffith-Jones was saturnine, swashbuckling, standing no nonsense with witnesses, indeed not above settling down to old-fashioned Serjeant Buzfuz legal bullying. He was fifty. After the second war (in which he had won an MC serving with The Coldstream, Gardiner having also been briefly a Coldstreamer in the first war), Griffith-Jones had been one of the Prosecuting Counsel at the Nuremberg Trials of War Criminals, where no doubt a savagely ironical manner had been easy to develop. He must, however, have had his less severe side, because *Who's Who* listed 'painting' as one of his recreations, and recorded the fact of his having notched up half-a-dozen one-man shows of his pictures.

Evelyn Waugh, who contrived to watch some of the Nuremberg Trials, told me he had stayed with Griffith-Jones during the visit. I asked what he was like. 'Not a very nice man,' said Waugh, but did not elaborate. It must be most emphatically added that no one was to be condemned out of hand on Waugh's evidence in that sort of connexion. Griffith-Jones may well have taken reasonable exception to something Waugh had done or said. Nonetheless I should have expected approbation from Waugh for a man of Griffith-Jones's outward complexion.

It was currently rumoured, I don't know with how much truth, that even apart from the professional role he was playing Griffith-Jones felt strongly as to the necessity of suppressing Lawrence's novel. I found him on the whole most enjoyable of the actors in the Old Bailey *mise en scène*. Once in Court, for the moment off duty and listening to the case from a faraway seat at the back, he winked at someone on the opposite side of the judge. I could not pin down Griffith-Jones's vis-à-vis, but, Dickens already in my mind from his demeanour, that deliberate closing and opening of the eyelid set up another train of thought.

Might not Sydney Carton have transformed himself into a counsel very like Griffith-Jones had he tired of devilling for Mr Stryver, given up drink‘ instead of wasting his life, decided to make a career at the Bar?

A reformed Carton (Shrewsbury School, Law studies in Paris, Inns of Court, Fleet Street taverns) was quite imaginable with a good war record and membership of White's. He had the same peremptory manner as Griffith-Jones. Carton's romantic attitude towards Miss Manette, the essence of propriety, by no means ran counter to disapproval of coarse language and irregular sexual relations.

Presumably Carton had learnt his bilingual French at the Sorbonne, knowledge of the language greatly facilitating the Far, Far Better Thing. To round off the parallel perhaps Griffith-Jones (the Welsh name not inappropriate to an Old Salopian) might have changed clothes with one of the War Criminals at Nuremberg; the latter now in consequence leading for the Prosecution in the Chatterley case.

Dismissing such fantasies from the mind one noted Griffith-Jones's emphasis was as much on adultery itself as on the 'four letter Anglo-Saxon words' (as with rather rough-and-ready etymology Lawrence's terms were usually called) used for describing Constance Chatterley's 'bouts' (another favourite designation); the last often accentuated as 'thirteen in number'; the baker's dozen somehow implying a particular viciousness.

Even in private among persons in general agreement about books, familiar with accepted modes of discussing them, literary criticism, especially when complicated by sexual ethic, may arouse violent argument. In a Court of Law, where much regarded as more or less axiomatic by those habituated to literary matters can be made to sound ridiculous under cross-examination, the simplest principles of writing are hard to affirm with credibility. Judges are apt to glory in their own ignorance of art and letters—no doubt often arid enough—and an atmosphere of unrelieved philistinism hangs by their very nature over all legal proceedings.

In consequence of these endemic handicaps in putting forward in

Court arguments based on widely accepted intellectual standards evidence for the Defence had perforce to take a line scarcely less in the nature of humbug than that of the Prosecution. Indeed the Defence's testimony well illustrated an innate aspect of British puritanism whereby some formerly condemned practice, once vindicated in the eyes of the Law and public opinion, cannot remain a matter of toleration only, but must be propagated as something actively beneficial. What is allowed must be good.

Accordingly the supporters of the book were some of them constrained by this national idiosyncrasy to plead that not only should Lawrence's novel remain uncensored, but that *Lady Chatterley's Lover* should be taught in schools and made the subject of organized discussion in youth clubs.

Lawrence, capable of an occasional joke in his letters, is consistently without humour in his books, a failing rarely if ever to be found in novelists of the highest class from Petronius to Proust. There was therefore a certain justice in the rights and wrongs of *Lady Chatterley* being hammered out without a vestige of humour on either side.

The Prosecution was hindered from laughing at some of the patently absurd assertions of the Defence, because to show jocularity might have cast doubt on the alleged harmfulness of the novel; while the Defence was equally in no position to allow any laughter at the Prosecution's ineptitudes of understanding, since the Defence's intention was to prove the high seriousness of the book.

Gardiner cross-examined a long string of witnesses, comparatively few of whom were re-examined by Griffith-Jones. Griffith-Jones, on the other hand, produced no 'expert' witnesses for the Prosecution (doubtless sagacious, a pity so far as pure comedy went), and kept masked the batteries of his most deadly anti-personnel weapon until his own closing speech.

Quite early on in the proceedings Griffith-Jones asked his now famous question: 'Is it a book which you would even wish your wife or your servants to read?'

The enquiry has now passed into history; together with the equally well remembered comment (attributed to a peer during the subsequent debate in the House of Lords): 'I should not object to my wife or daughter reading the book, but have the strongest objection to it being read by my gamekeeper.'

One of the most dramatic moments of the Trial I witnessed was when Francis Cammaerts (son of the Belgian poet Emile Cammaerts), Headmaster of a grammar-school in England, was giving evidence for the Defence. This was to be chiefly in connexion with his experience as a schoolmaster in the attitude of growing boys towards sex. As with all such witnesses Gardiner's cross-examination opened with a series of questions calculated to illustrate the credentials of the man or woman in the box to speak authoritatively of the matter in hand.

Gardiner's first question was an unexpected one:

'At the beginning of the war you were a conscientious objector?'

'Yes,' said Cammaerts.

The temperature of the Court perceptibly fell.

'Then you changed your mind after the war had been going on for two years?'

'Yes.'

'And you joined the army?'

'Yes.'

'And were parachuted into France?'

'Yes.'

'And later awarded the DSO?'

'Yes.'

'Together with the Légion d'Honneur and Croix de Guerre?'

'Yes.'

'And the American Medal of Freedom?'

'Yes.'

The list of awards may have continued even longer. This bit of staging was wonderfully effective. Cammaerts went on to declare his approval of *Lady Chatterley*. One might well ask why personal gallantry in war should be a recommendation for reliable literary or moral judgments, but that is the manner in which things are ventilated in open court; perhaps thereby providing some counterbalance to the often unjust and boorish reception of a purely intellectual approach.

Several clergymen appeared for the Defence. One of these, Canon Milford, Master of the Temple, made an interesting point. In principle well disposed towards the novel, he thought several of the scenes would have been 'indecent' had someone been watching Constance Chatterley and Oliver Mellors from behind a tree. In short Canon Milford considered that a reader of *Lady Chatterley* should not assume the individuality of a third party, but 'identify' with one or other of the lovers.

This optional approach to the narrative had not hitherto occurred to me. Professional novelists are more apt to reflect on how they themselves would have dealt with technical problems, rather than escape into a daydream of the imagination while they read another novelist's book. It is indeed one of the disadvantages of being a novelist that professionalism in that field is hard to shake off even temporarily; something that James and others writers have spoken of.

I saw at once that Canon Milford's distinction was an important one, although—speaking not so much morally as erotically—so far as making a choice between the two attitudes, not absolutely plain sailing.

The force of what the Canon asserted was vested not only in openly accepting the popular self-identifying approach of most novel-readers, but also in recognizing that important division of the human race between voyeurs and exhibitionists. In such a crude apportionment of temperament (in life rather than sex) I should, for example, grade myself as a voyeur, though, say, most of my Oxford contemporaries as exhibitionists.

Canon Milford's moral judgment on this differentiation might be thought even more pertinent in regard to those curious passages in *Lady Chatterley* where Lawrence appears to describe Mellors committing an act of buggery on his mistress; also suggesting that the gamekeeper had formerly been in the habit of behaving in a similar fashion with his ex-wife.

Although the language used to narrate these incidents (far from Lawrence's writing at its best) is less explicit than in recording more usual sexual intercourse, the actual term (admittedly not Anglo-Saxon nonetheless of respectable antiquity) not being employed, there seems little doubt the author intended this deviation to be understood; while at the same time momentarily abandoning his view that plain speech purified sexual action.

So far as Lawrence himself is concerned, both as novelist and sex reformer, no aspect of *Lady Chatterley* seems more a case of special pleading than these vague phrases that seem to indicate buggery. They possess all the highflown unstraightforward imagery that elsewhere he so strongly condemns. As to the practice itself, one can be sure that had Lady Chatterley's first lover Michaelis preferred this method of approach he would certainly have earned Lawrence's favourite epithet of sexual contumely 'doggy'; used not only in *Lady Chatterley*, but when speaking of Gals-

79

worthy's physically unexhibited pair of adulterers in *The Forsyte Saga*.

Griffith-Jones made no reference to sodomitical passages until his closing speech. At first this strategy seemed a miscalculation, since their innuendo would have been hard to defend in open court by those who put forward *Lady Chatterley* almost as a textbook for the young in learning about sexual relations. The comparative hesitancy of the Prosecution in pressing this line of attack early on had perhaps something in common with similar avoidance of deriding recommendation of the novel as an instructional work. In short the Jury might have been alienated by the overplaying of insinuations too oblique to be defined with absolutely certainty to the layman.

Another question only lightly touched on by the Prosecution was how extended a research on Constance Chatterley's part would Lawrence have approved had Mellors, notwithstanding his attractive exterior, proved a less than perfect lover. Was the implication that all wives whose sexual relations were not ideal should (as some do) leave their husbands?

Lawrence, no doubt sincerely, averred that he was against promiscuity, passionately on the side of marriage. All the same it is hard to see how the ideal Lawrentian spouse could be found without risking a process of trial and error. What would Constance Chatterley have done, for example, if Mellors, soon after the affair was begun, had in the course of his duties as gamekeeper at a shooting-party sustained from the gun of some unskilful guest a similar injury to that of Sir Clifford?

Lawrence himself would have been surprised, perhaps far from gratified, by the consequences of the Trial's verdict being defined in Philip Larkin's celebrated lines as 'Sexual intercourse began/In nineteen sixty-three . . . Between the end of the *Chatterley* ban/And the Beatles' first LP'; the conclusion drawn that the young to go to bed with each other *ad lib*. Certainly since that moment sex has been investigated in novel and on screen from every conceivable angle with the greatest frankness. How far that has advanced writing is another matter. Equally there is no turning back. Art is the true adjudicator, in its complicated relationship with taste. In the Courts of Art and Taste I should have thought Lawrence lost the case.

A footnote to the Chatterley Trial should be recorded. In 1967 a letter arrived from the Director of Public Prosecutions asking if I would give views on the propriety of publishing *My Secret Life*, an erotic Victorian work known to me by name but never sampled. Like *Lady Chatterley's Lover*, when prosecuted in the UK, *My Secret Life* had by then appeared without official objection in the US. On my replying that I was prepared to pass an opinion about *My Secret Life* I received a copy enclosed in a huge and all but impenetrable brownpaper envelope, marked in large letters *On Her Majesty's Service*.

My Secret Life turned out to be some 900,000 words long, that is to say more than half the twelve volumes of *À la recherche*; a bulk for which I had been altogether unprepared. To read nearly a million words conscientiously takes up a lot of time, which in my own case would otherwise have been devoted to ordinary reviewing. I saw at once that I had let myself in for more exertion than bargained for.

Written anonymously, the narrative chronicles every sexual action undertaken over certain periods of years by Walter, an upper-middle class Englishman born apparently towards the end of the first quarter of the 19th century. The manuscript is represented as having been bequeathed on Walter's death to a friend, who arranged to have half-a-dozen copies printed in Holland about the year 1882.

The bibliographer and art connoisseur Henry Spencer Ashbee (1834–1900) has been put forward as author of *My Secret Life*, chiefly on the strength of having compiled, under the pseudonym Pisanus Fraxi, a catalogue of Erotica called *Notes on Curious and Uncommon Books*.

This work was designed in three volumes: *Index Librorum Prohibitorum* (1877); *Centuria Librorum Absconditorum* (1879); *Catena Librorum Tacendorum* (1885). In less exotic fields Ashbee was among other activities an authority on the bibliography of Cervantes, art historian, traveller, collector of pictures, who left works by Wilson, Bonington, Turner, many other artists, to the National Gallery and Victoria & Albert Museum. Ashbee was in short a man of taste, and from the titles of his catalogue one would suspect by no means without humour.

From this external evidence identification of Ashbee with Walter of *My*

Secret Life is in the highest degree improbable, indeed ludicrous. So far as datable chronology exists there the narrative refers to the Great Exhibition (1851), friends of Walter killed in the Crimean War (1853/56), the battle of Solferino (1859), all of which were contemporary with Ashbee certainly, but seem viewed through the eyes of one born at least ten years earlier, which would mean that Walter died in his late fifties or early sixties.

My Secret Life is not included in Ashbee's own register of Erotica, to be expected both from an author's natural self-esteem, and requirements of completeness; an omission unthinkable in a man of Ashbee's scholarship. No erotic book is mentioned by Walter except the hackneyed *Fanny Hill*, indeed he indicates that he is not much interested in pornography. Ashbee wrote fluently on all sorts of subjects that attracted him; Walter's style, pedestrian to a degree, shows not the smallest literary facility. Finally, in an unremitting chronicle of casual sexual encounters none takes place in a bookshop or art gallery; unmatched locations for a pick-up.

Nonetheless, in spite of an appalling banality of outlook, and concerns other than sexual that never seem to have taken him further afield than his stockbroker's, Walter must in his way have been an unusual person. He lacked all imagination, his humour was the least subtle imaginable, he had no turn for expressing himself, yet he recognized his own exceptional sexual urges, and felt an inner need to set them down in terms that Lawrence might very reasonably have stigmatized as 'doggy'.

My Secret Life begins with Walter's earliest remembered sexual sensations, and carries his experiences through into middle life. The vast majority of the bouts (Griffith-Jones's term is appropriate) are with domestic servants or prostitutes. Allowing for occasional small vanities in matters of detail, what is written down carries all the mark of being substantially true.

Far the most remarkable aspect of this record is the need felt to undertake documentation combined with comparative tenacity of purpose demanded of an essentially unliterary temperament in assembling an enormous pile of manuscript jottings into some sort of chronological order, however unsystematic. It might be not inconceivable that Ashbee helped in arranging material, even gave advice about printing abroad, had Walter's work not been excluded from Ashbee's bibliography.

From time to time a few sexual deviations are touched on, but *My Secret Life* never begins to be anything like a pharmacopoeia designed to excite by description of out-of-the-way practices. On the contrary the un-satisfactoriness, even repulsion, of some of these when tried at the sugges-tion of women with whom he was on terms (e.g. flagellation) is commented upon quite objectively by Walter from the point of view of a man with few sexual fetishes.

On publication in America *My Secret Life* had been naively boosted as a 'revelation' of Victorian morals, although the profusion of prostitutes and brothel quarters in London of that period is well known to anyone with even a smattering of 19th century social history. Victorian straitlacedness was intended as safeguard against genuine surrounding licentiousness.

On this aspect Walter has interesting observations to make about changes taking place, such as decrease in availability of *maisons de rendez-vous* as the century wore on. These houses of assignation (one was in Blenheim Street off New Bond Street), where impatient arrivals were per-petually knocking on the door to enquire if current occupants had finished, seem at best to have been remarkably uninviting even for a relatively well-to-do fornicator like Walter.

After plodding through *My Secret Life* I sent the DPP a report of about a thousand words or more saying that the narrative seemed on the whole true, presented a most unalluring picture of promiscuity as there recorded, though one not without documentary interest, socially and sexually. I added that personally I had no wish to dip into the book again, and thought it unlikely to 'deprave and corrupt'; if anything calculated to have the opposite effect owing to the squalor of the picture.

This view was not, I think, followed, and *My Secret Life* was banned. At the close of our correspondence the DPP asked if I would consider accepting an honorarium for my trouble. The sum named, not insultingly small, was far from commensurate with time taken up. I replied that the amount mentioned would be agreeable to me, but—since in the first instance that department of the Law had come to me for guidance on literary matters—it was only right that the Director of Prosecutions should know for future reference that the honorarium represented at best half the amount an author in a position to be consulted on so vital a matter might be expected to receive were mere commercial dealings in question.

The DPP thanked me for this information when sending his cheque. Like Stroheim's White Russian Count in *Foolish Wives* pocketing the savings of the unprepossessing housemaid, I felt that it was not much for a man who, in ploughing through *My Secret Life*, had come within measurable distance of giving all for his country.

6

Like most of his opinions, whether one agrees with them or not, George Orwell's views on censorship are worth hearing. His response to what were often pent-up feelings of his time makes him a kind of Byron (less the sexual exhibitionism) of the Century of the Common Man; dragging through Europe the pageant of his washing-up at The Ritz; fighting in Spain instead of Greece and shedding a tear for the behaviour of Left Wing Spaniards, as Byron had done for that of Greeks in insurrection. In both cases 'thousands counted every groan/and Europe made his woe her own.'

In his younger days Orwell had written vigorously deploring British prudery, certainly laughable enough at the time where books were concerned. At his death nothing like the zenith (or nadir) of outspokenness in print had been reached, though laboured descriptions in novels of sexual goings-on were more common than formerly. Orwell used to say that the problem of what might or might not be said would disappear, when these sexually explicit passages took their place in literary history with the lusciously sentimental set-pieces demanded by the Victorians such as the passing of Little Nell or Paul Dombey.

The parallel seems apt, but there is small sign of persuasion that in many if not most circumstances in the arts restraint, anyway severe discipline, is more effective—if you like, even more erotic—than pedantically reciting the functioning of every organ and every emission. I don't think Orwell himself would at all have welcomed future developments. He had his prim side, being a little shocked (anyway on behalf of the postman) when I sent him one of his own favourite Donald McGill postcards in which a man in a shop asks a voluptuous-looking girl: 'Do you keep stationery?'; to which she replies: 'Sometimes I wriggle a little.'

Meanwhile, freedom of literary expression having shaded effortlessly into 'hard porn', what should or should not be published continues to arouse strong feelings; more especially as a public for the latter has become immensely widened by an increased egalitarianism. Erotica, even if frowned on by the Law, was formerly procurable by anyone requiring that stimulation who was prepared to take a little trouble and spend slightly more than the price of an ordinary novel.

Nowadays not only is Erotica less hard to come by, but many more people can afford to indulge the taste; which turns out to be by no means limited to a few decadent and ageing bourgeois furtively glancing each way before making the purchase. On the contrary the 'affluent society' has shown that pornography can appeal to the population at large, the younger groups at that. Does that matter? Should not grown-ups be allowed to decide what they want to read? Yet those who object to over lavish windows displays seem reasonable enough; while not all social side-effects of pornographic big business can be dismissed as absolutely harmless.

But how to prevent the puritans from banning *Ulysses*? To declare that any person of intelligence can tell the difference between a 'serious writer' and a pornographer is not as easy as all that; indeed rendered even more difficult by the former sometimes deliberately usurping the functions of the latter.

Guillaume Apollinaire, a favourite poet of mine, is a case in point. Apollinaire, poet *par excellence* of romantic love, produced a couple of volumes of the hardest of hard porn. He did that at a moment when he was earning a meagre living as clerk in a dubious Paris bank, and (if the metaphor is not contradictory) trying to keep the wolf from the door. I know only one of these works, but have no reason to suppose the other greatly differs.

An inescapable falling short of pornography is its sameness, the limitations of expression:

> Ah, where shall we go now for pastime
> If the worst that can be has been done?

The question, no doubt a burning one for former lovers of Dolores, is equally ineluctable when applied to Apollinaire in this unedifying field. Even for a poet who might be called the St Paul of Cubism, Surrealism's John the Baptist, pornography's imaginative bounds are soon set, notwithstanding inclusion of material that (unless the reader's particular 'thing') the least prudish would have to admit to be fairly unappetizing: a sadistic Pelion piled on a scatological Ossa.

Even so Apollinaire is not able to suppress all trace of himself and his intelligence. In *Les Onze Mille Verges où les amours d'un Hospodar* (1907) no hack pornographer would have brought in references to the recent murder by Serbian officers of the wanton Queen Draga in the Royal Palace at Belgrade (another incident crying out for Stroheimian treatment), nor (to be touched on later in these memoirs) the sea battle of Tsushima in the Russo-Japanese War of 1904–5.

These attempts to earn a dishonest penny on the part of a poet whose own verse is full of tenderness and humour in one aspect underlines, perhaps intentionally, the aridity and brutality of pornography. In that respect anyway Apollinaire deserves to be given the benefit of the doubt. These less reputable works of his also demonstrate the Nietzschean dictum that the comic is artistic delivery from the nausea of the absurd; as usual one touch of Nietzsche making the whole world kin.

7

Before leaving the subject of books regarded as erotic, a word about a writer I greatly admire whose name is associated with that end of literature; not altogether justly, because, although clinical in some of his descriptions, and not afraid to laugh about sexual matters, he is never deliberately pornographic.

The literary standing Giacomo Casanova (1725–1798) has long held on the Continent has never been his in Great Britain, where it is still not generally understood that Casanova is a writer of immense talent who was also an adventurer, and had copious affairs with women; not a professional womanizer and gambler who happened to leave some odds and ends memoirs which have survived.

In fact only about thirty named women occur in Casanova's *Memoirs*, a number that some of one's own acquaintances would regard as risible in its smallness, though admittedly Casanova was addicted to prostitutes as well. Even so far as these commercial relationships are concerned accounts of them are light-years away from the squalid dullness of *My Secret Life*, the sort of chronicle with which the *Memoirs* of Casanova are sometimes confused.

17. Ivan Morris, Violet, Yaki and AP at Delos, 1963

18. Violet and AP (scene like a movie 'still') in Cairo night-club, 1964

19. Violet and AP, Iran, 1970
(taken by Bill Robinson)

20. Violet, Taluca, Mexico, 1973

21. Congress in Sofia, 1977. AP (reading) in back row, Gore Vidal in dark spectacles, Indian delegate, Peter Elstob

22. AP with Trelawney

The handling of the *Memoirs* is masterly. Casanova has the instincts of a novelist in presenting a succession of autobiographical episodes in such a manner that substance is imparted to the other characters concerned. This is rare in the reminiscences of men of action, usually too egotistical to achieve personal portraits, especially those of women. A dramatic suspense is also imposed on the reader as to what will be the outcome of events with all the ability of a well organized thriller or detective story.

This very facility has suggested to some that the Memoirs have been invented from start to finish, the whole story imagined. To do that for a million words in Casanova's manner would be an even more extraordinary achievement. In fact modern research has established the truth of all sorts of incidents that might have been supposed, to say the least, highly improbable. If Casanova knocks off a few years from the age of many of his ladies (as has been shown more than once) he is not the only man to have done that when retailing a sexual exploit, and he never attempts to conceal or diminish his own failures with women.

The rarity consists in a man of Casanova's temperament possessing the wish or ability to write. In fact he used to describe himself as man of letters, and his scholarship in both literary, economic and scientific areas was considerable. Referring to his famous escape from the Venetian prison of The Leads, one of the most intensly dramatic incidents of its kind in existence, Casanova says: 'I had read in the great book of experience that in important schemes action is the great requirement, and that the rest must be left to fortune.'

That was the principle upon which he ran his life. The fact that he was able to combine this principle with a narrative gift and objective view of himself puts him among very few writers. He is vain, but well aware of his vanity, quite open about cheating at cards, or once in a way jumping the gun when involved in a duel. At the same time he is aware of honour and of what honour consists. The picture he gives of the worlds through which he moves (they often varied) is so vivid that the scenes can be almost perceived, heard, smelt.

He was probably bastard son of a Venetian nobleman, not the actor supposedly his father. That does not altogether explain the three rather sinister old gentlemen (of whom the chief was Matteo Giovanni Bragadin, a Senator), who kept Casanova going by paying him a small allowance. In return he operated for them a bogus system of fortune-telling which he invented; a form of sortilege which sometimes surprised Casanova himself by producing answers that fell out to be true.

We still do not know the motive for Casanova's perpetual flittings backwards and forwards across Europe, nor often for his frequent expulsions. It has been suggested that he was a spy. For whom? The Freemasons? The Jesuits? How did he find time to acquire his undoubted knowledge, say, of metals? He was put in charge of the French lottery, a job others must have coveted. He came to England (a country he admired but never quite got the hang of) with the idea of setting up a similar system of public lotteries there. Casanova may also have collaborated in writing the libretto of Mozart's *Don Giovanni*.

The force of Casanova's work is not to be appreciated by extracts of such self-contained incidents as the escape from The Leads. The *Memoirs* must be read in their entirety like Shakespeare's Sonnets, Ariosto, Proust. They have the coherence of a well-constructed novel, one of the striking features being the manner in which individuals with whom the writer has been involved crop up again in his life, emphasising those disregarded coincidences referred to earlier.

The finely phrased exchanges of stylized dialogue (which often retain their wit) must be accepted as a literary convention of the age; like occasional sententiousness and, it must be acknowledged, intermittent clichés. Understandably, a tendency to philosophize dilated with old age. That may be forgiven in a writer for whom the French Revolution had terminated the epoch in which he had so consciously had his being; a writer who was slowly dying of boredom and irritation as librarian at Count Waldstein's castle of Dux in Bohemia. During these tedious years Casanova had nevertheless forgotten little or nothing of what had actually happened under his eyes.

In this last period of decline he found consolation in his fox terrier Melampyge. The dog's name had been chosen, one presumes, from a surname sometimes given to Hercules on account of the hero's black and hairy back. Casanova must have been on the look-out for visitors sufficiently highbrow to recognize the allusion. Alas, Melampyge died. Casanova wept long, and composed a Latin elegy.

An absorbing sequence in the *Memoirs* is that which deals with the two (mutually lesbian) nuns CC and MM (the first now identified, the second possibly), whom Casanova used to visit in the parlour of the Convent of

Santa Maria degli Angeli on the island of Murano; later have fun with them both on the mainland of Venice (sometimes as voyeur) in the company of that broadminded prelate François-Joachim de Bernis, French Ambassador to the Serene Republic, in due course Cardinal.

In the spring of 1972 Violet and I made an excursion to Murano. Although the day was wet we found our way to the former conventual church of Santa Maria degli Angeli. Dilapidated to the point of being derelict the buildings retained a crumbling dignity. There was clearly easy access to the water for those clandestine journeys by boat to the love-nest in Venice.

One of these trips had nearly cost Casanova his life on account of the storm that had blown up. He often chronicles bad weather in Venice, especially extreme cold. While the rain poured down, making the story of the sudden squall on the lagoon very believable, I reflected that Casanova, in spite of his romanticism, remained on the whole the philosopher he liked to think himself. Incidentally, when the State Inquisitors impounded his books before incarceration under The Leads, one manuscript volume was entitled *Le Philosophe militaire*.

V

Transatlantic Reconnaissances

A Question of Upbringing was bought for America by the long-established New York house of Scribner, this first volume of *Dance* appearing in 1951, the same year as British publication. The Scribner connexion was arranged by John Carter (known on and off since Eton), who, as an accomplished bibliographer had begun life on Scribner's antiquarian book side. He now to some extent concerned himself with the firm's publishing activities.

After *Upbringing* had been taken on I met Charles Scribner (the Third) when he came to London. Charlie Scribner, who figures a good deal in Hemingway's *Letters*, was a courteous engaging figure, very much of the old school of American publishers; as was another member of Scribner's who appeared in London, the poet John Hall Wheelock, whose handle-bar moustache made him look like one of Peter Arno's *New Yorker* clubmen. I should like to have completed the Scribner picture by corresponding with Max Perkins (who never ventured beyond his native shores), midwife of so many American writers, but Perkins had died a year or two before.

Though the critical reception of *Upbringing* in the US was on the whole friendly, sales were far from exciting, so that when *A Buyer's Market* came along the following year Scribner's only bought a thousand 'sheets', a gloomy omen for an author conversant with the book trade. Perhaps I should have lingered on in a state of suspended animation, kept alive in the US on a starvation diet of sheets, had not Charlie Scribner himself died, and one of his sons been killed in a motor accident. The consequent re-organization of the business resulted in my name being dispensed with from the Scribner list.

Meanwhile an unexpected flicker of transatlantic attention showed itself in a quarter quite other than that of wellknown New York or Boston publishing houses. At the beginning of 1952 the young proprietor of two New York bookshops, The Holliday and The Periscope, wrote to say that he was contemplating a small publishing venture on the side, which he would like to take the form of reissuing one of my pre-war novels.

This was Robert Vanderbilt Jr. His project was naturally an extremely agreeable one to myself. With the exception of *From a View to a Death* (republished by John Lehmann in 1948) all these books were out of print even in England. The matter was further discussed in correspondence, then Vanderbilt himself, with his bride Virginia, appeared in London. They were a very congenial couple, and it was arranged that not one but two of these early novels, *Venusberg* (1932), *Agents and Patients* (1936), should be published in one volume, marking in both cases a first appearance in America.

The Vanderbilt venture, given the title *Two Novels by Anthony Powell* (ND), came out in New York a few weeks before Christmas 1952 under the imprint Periscope-Holliday. Vanderbilt's own energy and enterprise stopped not much short of hawking *Two Novels* from door to door on a barrow. He managed to dispose of nearly three thousand copies, no bad sale at a period when the wartime boom in reading was over; more especially in disposing of a two-decker of this kind, emanating from an unorthodox source, and containing a couple of novels for twenty years wholly defunct as a selling proposition in the country of their origin.

This *jeu d'esprit* of Bob Vanderbilt's played a part not at all to be disregarded in the lumbering process of getting my books on the road in America.

2

A long-term side-effect of Vanderbilt's enterprise was a publishing row in England fifteen or more years later, insignificant in itself, but receiving a certain amount of publicity at the time, though never I think properly understood. At the risk of being a bore about publishing 'shop' I shall rehearse the story just to get the record straight.

Bob Vanderbilt, an admirer of Osbert Lancaster's cartoons, was anxious that Lancaster should design the wrapper of *Two Novels*. They met, and it was agreed that two pictures should be executed, one for the front of the jacket, one for the back, illustrating scenes from both novels.

I was very pleased by this arrangement, and grateful to Lancaster, a man overwhelmed with work—not only a diurnal pocket cartoon for *The Daily Express*, but innumerable commitments in the Theatre and elsewhere—who had something better to do than earn a few guineas drawing book-jackets.

A dozen years later my then paperback publisher asked permission (given free of charge) to use the same two Lancaster designs for new editions in paper of *Venusberg* and *Agents and Patients*. The paperback publisher followed up this request by approaching Lancaster directly to design further covers for *Dance* when the sequence began to appear. I should not have asked that myself, knowing how busy Lancaster was, but again was delighted that he once more agreed.

When half-a-dozen paperback volumes of *Dance* were published, aware another was on the way Lancaster mentioned to me that he was going abroad, and would like to have the date by which the next cover for the sequence would be needed. My first letter requesting this information from the paperback publisher remained unanswered. A second one received a couple of lines from a secretary saying it had been decided to use other—a characteristic publishing phrase—'art-work'.

This casualness made me angry. On the whole I regard it as a publisher's job to decide what is the best cover to sell a book, and, having taken a keen interest in book production in my own publishing days, I would even admit to a kind of revulsion from interfering in that area now myself; anyway beyond a certain point, or making decisions when asked to do so. In short, I was far from insistent that Osbert Lancaster should for ever after design the covers for *Dance*.

What made me cross was that the good nature of a distinguished artist should be abused in this loutish manner by a publisher after Lancaster had been kind enough to take on what was for him a very minor assignment. He and I could perfectly well have been written a letter announcing the decision. There was a brisk exchange between myself and an executive (now deceased) of the paperback firm, who seemed altogether incapable of taking in this aspect of his behaviour. I went elsewhere, and found myself much more happily placed. The point I want to make is that my plea was not against another sort of 'art-work', but for better manners.

Enough about such things. Vanderbilt told me that when he dined with Lancaster he learnt from his host that Osbert Sitwell had at first resented that another Osbert should have entered his *monde*. In due course Sitwell and Lancaster had become friends, so that when Osbert Burdett, a man of letters of a somewhat older vintage who wrote of the Nineties, passed away in the 1930s they lunched *à deux* to celebrate being left as the sole Osberts (now, alas, reduced to one) in the field.

3

Meanwhile further tribulations as regards sales had been taking place along more orthodox American publishing paths. Parting with Scribner's was followed by even less luck with Farrar, Straus & Cudahay, who issued *The Acceptance World* in 1955; also producing an American paperback that must have become quite a bibliographical rarity.

When *At Lady Molly's* appeared in 1957 American rights were bought by Little, Brown of Boston, another historic house, who did much of their business through New York, though that was soft-pedalled. Little, Brown were to remain my American publishers for twenty years, those I dealt with there all the most agreeable of men; the last known to me personally being Harry Sions, who died suddenly in 1974.

During the next few years considerable changes took place in the firm, and when the first volume of these memoirs came along Little, Brown enthusiasm for them was so restrained (a sheet offer) that I moved on to Holt, Rinehart & Winston; Holt having in fact been my first American publisher when *Afternoon Men* had appeared in the US the best part of half a century before.

Until quite recently (when individual popularity of *Dance* volumes has become less easy to estimate) *Lady Molly* has always shown a tendency to keep a short way ahead of the others. Whether on account of that, or simply because the sequence was getting more widely known, perhaps better marketed, transatlantic sales began to look up when Little, Brown took over. The comparatively large jump (in terms of what have always been modest sales) happened when they put the first three into one volume; followed up until the whole of *Dance* was available in that format; as now in paperback in America.

The experiment was then tried by Heinemann, but with less success; accordingly abandoned. This is one of the differences between American and British publishing; the Americans feel drawn to a thick mass of printed matter; the British preferring a slim volume which, while giving money's worth, does not threaten too long commitment. My sales in the US tend to be much the same as in the UK, possibly a shade higher in the former.

4

T. S. Eliot once remarked to Violet that, when you have to do the washing-up, the vital question to decide is the best moment to drink coffee. Life is weighed down with such problems, solved by nations and individuals in different ways. The subject is allied to a comment of Arthur Mizener's (credentials Princeton, Harvard Business School, Professorship at Cornell, almost annual visits for many years to Great Britain) that 'in England there is more formality, in America more etiquette'. Even in England I would hesitate to speak on the subject of formality now, but in the US twenty years ago the Mizener precept was always worth a thought for the traveller there.

Except for the encounter with Scott Fitzgerald, such contacts as I had made in Hollywood in 1937 were not on the whole of a kind to throw much light on American ways in any but the most superficial aspects, the movie background being one from which few generalizations are to be drawn. Fitzgerald himself was keenly interested in American characteristics as such, and would certainly have shown himself alert to the distinction between formality and etiquette.

Fitzgerald's shade presided over my coming to know Mizener, whose biography of the novelist, *The Far Side of Paradise* (1951), I reviewed for the *TLS*; subsequent correspondence bringing us together. Since then Violet and I have been seeing something of Arthur and Rosemary Mizener on and off for the past thirty years.

In reply to some now forgotten observation of mine Mizener once answered: 'I quite see the logic of what you say, but cannot agree, because if I agreed I should cease to be an American.' These words much impressed me, confirming as they did what I had long suspected, that the concept of 'being an American' inseparably combined a sense of nationality with a kind of metaphysical creed. This is something of which a European visitor to the US is often subtly aware, and should always bear in mind.

To undertake a presumptuous investigation into American habits is far from my intention here, but over the years certain of these have inevitably made an impression. For example, another American friend Bill Davis (*Faces*), whose wife Annie was sister to Cyril Connolly's first wife Jean, speaking of Connolly's occasional peevishness about acquaintances who seemed to be doing rather too well, once said: 'But I *like* my friends being successful'.

This is, I think, a point worth attention; an engaging counterpart to what is sometimes decried as American success-worship. I don't feel at all confident that I could produce more than a few persons known to me in my own country who could truly echo that sentiment, but here again feelings antipathetic to ambition are not necessarily ignoble ones.

How far Bill Davis's remark represents a general American reaction I do not know, but a concrete example of contrast between American and British feelings about failure have been more than once provided by reviewers of these memoirs when they speak, say, of the memorialist having been sacked from a job or otherwise suffered a reverse. American reviewers sometimes sound genuinely shocked and surprised by the admission; British ones, on the other hand, are relieved and diverted bya ny story of rejection.

After the Hollywood interlude I did not cross the Atlantic again until the autumn of 1961, when I found that even if far from a bestseller, the fact of being not wholly unknown as a writer created a greatly preferable ambience to that attaching to a young man who had published only three or four novels, and was seeking employment as a scriptwriter in the film industry.

Here again, even in relatively intellectual circles in London (I mean very relatively), I have sometimes been appalled by the casual treatment dished out to wellknown American writers; but that is the English way, and no doubt the more intelligent Americans would wish it to remain so.

The second American visit, this time to the Eastern Seaboard, grew out of a letter received from the Vice-President of Dartmouth College, New Hampshire, the late John Meck, who invited me to visit that foundation, perhaps lecture there.

This invitation was expressed in terms that might have flattered King Arthur had he been bidden to the Court of the Yankees rather than the reverse, but I do not care for lecturing, which—unless undertaken in dire need of money—seems no part of a novelist's obligation. Apart from that I foresaw that any such transatlantic jaunt would impose an extortionate toll on 'writing time' mentioned earlier. Accordingly I was at first unwilling to accept this otherwise tempting proposal.

Meck was, however, a man of considerable firmness. He unfolded a prospect from the Arabian Nights in which I should be conveyed by magic carpet (operated through a Dartmouth man in PanAm), and (without reference to myself) arranged that Little, Brown should take me under their wing at The Ritz in Boston, then The St Regis in New York, after the Dartmouth or other commitments were at an end.

Recognizing that, if lecturing were to be abjured I should have to substitute an alternative manner of singing for my supper, I agreed to be publicly interrogated about my own books and writing generally (a test of endurance I was also to experience in Japan). Dartmouth was apt to share sporting and other activities with Amherst College over the border in Massachusetts, a foundation I concurred in also visiting with a similar programme.

From Amherst I myself arranged to pass on to Cornell University at Ithaca in upstate New York. That was not so much because I wished to prolong what the girl at the US Consulate in London endorsed on my passport as 'informal lectures at Ivy League Colleges' as in order to see the Mizeners, who were in due course kind enough to put me up in their house at Ithaca. It was already in my mind that our younger son John might attend an American university, probably Cornell, and in the event he became an undergraduate there a few years later.

3

When Violet and I both stayed in Boston (again as guests of Little, Brown) in 1965 the restaurant of our hotel (The Ritz was out of commission being redecorated) was called *The Hungry Pilgrim*. Outside stood an examplar of esurient puritanism dressed in a black-and-white Cromwellian costume with hair in a pigtail, which was a shade anachronistic and had not yet become at all chic for men. From time to time, looking as if he had just landed from *The Mayflower* and was in urgent need of a square meal, this gaunt figure would ring a bell.

In general, however, Boston, a city of considerable charm, suggests a date later than the 17th century, though there are fine buildings of that period. The Common, a green stretch sloping steeply down from the red-brick houses of Beacon Hill (for which the cliché mellow is inescapable), ends in the more modern lower town with its somewhat Austrian or Swiss air. The ensemble gives a touch of a more metropolitan Tunbridge Wells.

Boston does not disappoint. Even on the briefest visit one can detect layer upon layer of the Bostonianism celebrated in such a long American literary tradition. When I was there in 1961 Little, Brown's, with much other entertaining, gave me luncheon at that haunt of ancient peace, shrine of Boston brahminism, the Somerset Club. The party on that occasion consisted of my host Alex Williams, another director Randall Williams, John Cushman my 'editor' (the American term always carries a slightly ironic ring for one who has himself worked in an English publishing firm), Bob Fetridge the PR man (my constant companion at meals with journalists in the high-backed wooden seats of Locke-Ober's), and the late Edwin O'Connor, an American novelist I had already come across in England.

The Somerset Club is deservedly famous. I doubt if any club in London could equal—certainly none surpass—the inspissated and enveloping club atmosphere of The Somerset. Ancient armchairs and sofas underpropped one or two equally antiquated members, ossified into states of Emersonian catalepsy in which shadow and sunlight were not only the same, but had long freed them from shame or fame. It was comforting to see so splendid a haunt from the past surviving intact in a widely disintegrating world. I hope the Somerset Club still remains untainted by modern barbarisms.

Ed O'Connor, large, talkative, master of a quiet but lively conversational style, was a fellow Little, Brown author. His novels, notably *The Last Hurrah* (1956), were about Boston political life, and he himself, as celebrator of a very different sort of Boston to that surrounding the party at the Somerset Club, was without Bostonian reserve. He produced a story about Evelyn Waugh which, although turning out to be wholly chimerical, deserves to be put on record for its surrealist overtones.

O'Connor said that a few weeks before he had been chatting with a senior member of the firm, 'old' Mr Thornhill of Little, Brown's, a publisher, like Charlie Scribner, very much of a former generation. Mr Thornhill had suddenly expressed aloud to O'Connor what sounded like a long bottled-up grievance.

'You know, Ed, I don't like writers.'

This was a painful admission from a lifelong publisher, one not altogether easy for an author to answer off the cuff. O'Connor temporized.

'You don't, Mr Thornhill?'

Mr Thornhill relented a little. At least he qualified his earlier unmitigated detestation.

'I like you, Ed, and I like Marquand, and I like Thornton W. Burgess, but I don't like most of them—and *I don't like Evelyn Waugh.*'

John P. Marquand (a writer to whom Violet is much addicted) is less known in the UK than in the US, perhaps surprisingly because Marquand more nearly represents an English tradition of writing, the novel of manners, than many American novelists. Marquand books deal with the Harvard end of American society, he also wrote successful detective stories, and it was no surprise to find that Mr Thornhill approved of so respectable, well-informed, patrician, disillusioned, an author.

Thornton W. Burgess, unread in Great Britain, but so far as I know still looked on as a popular writer of children's books about animals in his own country, might be compared with Beatrix Potter. Here again Mr Thornhill's approbation gave no cause for surprise.

A story no doubt lay behind Mr Thornhill's strongly expressed objection to Waugh. O'Connor pressed the matter further.

'What makes you feel that way about Waugh?'

'He behaved in a very silly manner.'

'Where did that happen?'

'He dined with me.'

'And it didn't go well?'

'He ordered all sorts of ridiculous things.'

'To eat?'

'Yes.'

'I believe he looks upon himself as a gourmet.'

That was too much for Mr Thornhill. He spoke with loud indignation:
'*Three soups!*'

On my return to England I told Waugh this story. He was delighted.

At the same time, although Little-Brown's was certainly his American publisher he had no recollection of ever having met Mr Thornhill, still less dined with him and ordered three soups.

'Obviously this is a very important incident in my life,' Waugh said. 'I should like a full record of it for my memoirs. Would it be a great trouble for you to obtain further details about the occasion, and pass them on to me? I should like to know all the circumstances.'

I opened up an investigation. Unhappily it turned out after careful enquiry that Mr Thornhill Sr said he would have very much liked to meet Evelyn Waugh, but had never had the honour of doing so; his certainty that they had never been introduced to each other being even stronger than Waugh's. In short there had been no confrontation. O'Connor must have fabricated the anecdote or forgotten that it was two other people who were concerned. All the same 'Three soups!' must be admitted to be a good pay-off line.

4

John Meck picked me up at the hotel to continue the journey from Boston to Hanover by road. He was a tall lean New Englander, a figure from a James novel, quiet almost to the point of complete taciturnity, at the same time practical to a degree, and quick to pick up a literary reference. He said we were stopping for luncheon at Andover, one of his sons (aged fifteen, I think) having just entered this well known American boarding-school for boys.

Shared two-and-two, the boys' rooms at Andover were remarkably like those of an Eton house; indeed the whole atmosphere of the school reminded me of Eton in what appeared to be its unstrained easygoing tone. The impression could hardly have been more superficial, nor were all Eton houses easygoing. One just had that feeling. A small incident suggested a national difference. Meck asked: 'Are you allowed to drive with us as far as the restaurant?' His son fumbled in a pocket, produced a book of school rules, glanced at them, then said: 'That's OK.' Afterwards I could not decide in my own mind how an English schoolboy would have answered the question; somehow not quite like that.

The pleasing buildings of Dartmouth College date back to the 18th century. A charter was granted by King George III. For six months of the year New Hampshire is under snow; the Dartmouth Winter Carnival a famous institution. Here again Scott Fitzgerald crops up with his calamitous visit to Hanover in February 1939.

Fitzgerald and Budd Schulberg the novelist (*What Makes Sammy Run*), then a young script writer, were to seek local colour for a picture about the Carnival, the 'treatment' for which was already under way. The two of them had stayed at The Hanover Inn, where (while at the same time enjoying a great deal of hospitality at the home of John and Jean Meck) I too put up.

The Fitzgerald débâcle was later made subject of a novel, *The Disenchanted* (1951), by Schulberg, a Dartmouth man himself, considerably junior in age to Fitzgerald, whom he revered but supposed dead before embarking on their collaboration. Subsequently Schulberg denied that the Fitzgerald-type in the novel was by any means wholly modelled on his companion, and certainly the admiration which this character shows for the Schulberg-type hardly fits in with Fitzgerald's estimate of himself.

While on the ever fascinating subject of novelists' models it might be noted that Schulberg, son of a head of production in one of the big studios, born and bred in Hollywood, may for his part (*en travestie*) have contributed a few hints to Fitzgerald for Cecilia Brady in *The Last Tycoon*, who had a similar Hollywood upbringing.

Setting out together in the first instance by air to New York, thence by train to Hanover, Fitzgerald and Schulberg opened up an extensive carousal from the moment they stepped on to the plane from Hollywood. Even had they arrived sober things would have gone badly from the start, since they had omitted to make reservations at The Hanover Inn, where they had to sleep in an attic equipped with a double-decker bunk; austere couch for Hanover hangovers.

The final *Götterdämmerung* of Fitzgerald and Schulberg as employees of the film company concerned (although in fact Schulberg was later re-hired) is said to have taken place in the snow on the steps of The Hanover Inn; comic in its parody of oldtime melodrama; tragic in long term consequences for Fitzgerald. This Nemesis was also a happening far more lurid than anything likely to have been achieved by the projected Winter Carnival picture. I was glad to see the historic spot where banishment had been pronounced by the movie mogul locally in charge.

4

The organization of the sessions I attended at Dartmouth, and other foundations visited, impressed by the manner in which the participating academics were schooled. In questioning they would work like a team, never interrupting each other, nor allowing an awkward pause to take place. I think similar convocations in England would have been less disciplined, dons harder to keep in order, but perhaps at the same time more given to discussion afterwards when the official business was over.

At one of these public interrogations (I am not sure which college) a professor prefixed a question by saying—rather archly—that he was uncertain how to pronounce my name. As an inspiration of the moment I replied that like the Boston family of Lowell I rhymed it with Noël rather than towel.

I was later surprised at the manner in which this off-the-cuff comment spread ahead of me wherever I went, as things do in America. I feel no bigotry as to the usage in which I was brought up, certainly by no means universal, but the practice is not mere affectation. The sound made in Welsh when the names Powell and Howell are spoken in that language is not easy to transliterate into English pronunciation, and the fact that 16th and 17th century documents about Wales and the Marches often spell Powell as Poel must record more or less what the clerk heard. The tilting spears in the arms of the Norfolk family of Powell (no relation) may be a pun on 'pole'; certainly the case in their Welsh motto where 'pwyll' (sense, discretion) appears: Pwyll being also the name of the Prince of Dyfed in *The Mabinogion*.

After a very agreeable time at Dartmouth I was dispatched to Amherst in the collegiate automobile driven by an ex-Marine, what's called in the army a good type. He had been in the Corps during the second war, and served beside British Commando units, about which he was complimentary beyond the needs of politeness. He particularly praised their lack of fuss.

I spoke in return of the prestige enjoyed by the US Marine Corps, which seemed so much in contrast with the all but anonymous regiments of the American army. I said it always seemed odd to a European that, apart from the Marines, no US regiment appeared to possess a public 'image'; yet many units must go back, if not to the Revolution and 1812, at least to the Mexican War so far as traditions went.

The driver laughed. 'Sure the Marines are a crack corps,' he said. 'On pay day most of the men contribute a dollar or fifty cents to the collection box for the Marine Corps Publicity Fund.'

And after all why not?

At Amherst I stayed at The Lord Jeffrey, named after Jeffrey 1st Lord Amherst, much associated with the North American wars against the French, in due course Field Marshal. I was shown round the College, in general looked after, by Ben DeMotte, himself a writer, and a man with a proper regard for not always being too serious.

Among other things DeMotte took me to an informal talk on Zen philosophy given to a group of star undergraduates by the President of Amherst. The President read aloud some Haiku. He did not include any practical demonstrations of Zen taking a violent form, but the experience was nevertheless an interesting one. Afterwards I tried to imagine which head of an Oxford house known to me would have been most unexpected expounding Zen.

I also sat in on a class for that strange subject 'Creative Writing' conducted by the American poet Rolph Humphries, then approaching seventy. He read his students passages from various books, more or less wellknown, which they had to identify. I should have been quite at sea. Afterwards Humphries showed me examples of their work, prose and verse, perhaps twenty or thirty of each.

The prose was decidedly ragged; the poetry, on the other hand, varied and alive. I found this contrast surprising, wondering if the same would be true of a chance group of undergraduates in the UK. The prose of the Amherst class made clear long American abandonment of Latin, even a smattering of that ancient tongue a help in dealing with a language like English. Constant Lambert used to say that he found the small amount of Latin he knew helpful even in knocking off an article for a daily paper.

But this survey of mine was all twenty years ago. No doubt changes have taken place in teaching everywhere, one suspects not always for the better.

Another member of the English Faculty at Amherst was William Pritchard, who has since written several acute critical works. I was having a drink with Pritchard and another of the younger Amherst dons when two elderly professors dropped in by chance. We talked about English writers. I happened to mention my own liking for Surtees, who always seems to me one of the best no-nonsense social historians for the first half of the 19th century in England. When the two older men left Pritchard and the other young don said almost in the same breath: 'How marvellous that you talked about a Victorian novelist like Surtees. It's always suspected that no one whose books we like reads anything but the latest literary fad. This will do us a lot of good.'

I found that as unexpected as the students' poetry being better than their prose.

On proceeding to Cornell I stayed in Ithaca with the Mizeners, who were later boundlessly kind to John when he attended the University in 1965. Mizener, as a friend, was in a position to blackmail me into an exertion I had hitherto avoided, that is to say giving a lecture. In preparation for that contingency taking shape I had in fact brought with me a draft of some sort of talk on The Novel delivered under duresse on one or two occasions before.

I fought back to the extent of saying that if I were forced to give a lecture I could do so only by including a reading of certain passages translated from the *Satyricon* of Petronius, as these were part of the argument in illustrating how novels are written. A search was made. It turned out that the only English translation of the *Satyricon* to be found in the libraries of Cornell was a comparatively recent one rendered in Twenties gangster slang. I was told afterwards that Petronius read aloud in an English accent, and transferred to the language of an Edward G. Robinson or George Raft gangster movie, was bizarre in the extreme.

Perhaps in connexion with this Petronian reading I remarked to Mizener that as protagonist (if that much abused term may be used in the context) of these public appearances in American colleges I was surprised never to have had my leg pulled by undergraduates; something that would almost certainly have taken place in a British university. Mizener replied to the effect that the American student went to college to get an education, and expected to do that in a serious manner.

There was a certain irony in this explanation (though true that again in one sense seriousness rather than frivolity was in question), because American academic life (European too for that matter) was on the brink of some of the worst student troubles known to history.

Nonetheless one recognizes the fundamental truth of Mizener's comment. The student disturbances of the 1960s, both in Europe and America, were largely the consequence of the romanticism of youth, urged on by the international cult of self-pity, essentially humourless, without any of that lightness of touch which universities should impart to the young, thereby giving understanding of life.

5

At one of the parties I attended at Cornell a lady said: 'There is a very shy girl who wants to meet you, and would never dare, etc. etc.' This was my introduction to Alison Lurie, then married to a Cornell don, Jonathan Bishop, son of the poet John Peale Bishop, contemporary of Scott Fitzgerald at Princeton.

Since Alison Lurie is one of the most determined personalities I know, her presentation as the essence of diffidence has always appealed to me. I was not told that she had already written a privately printed work *V. R. Lang: a Memoir* (1959: reprinted in *Poems and Plays by V. R. Lang*, 1975), and that her first novel *Love and Friendship* (1964) must have been on the way to being fixed up with Heinemann (one of the peculiarities of Alison Lurie's literary career being that first publications were in England). After ten minutes conversation I saw that undoubtedly one would hear more of this supposedly shy girl. I can't remember whether we met again on that visit to Cornell, but we have done so on many subsequent occasions.

V. R. Lang is an evocative piece in its genre, well suggesting a dead friend and young people's group intellectual life, but in general Alison Lurie's theme is marital discord, the various forms that takes. My own favourite is *The Nowhere City* (1965), set in Hollywood, though not primarily about movie people. The horrors of married life in academic surroundings reach a crescendo in her best known and longest novel *The War Between the Tates* (1974).

Uneasy marriage is also hinted at in *Real People* (1969), which preceded *The Tates* and deals with a 'retreat' for writers. Perhaps her most unusual novel is *Imaginary Friends* (1967): two professors set out on a sociological project to study an obscure sect believing itself in touch with beings from Outer Space, one of the investigators himself becoming a convert.

Alison Lurie was with us once on an Hellenic cruise. The ship was sailing by that stretch of Greek coastline ornamented by the monasteries of Mount Athos. She passed when I was standing by the ship's side talking to General Sir John Hackett, one of the guest lecturers. That night at dinner she said: 'I heard the General say to you *Of course the first thing to decide is whether meditation is an action or a condition.* You know that's not the way American generals talk.'

When I suggested (p. 100) that Budd Schulberg may have contributed to the picture of Cecilia Brady in *The Last Tycoon* I had not read M. J. Bruccoli's *Some Sort of Epic Grandeur* (1982), in which Fitzgerald is recorded as saying that Cecilia was a combination of his daughter Scottie and Schulberg.

VI

Thespian Moods

After spasmodic comings and goings in the theatrical world extending over about two years a dramatized version of my first novel *Afternoon Men* was given a four weeks' run at the New Arts Theatre Club (just off Charing Cross Road) in the summer of 1963.

This fulfilment was principally due to the energy of a young American director Roger Graef, who entered the field after the project of staging *Afternoon Men* had been virtually abandoned, at best postponed *sine die*. By that time an adaptation of the novel had already been made by Riccardo Aragno, an Italian scriptwriter based on London. The presentation of the play was undertaken by a company called J. B. Productions of which I knew nothing.

Written when I was twenty-three or twenty-four *Afternoon Men* can possibly claim some of that first-novel *élan* which, whatever other existent faults, can never afterwards be quite recaptured, but the story, so far as there is one, was not in the first instance designed with any thought of subsequent transformation into a play. The book is not without all pattern (in the light of being a first attempt), but scarcely any plot as plots are usually thought of is to be found there, while the moments of dramatic action take place in the middle rather than as a final climax.

Indeed the title of the third and last section *Palindrome*, applies to the whole novel, which opens and closes with the same situation; the anti-hero Atwater about to set out for a bohemian party of the kind he has attended in the opening pages of the book.

Plenty of plays begin and end with the same or similar situation, but usually these have been constructed in such a way that the termination makes a sharp impact on the audience. The techniques of the novel are very different. James's exhortation: 'Dramatize, dramatize' is almost always good advice for novelists, but drama in a novel can be powerful even if long drawn out and underemphasized; sometimes even the better for that. In the case of *Afternoon Men* the palindrome—so to speak the drama—reasonably apparent on the printed page, could easily be overlooked in the theatre.

In short it was clear that considerable demands would be made on the skill of any adapter, probably on the good will of the audience too. The theatrical passport to the sort of play *Afternoon Men* was likely to make is apt to be endorsed with the visa 'Chekhovian' (however different in content and feeling from the work of that dramatist). In fact Chekhov abhorred the manner in which his own plays were usually produced, even in Russia, disapproving of the label 'frustrated' that was applied to his characters, and always insisting that *The Cherry Orchard* ought to be played as a rousing comedy.

Riccardo Aragno (who came from Turin), tired of politics after fifteen years of being London correspondent of *La Stampa*, had turned with success to stage and screen. He had complete and fluid command of English, combined with thorough understanding of late 1920s atmosphere, the world the novel depicted, where individual romanticism fights a losing battle in the no-man's-land of sub-intellectual life. Aragno and I had no disagreements whatever about his treatment of the book, and throughout ups and downs of presentation no one could have been a more sympathetic associate.

Roger Graef, ardent in devotion to the project itself and tireless in the work he put into the play, never, so it seemed to me, quite got the hang of *Afternoon Men*'s period (naturally before his own), nor the London scene that provided its background; a parallel with which he had probably never run across in American life. Thus the sceptical tone of the characters, perfectly familiar to Aragno, always seemed alien to Graef, who among other misapprehensions inclined to upgrade them all socially.

For Graef, for instance, the girls were debs, rather than artists' models and 'mannequins' living on their wits, and a similar tendency took place throughout all the directing. There were also occasional disharmonies between director and hard-worked cast, though no doubt such are far from unknown in most productions. Nonetheless, without Roger Graef *Afternoon Men* would never have been put on at The Arts, an experience I should be sorry to have missed.

Let me repeat that I have never been in the least stage-struck, but as the preliminaries of production began to take shape I became very conscious of the fascination which the Theatre exerts. This was not only in the technical antitheses spoken of above—the contrast of what is dramatic in a novel, what dramatic in a play—but also in the actual physical effervescence generated round one by all that goes with mounting a theatrical performance: the transformation of ideas into the physical actions of men and women; the changes in one's own apprehensions which such visual vitalizings effect; the complicated human relationships which immediately come into being among the various individuals concerned with the whole operation.

A pleasant aspect of The Arts as a place of presentation was the personality of the Club's general manager Richard Schulman, an old hand at the Theatre, who knew every move of the game and trick of the trade. Schulman was always goodnatured, always enthusiastic, above all always ready for a good laugh (though confessing that what he really enjoyed at a play was a good cry), particularly a good laugh on the subject of the foibles of actors, directors, anyone else in showbiz, not least at their foibles where sex was concerned.

Afternoon Men did not demand much in the way of staging (an ingeniously stylized set with a staircase worked equally well for parties, restaurants, night-clubs, flats, country cottages). There had been some discussion earlier as to how much the play should be represented 'in period'. Finally 'costumes' were designed to fit the Twenties without too much stress on that era as such. Long hair for men, which would have complicated the question, had mercifully not begun its years of Absalomian luxuriance.

Rather incongruously, however, certain lines were added which referred to such contemporary preoccupations as Guided Missiles and dancing The Twist. I am not sure whether Aragno wrote those in—actors cannot be prevented from uttering scraps of improvised dialogue or gags of their own —as there had been general agreement that the characters of the play were not at all dated, nor for that matter the circumstances. The view was flattering to myself as author, but looking back I am inclined to think that even relative modernization, however minor, was in principle unwise.

The cast of *Afternoon Men*—additionally with the passing of time—could reasonably be called distinguished in its names. The anti-hero Atwater, languishing for love of the beautiful Susan Nunnery, but consoling himself with Lola (unsurnamed in the novel) was played by James Fox: Susan by Georgina Ward: Lola by Pauline Boty.

James Fox seemed to me everything that was required, and, unlike so many actors, was capable of speaking the throwaway line effectively. Georgina Ward in looks and temperament was ideally suited for the part of Susan. Pauline Boty, immensely funny in the seduction scene, was really too pretty and charming for a character intended to be a trifle grotesque, for whom an actress in, say, the tradition of that incomparable comic film star Zazu Pitts would have been preferable. Pauline Boty was in truth a painter (Lola a poster-designer) as well as a talented actress. It was tragic that she should have died suddenly a year or two later.

The rest of the men in the cast have all made names for themselves, indeed were far from unknown then. Peter Bowles played Pringle (also a painter, owner of the country cottage where much of the action takes place). Jeremy Kemp played Barlow (another painter, who seduces Pringle's girl Harriet at the cottage). Alan Howard played Fotheringham (the drunken commentator on life), whose performance specially struck me, though all were admirable.

Harriet's part was taken by Imogen Hassall (rather an unhappy figure later to get a good deal of publicity and die of an over-dose), a beauty undoubtedly, but not *gamine* enough for what she had to do. She was daughter of the poet and librettist Christopher Hassall, protégé of the art patron Sir Edward Marsh, whose biography he wrote. We had seen something of Imogen Hassall's father on the *Canada* when sailing to California via Panama (*Faces*). He had been decidedly stand-offish on the ship. I gathered from his daughter that it had been a moment of great nervous tension for him as to whether or not he and her mother would marry.

2

At an early rehearsal of *Afternoon Men* an incident took place—no doubt common enough in the life of the practised dramatist, but new in my own case as a novelist without theatrical experience, which greatly impressed me. It is one I have often pondered. Alan Howard, trying out a long rambling drunken speech uttered by Fotheringham, said: 'I can do this several ways. Which would you like?'

Howard then proceded to demonstrate three altogether different styles which he could adopt in playing the part. I found of absorbing interest that a character I had invented might, by the art of a brilliant actor, be so to speak split into three, perhaps expanded almost indefinitely. The fact that Fotheringham was somewhat modelled on Bobby Roberts added to the interest, as Roberts, the model, might move closer or farther away, but the essentials of Fotheringham remained the same to be variously mimed.

The question at once posed itself: to what extent does the novelist 'realize' the characters created on paper? The dramatist is in rather a different position. Even in the first instance the dramatist knows that an actor (I use the term to include the always slightly suspect noun actress) will add something to what has been specifically written for that medium. Although even in the case of the dramatist differences of opinion can obviously arise with actor or producer, the dramatist's work has something in it of the painter who, knowing colours will slightly fade or change, allows for that in the chiaroscuro.

The novelist, on the other hand (if satisfied with what has been written), sees the characters as complete when the novel is finished. Even with the novel that cannot be so absolutely on account of the deep abyss between writer and reader. This is something often brought home to the novelist; never more so than when readers suppose a character in a novel is based on an existing individual known to the writer, thereby revealing a vision quite other than the author's.

Even in the case of a play written for the stage, when by definition, actor and director have their say before the consumer is reached, how far should these two elements be conditioned to interpret what—perhaps only what—the writer himself is aware of? Should an actor not only develop the part, but perhaps even represent it in opposition to the author's point of view; thereby accepting that a fictional character, as in the case of a 'real human being', is sufficiently alive to make more than one judgment possible? One thinks of Pirandello.

Chekhov, chosen as an example not only because referred to above, also because his own views on the matter were uncompromising, opposed any such thing. Chekhov knew precisely what he wanted. His aim was to extract from actor and director all that his own intensely professional workman-ship had laid down. Most other writers with whom I have discussed the question take in principle the Chekhovian line; characters must be re-presented as closely as possible to the author's original concept.

These writers presuppose an unalterable view of the actor's subordinate role. No doubt that is safer. I myself remain a little uncertain as to whether it is immutable.

When from time to time a novel of my own has been adapted for radio I have sometimes thought an individual actor 'wrong' in the manner the part has been tackled. Usually, however, the wrongness (from the author's point of view) is due not to the actor having brought a new interpretation to the character (one of which as author I might disapprove), but because the actor in question seems to have been miscast, or simply given an indifferent performance. Indeed such reservations as I have occasionally felt have been (unexpectedly to myself) because characters in the novel have been underplayed rather than acted in too corny a style.

On the other hand, having admitted to occasional dissatisfactions with metamorphosis from novel to dramatic form, I am at the same time attrac-ted by potential development (even if necessary change) of the original character placed in the hands of a talented actor; though certainly nothing short of an actor of the highest gifts. After all *Hamlet* can be played a hundred ways, something that enhances rather than diminishes the genius of Shakespeare; though it should be remembered that Hamlet himself said: 'Let them that play your clowns speak no more than is set down for them'; indicating that The Bard as much as anyone else suffered from intruding gags.

When actually writing a novel one is at times conscious of an external agency taking over the job, something beyond the processes of thought, conscious planning, or invention. In a similar manner could not an accom-plished actor draw out yet more from a character and situation than the author has been aware of; subtleties of human personality revealed only to an expert practitioner of the actor's art?

In saying this I certainly do not mean that (as customary in Hollywood) the structure of a novel should be altered, its tone popularized, but that within the sphere of the relationships laid down by the novelist much may be opened up in another creative field.

No doubt the answer as usual abides in the potency of the art available. If the art is there in actor and director I incline to think it should be so far as possible uncircumscribed within the terms of reference; the extent of its possibilities being in the last resort gratifying to the author.

In this connexion Aragno used to say that there were certain lines no actor, not even the best, could speak. An author had to face that. The actor's training, designed to get the most out of every word or lack of words, every gesture or rejection of gesture, causes (said Aragno) the re-presentation of various types of individual or throwaway line of speech impossible to obtain on any stage; the very personality of a first-class actor, even before speech, in itself militating against an underplaying that may in fact be required.

The cast of *Afternoon Men*, an accomplished and delightful crowd, showed an inflexible loyalty and gaiety throughout what was, from door to door, a far from untroubled run. Their understanding and good sense were a revelation to me. One often reads of the 'sterling qualities' of those usually styled in such eulogies 'theatrical folk'. I had remained unconvinced. Such qualities are sometimes less apparent off the stage on unprofessional occasions, liable to be mistaken for gush. I was now made to feel ashamed of such doubts. The sterling qualities were outstandingly demonstrated in unpropitious circumstances.

3

I was not able to be present when the curtain was rung up on the First Night of *Afternoon Men* at The Arts on 22 August 1963. The date of that *première* had for one reason or another been chopped and changed about so often that the play eventually opened on a day we had irretrievably arranged to fly to Venice for embarkation on a fortnight's Hellenic cruise. The best I could do was to send an encouraging telegram to the cast.

At a comparatively early hour (we were still in bed) the following morn-ing Aragno telephoned our Venetian hotel room to report on preliminary notices. They were reasonably long but considerably less than rapturous. I had the impression, a correct one, that the show had not got off to a good start, even if one or two of the critics were more amicable than others.

As a veteran of literary criticism on both sides of the fence I had not before experienced critics of the drama. Although, as individuals, some of these combine or have at some time combined both vocations, theatrical critics remain on the whole a very different race from literary ones, anyway while following the former calling.

By the nature of their job dramatic critics are more powerful than literary critics. The latter can—indeed often do—make foolish misjudgments in the way of praise or blame, but their effect on a book is except in rare cases very relative. An exceptionally popular reviewer (Arnold Bennett is customarily trotted out as an example in the past) may sell a few hundred copies of a book that has been overlooked, a few thousands of one that is already doing pretty well, but even the rudest notice can usually do no more than put a slight break on sales if a book is really 'what the public wants' or seems worth reading for more recondite reasons. Dramatic critics, on the other hand, can, anyway in bulk, wreck a play. The egos of dramatic critics accordingly grow proportionately inflated, their judgments more erratic.

Dramatic critics, unlike literary critics, must also make up their minds rapidly, probably dictate an article immediately over the telephone, when at worst a book-reviewer can sleep a night digesting what has been read before the morning excretion of views. There is a certain rightness in this. If the rest of a theatre audience register an immediate reaction, it is putting dramatic critics on the same level as the public for which they are catering in having no opportunity to turn the play over in the mind before passing an opinion; a process in all the arts which can often modify judgment one way or the other.

In addition to these things book reviewers rarely discuss the book in hand with a dozen other members of their profession, all reviewing the same book, in a bar while consuming drinks between chapters.

In the case of the *Afternoon Men* adaptation many of the dramatic critics—while sparing a crumb of praise for the novel itself—deplored the subject of a play dealing with drifting purposeless promiscuous young bohemians. That was not the way young people ought to behave. If they did behave like that plays should not be written about them.

This was precisely the condemnation visited on the novel in 1931. Now the novel seemed to have become morally exculpated from this particular form of censure, but in 1963 the play was still reprobated by exactly the

113

same puritanical standards as those of thirty years before. I record this simply as a fact of social rather than aesthetic note, that dramatic critics as a class stubbornly maintained an old fashioned morality that the apparently laxer literary critics had long abandoned.

Qui s'excuse s'accuse is never more applicable than when writers try to justify their own writings in whatever form. I attempt no 'defence' of *Afternoon Men* as a play (a medium for which it was not written in the first instance) beyond saying that when we returned to London, and I attended several performances, I found myself, admittedly an interested party, amused rather than bored.

Moreover that appeared to be the feeling of the rest of the audience, though the theatre, small as it was, remained always three-quarters empty. Some of the critics' complaints were undoubtedly valid, for example, that there were far too many short scenes, and that a wholly miscalculated comic waiter had been disastrously inserted to ruin a love scene. Even so the impression remained that the show was not as bad as all that; in fact rather funny.

The Arts being a club the public could not queue up at the box-office and buy a ticket, to be purchased only by a card-carrying member of at least twenty-four hours' standing. Membership was attainable for some quite modest sum, but one's friends, who would certainly have turned up at any ordinary West End theatre, were on the whole understandably reluctant to make a decision as to how an evening might be spent twenty-four hours in advance. In consequence houses were thin, not to say gaunt. It was then that my admiration for the cast took shape. They played every night with the spirit of a Command Performance at The Haymarket or Drury Lane.

One of the two or three critics who spoke warmly of the *Afternoon Men* adaptation was the anonymous representative of the *Times Educational Supplement* (6 September 1963) in a longish piece headed *Latecomer's Luck*. Perhaps I may be forgiven for quoting some of its paragraphs, not so much for the praise, however acceptable, as for the comment on why the show was displeasing to some of the journalists who panned it.

The writer began by remarking that he had been unable to attend the play's First Night, having had to cover the Edinburgh Festival. He went on to say:

'In general this [*Afternoon Men*] was given a pretty rough passage from the critics: it did not hang together as a play: it was just a string of inane, empty conversations, which might have some point given the ironic content of the novel but did not begin to stand up by themselves. It was outdated and irrelevant . . . So in some trepidation I went along, and to my great surprise found a witty, sophisticated and wholly delightful entertainment, remarkably well acted by everyone and admirably staged . . . Far from being dated and irrelevant, it was all too uncomfortably relevant: the horrifying thing is the way that everything Mr Powell wrote thirty years ago is immediately recognizable today . . . but nobody is there to say tut-tut or moralize about the Bomb . . . no humanist heart is being worn on a liberal sleeve, and that, it seems, is for most of our serious theatre critics the one unforgiveable sin in a play about modern society.'

I was grateful for this exposé, however long after the ball it appeared. Another postscript was written fifteen years later.

When we toured India we made two American friends, Bill Robinson and his wife Virginia, who were again in the same party as ourselves in Iran. Bill Robinson once delighted me by repeating a formula used by a fellow Kansas lawyer when lunching with him *à deux*: 'Separate checks, waiter, we ain't romancin'.'

The Robinsons, in London in 1978 doing a round of theatres, rang up to say hullo. Almost the first words Robinson spoke were: 'I knew you wrote novels, but I'd no idea you'd had a play running in London that was a great success.'

I made some deprecatory remarks as to the dramatization of my first novel having been staged for a week or two at a theatre club, where it had been received without much enthusiasm. I could sense on the telephone that he supposed this comment a piece of typically British understatement.

'But it must have gone pretty well,' he said. 'There was a very complimentary reference to it in our theatre programme last night. I'll send the programme along before we leave.'

He did. Sure enough an item in the magazine part of the programme referred to the 'now celebrated performance of Anthony Powell's *Afternoon Men*'. In some mysterious manner the wine seemed to have matured.

4

The Kindly Ones (sixth volume of *Dance*, and that which linked the two wars) had been published the year before the staging of *Afternoon Men*. That was a juncture in the sequence when clearly plans had to be made for dealing with the period of the second war. I decided the war would require three volumes of narrative to cover its various aspects and their effect on the characters of the novel. Accordingly, making a rough estimate of the age I should be when the last of the war trilogy had been completed—and not wanting the engine to run down before the end of the journey—I settled at this point that *Dance* should be contained within twelve volumes.

In due course *The Valley of Bones* (1964), *The Soldier's Art* (1966), *The Military Philosophers* (1968), appeared at what had been the normal rate of one every two years, but I was now prepared for the moment to break that routine. After *The Valley of Bones*, the first following the halfway line, I felt a change might be worth trying, anyway for a short time.

Twelve volumes left a year or two in hand (if I remained alive) so far as Time was concerned; Time dominating not only the atmosphere of the novel, but also, inevitably, the techniques of its composition. A brief change in employment might fend off risk of growing stale. In short I wanted to try my hand at a play.

Among the hypnotic influences exercised by the Theatre none is more intoxicating than to hear one's own dialogue spoken on the stage. I had by then listened to adaptations of my earlier novels on radio, but for some reason radio in that respect has less fascination than 'the legitimate'. When *Afternoon Men* was performed I fell an easy victim to this contagion, particularly in the field discussed earlier of an actor being able to give wide variation to words I had written. In the event I wrote two plays, while as things turned out the regular biannual volumes of *Dance* kept up steady publication.

When the show came to an end a nucleus of those who had been in-volved in *Afternoon Men* continued to meet. Riccardo Aragno was still professionally interested in the play's possibilities, and, with a view to having another shot at placing it in the West End, talked of polishing up his adaptation in the light of what was to be learnt from the staging at The

Arts. Richard Schulman always loved to discuss any theatrical venture however remote. Georgina Ward, whose forceful personality had done much to help the production through some of its more troublesome interludes, was not only keen to appear in a new version, but continually urged me to write a play with a good part for herself.

All these elements had their effect in creating an accumulation of exterior pressures which, strangely enough, can sometimes assist in stimulating certain forms of inventive writing. They are capable of setting the imagination working from new angles. There was also a sudden perceptible relief in getting away from the novel—ceasing to ponder novel writing at all—for at least a short while.

Georgina Ward loved to talk about herself, her feelings, her relations, her career on the boards, half-consciously creating a dramatic personality, not necessarily her own in truth, but suitable to work over as a character in a play. Her firmness of personal definition was allied to an often acknowledged waywardness, which, in spite of much hard work, would always, I think, have caused her to stop short of that easy malleability, total dedication, required of an actor: the condition of having no other life but the Theatre.

In fact her instinct for the Theatre was at least equally an intellectual one, which made her of great assistance in criticizing a script. She had strong opinions, not only experience of acting but of employment on the play-reading side of a literary agency. Her advice about getting the two plays into shape made me want to dedicate them to her. As neither achieved production, nor were they published in book form until 1971, in place of that *The Military Philosophers* had to be the dedication; but the Plays were meant.

5

The first play *The Garden God* was a fantasy. Its theme emerged, I suppose, from the many archaeological sites visited at one time or another on Hellenic cruises. Priapus, Roman deity of Procreation and Horticulture, is by chance conjured up by a group of archaeologists excavating one of his shrines on a small Greek island. Enraged by their ineptitudes Priapus makes himself manifest. The disturbed god angrily investigates the sexual habits of these intruders, notably their failings in the light of the physical worship they owe him.

Richard Schulman, whose opinion was worth having, showed himself well disposed towards *The Garden God*. He set the wheels in motion by introducing me to a friend of his who turned up the very moment after Schulman had read the play. This was William Donaldson, who had been in the past concerned with various theatrical projects, but absented himself from that world for several years. Now he felt a growing desire to return.

Donaldson, a pale fair-haired young man of decidedly raffish appearance, educated at Winchester and Cambridge, had been mixed up with the production of *Beyond the Fringe*, *The Bed-sitting Room*, *An Evening of British Rubbish*, the first of which especially made a hit. Donaldson had for some reason never managed to cash in on these former good connexions, and now hoped to re-establish himself.

Schulman suggested that he read *The Garden God*. Donaldson did so, and liked the play. He and Schulman put forward a few minor alterations in the script. These were made without difficulty. An option was arranged through my agent with a company Donaldson knew of. The first step towards staging *The Garden God* had been taken.

Throughout the first half of 1966 Willie Donaldson, Richard Schulman, and myself, used to meet regularly at different London restaurants, each choosing a rendezvous and paying for luncheon in turn. We would discuss ways and means of getting the play afloat, with such matters as director and cast. These lunches were thoroughly enjoyable. They also added to a sense of escape from novel-writing routine, though far from valueless in covering ground which in one way or another might be employed as novel material at some future date.

As time went on it really looked as if *The Garden God* would be up in lights one day. Before proceeding to its production Donaldson was committed to putting on another show to be called, so far as I remember, *Knights of the Comedy*. This was to be an attempt to revive the glories of the oldtime English music-hall, of which many people (for instance Leslie Marsh on *Punch*) had always remained devoted fans. Donaldson took me to see some of the scenes which were being rehearsed at The Arts.

'This is going to set the London Theatre back ten years,' he said amiably.

23. Violet, AP and Sir Mortimer Wheeler, Delhi, 1969

24. Violet on the road to Swat, 1966

25. Kingsley Amis, 1958 (taken by Philip Larkin on the outskirts of Soho)

26. Rupert Hart-Davis, at a Duff Cooper prize meeting at New College, Oxford, 1961

27. V. S. Naipaul at The Chantry, 1963

28. Roy Fuller at The Chantry, 1968

29. AP Hon. D. Litt, Oxford, 1980.
Balliol Chapel in the background

30. Robert Conquest and
Bluebell at Golden Gate, 1977

31. Violet, Royal Wedding celebration aboard *MTS Orpheus*, 1981

32. AP, Royal Wedding celebration aboard *MTS Orpheus*, 1981

The merits of the show were hard to judge critically from the few knockabout numbers I watched, but they seemed amusing enough. Certainly I had no impression of imminent disaster. I think had all else prospered *Knights of the Comedy* might well have been a success.

Before the West End opening a try-out was to take place in Liverpool. Everything was arranged for the First Night when a series of blows began to descend.

In the beginning the Liverpool theatre had a much larger stage than The Arts, so that the cast required a day or two's extra rehearsing over and above time allowed. Meanwhile a car containing certain essential props for some of the scenes was stolen on the way up to Liverpool. New props had to be acquired, or some rearrangements of scenes devised. In consequence of these mishaps—there were at least two or three others, including, I think, the leading lady falling sick—the First Night at Liverpool had to be postponed for at least a week.

This delay naturally meant that more money was needed. Donaldson travelled south to see his usual 'angel', who lived far enough from London to necessitate a whole day's visit. After spending morning and afternoon talking things over the angel came to a negative conclusion. He would advance no more money. That was flat. Donaldson, much cast down, left the angel, but with one last trump up his own sleeve.

Like Maclaren-Ross (though I imagine on a larger scale) Donaldson came from a shipping family, and a respectable amount of money was entailed on him at the death of an aged uncle. The Trust in which the capital was vested was controlled by this uncle, with whom Donaldson himself was on the worst of terms.

In a crisis such as this delicacies of family feeling had to be disregarded. Donaldson went to see his uncle, to whom he explained what a mess had come about. He asked that in order to be tided over this awkward period a comparatively small sum should be put at his disposal (if necessary to be paid back later) as legatee of funds that he would in any case ultimately inherit.

After much persuasion the uncle agreed that the requisite amount should be made available at a Liverpool bank by the time Donaldson returned there.

Donaldson took the train back to Liverpool thinking that anyway for the moment the problem was solved. The following morning he went to the bank named as that from which the money was to be drawn. He was taken in to the manager. The manager explained that Donaldson's uncle had indeed made arrangements the previous day for the sum in question to be advanced. That very morning early—in fact first thing—the uncle had rung up to say that he had changed his mind. He wanted the previous instruction cancelled.

This unhappy story was retailed to me by Richard Schulman. Even he, I think, had received it secondhand, possibly from a former girlfriend of Donaldson's. Donaldson himself now withdrew from general circulation. No one seemed to know where he had gone. I never set eyes on him again in the flesh.

A long time later, however, I once or twice saw Donaldson's name in a gossip-column accompanied by a photograph, and in 1975 a firm of publishers unknown to me by name sent a work in paperback entitled: *Both the Ladies and the Gentlemen: the Memoirs of a London Brothel-Keeper in the 1970s*, by William Donaldson. On its blurb the author was quoted in giving an opinion that 'as I might be the only ponce with a pen, it was of some importance that I kept a record of various comings and goings.'

That seemed a perfectly allowable claim, though perhaps importance was not quite the word. I saw no reason to disbelieve the gist of what this volume chronicled about the author's activities in the sphere specified.

Some years after the publication of these autobiographical gleanings Donaldson surfaced once more in print, this time not precisely as author. Under the *nom de guerre* of Henry Root he published two volumes of spoof letters he had written, signed with that equivocal pseudonym, to various persons of eminence or notoriety, together with answers received from them. These collections of Letters were frequently quoted in newspaper Bestseller Lists.

On the matter of these Lists I should like to interpolate a reminiscence of my own. When I was at Duckworth's the firm published 'on commission' (i.e. paid for by the writer) a volume of verse in the manner of Swinburne put out after release from prison by a financier called Gerard Lee Bevan, who had in some manner transgressed in City dealings. Bevan's Poems appeared at least once if not more in the Bestseller Lists, when in fact Duckworth's had disposed of only three copies. That, however, is by the way, and I am sure did not apply to *The Root Letters*.

The Root Letters seemed to me of less interest than Donaldson's account of life as a souteneur. Everyone who has ever worked in almost any sort of office, let alone a governmental organization, knows that letters from crackpots arrive all the time and have to be given a formally polite answer.

Nevertheless Donaldson's literary output up to date does prove that it takes all sorts to create Old Wykehamists; both publications in their different ways emphasizing the truth of the school's motto that *Manners Mayketh Man*.

6

The shipwreck of the show in Liverpool, which took place in 1966, naturally brought on a miscarriage in the state of gestation reached by *The Garden God*'s theatrical pregnancy. In due course other producers and directors read the play, some expressing temperate interest, but nothing material ever resulted. I have myself sometimes wondered whether *The Garden God* might not make the basis of a 'musical'.

The Rest I'll Whistle was written quite soon after finishing *The Garden God*. The title is a quotation from *King Lear* (Kent in the stocks) but borrowed at closer range than Shakespeare, in fact from one of the chapter epigraphs in the Maclaren-Ross novel *Of Love and Hunger*.

The play is set in a small rarely visited manor house in remote country, administered by the National Trust or made in some similar fashion more or less a museum. It is looked after by a custodian in late middle-age, an intellectual who has been a failure in life, and is tormented by incestuous feelings towards his hippy daughter. There are other complications such as an alcoholic wife from whom the father is separated, and a bisexual American research student who becomes involved with the girl.

The lady then dealing with plays at my agent's thought *The Rest I'll Whistle* not only 'unpleasant' (shades of what was soon to come in the way of theatrical unpleasantness), but what was more important, unsaleable. She and I were on the best of terms. I saw her point on both issues.

It fell out, however, that the young man in principle dealing with film rights in the same firm read *Whistle*, and, while agreeing that some people might be shocked, was by no means convinced of the play's unsaleability. He suggested I hand it over to him with a view to having a look for the

121

right management. I pictured that at best to be something like *Afternoon Men*'s run at The Arts, or perhaps an 'off West End' theatre in Hampstead or the like.

This was in the late summer of 1966. That autumn Violet and I went on a trip to the Indian subcontinent led by Sir Mortimer Wheeler, of whom I shall speak in a later chapter. We were staying at Bangalore, in one of those detached bungalows characteristic of Indian and Pakistani hotels, when very unexpectedly one afternoon I found a cable thrust under the bungalow's front-door.

The cable was from my agent and announced that an option on *The Rest I'll Whistle* had been taken up by the theatrical management company of H. M. Tennent.

This news not merely surprised but astonished me. As I have said, I had allowed myself to envisage a few weeks' run in some very modest theatrical circumstances, scarcely considered a West End production of *Whistle* in the face of all that had been said against it by those calculated to know the form. Here was the most powerful management in London displaying interest. On return to England I immediately got in touch with my agent, congratulated him on this coup, and within a matter of days an interview was arranged with the redoubtable Binkie Beaumont of Tennent's.

Hugh Beaumont—never referred to as otherwise than Binkie—famous in song and story throughout the London theatrical world, hero (or anti-hero) of a thousand stage anecdotes, was virtual dictator of the West End Stage. Whatever befell I was glad to have an opportunity to cast an eye on so celebrated a figure, who in the normal course of events, as one rarely frequenting theatrical circles, I should have been unlikely to encounter.

I set off in the company of the young agent who had arranged the option. H. M. Tennent's offices were established on the upper floors of the Globe Theatre. To gain these topmost reaches of the building it was necessary to ascend in a lift—a legendary lift I discovered later—that might have been thought not specially roomy for a service lift in an hotel.

My agent and I could only just squeeze in. We found ourselves at once making apologies for the cramped nature of our proximity, which seemed to presume on a mere business relationship. In the same breath we both remarked on the convenience of such a vehicle for Binkie Beaumont to exercise snap judgments on the potentialities of young and unknown actors suddenly called upon to show their mettle at the closest of close quarters.

On extracting ourselves one by one from this funicular sardine-tin we entered Tennent's outer office. A moment later we were ushered into Binkie Beaumont's room.

He was then, I suppose, trembling on the brink of sixty, the embodiment of brisk genial well-preserved well turned out theatrical camp. His courtesy was quite overpowering. After we had sat down Binkie Beaumont began by saying that he had scarcely looked at the name on the typescript which 'they' had set in front of him; a faraway state of mind no doubt induced by the weighty responsibilities of showbiz that were his daily lot. He had languidly begun to scan a page or two.

'After a few lines I asked myself,' said Binkie Beaumont, 'but *who* has written this dialogue?'

Either he must have turned back to the title-page, or—more probably— an attendant sprite, hearing the strangled cry of excitement, had stepped forward apologetically to assist or enlighten the great man. '*Then I read your name . . .*'

I bowed some sort of embarrassed and quite inadequate acknowledgment of such commendation from such a source.

'I'm thinking of a *special* director for this play,' said Binkie Beaumont, speaking now very seriously. 'Not one of my usual ones.'

His voice suggested that such prosaic underlings as his 'usual ones' would fall far short of so exalted a task. He then mentioned the name of the director he had in mind.

I confess my heart sank. Was he quite the man? I had a twinge of doubt. I had heard more than one disconcerting story about him. Nevertheless who was I to mistrust the opinion of a figure who in theatrical matters was not only omniscient and omnipotent but not far from being omnipresent.

By this time Binkie Beaumont was enlarging on the cast of superlative talent that *The Rest I'll Whistle* would need to be at all adequately presented, toying with a series of great names in the Theatre, commending here, disparaging there, jettisoning not a few of both sexes whom he judged wanting in relation to matching their powers in so enviable an opportunity to display histrionic genius.

At last, more than a little overwhelmed, I said goodbye. My agent and I returned to the involuntarily chummy lift, scarcely noticing its restricted confinement after such a reception.

That was the last I ever saw of Binkie Beaumont; the last my agent or myself ever heard of the projected staging by H. M. Tennent of *The Rest I'll Whistle*. Letters remained unanswered; Mr Beaumont was always too momentously engaged to speak on the telephone: no one else in the office seemed to know anything about the negotiation.

In the end I put *Whistle* away in a drawer beside *The Garden God*. Both by then had admirable sets designed by Osbert Lancaster, which combined to illustrate when published *Two Plays by Anthony Powell* (1971).

Some years before that, indeed not very long after our meeting, Binkie Beaumont himself starred in that widely produced one-man show for which no option has to be arranged, no curtain calls are taken.

VII

Heyst's Magic Circle

In 1964, four hundredth anniversary of Shakespeare's birth, the Japanese, who possess boundless enthusiasm for the arts of the West, prepared appropriate celebrations. As part of these festivities the British Council in Tokyo organized a Book Exhibition. Also under the Council's auspices three writers were chosen as anthropological specimens of that trade in the United Kingdom to be dispatched to Japan for display.

I was one of these. The other two examples selected were Alan Pryce-Jones, an old friend for whom I had worked when he was editing the *Times Literary Supplement*, and Muriel Bradbrook, whom I had not met (in the event a wholly sympathetic companion for a jaunt of that sort), Cambridge Professor, authority on Shakespeare and the Theatre of that period.

Pryce-Jones had by then resigned from *TLS* editorship, and taken up residence in Newport, Rhode Island. Neither he nor Muriel Bradbrook was on the aircraft (Tokyo via Istanbul and Kuwait), which for some unexplained reason took off from London Airport four hours late.

Reasonably enough for so long a journey the British Council had provided accommodation in the First Class, the rest of the compartment being filled with pretty Chinese girls from Hong Kong undertaking their final initiation as BOAC stewardesses, which included receiving all the gifts handed out on a long trip of this kind. Helen, the one next to me, said that on arrival in Hong Kong her mother would see her for the first time in 'western costume'. Helen suffered some slight malaise at one stage of the journey, and I was able to provide a digestive pill. Otherwise our relationship was uneventful.

125

On leaving Bombay, ostensibly to collect spare parts, the plane flew a thousand miles or so off the route to Colombo, in consequence of which touch-down at Tokyo, instead of some quite undemanding hour the previous afternoon or evening, took place at 3.15 a.m.

Frederick Tomlin, head of the British Council and Cultural Attaché at the British Embassy, had nobly sat up to greet my arrival. He was a philosopher by profession and must have needed all his philosophy to survive so weary a vigil. He was as nice about that as about all else during our collaborative tour of duty, and took me to the New Japan Hotel.

Owing to this nocturnal advent only a 'Japanese style' room was available at The New Japan, a de luxe establishment, rather far from the central part of Tokyo; if that sprawling city can be described as having a central part. The young night-porter shook with laughter when I omitted to remove my shoes on first crossing the *tatami* matting of the bedroom (rather like getting into your bath with your clothes on), a rite of which I had been forewarned, in a state of jet-fatigue forgotten.

The bed, together with the rest of the room's appointments, was on the floor. I found this mode of sleeping most agreeable, and on the following morning asked to be allowed to stay in the Japanese style room. As so often in the Far East, where perhaps justifiably Westerners are usually forced to be Western whatever they may wish, the request was not granted. I was firmly allocated to a Western bedroom.

Tokyo, a huge proliferating jumble of streets without names and houses without numbers, gets a bad press as a capital city. All the same Tokyo is not without all fascination; perhaps rather sinister fascination. The excess of population is immediately apparent. No one who has failed to see a Japanese commuter train arrive at the railway station in the morning knows what a commuter crowd can look like. Traffic in the main streets is slaughterous, all drivers *kamikaze*, universally hooting furiously long before the red light turns green.

Out in the country, every inch cultivated, one is struck by the uniqueness of the landscape's hue, or rather its variety of shade that seems made up of infinite variations on more or less the same colour. The pink cherry tree —hideous in England where of recent years it has unwelcomely begun to disfigure pleasant country towns—suits the Japanese drop-scene, with its subtle mutations of mauve, violet, purple, crimson, magenta, which trace what seem deliberately pigmented patterns across superabundantly crop-laden fields; a foreground with all the air of being designed to set off to best advantage the sharply pointed mountain peaks of distant blue-grey ranges.

The whole country falls in with the aesthetic conventions of a Japanese print; even those three short black parallel straight lines, each placed a little below and beyond the other, that are a favourite stylized typification for clouds, actually appearing in Japanese skies as if placed there by one of their artists.

2

Not long before this our friends and country neighbours Lees and Mary Mayall had been *en poste* at the British Embassy in Tokyo. They provided a sheaf of introductions. Through the Mayalls we had already made a Japanese contact in Ivan Morris and his wife Ayako (Yaki), a Japanese dancer, both of whom had been with us on an Hellenic cruise taken in 1963.

Ivan Morris (who later parted with Yaki, and died in 1976 at the age of fifty, a tragic loss to Oriental scholarship) was a remarkable figure. Half-American, half-Swedish, he had been brought up in Europe, chiefly Great Britain, and become foremost student and translator of Japanese literature in the generation after Arthur Waley, whose prize pupil Morris had been. Waley is best known for his rendering of *The Tale of Genji*, 10th century novel by The Lady Murasaki (*Anglicé*, Lady Violet), and Morris's crowning work, *The World of the Shining Prince: Court Life in Ancient Japan* (1964) also deals with the Heian period; roughly that of Aethelred the Unready at home.

The Shining Prince was published during the years when I was on the board of the Duff Cooper Memorial Prize (to which I was co-opted by Rupert Hart-Davis), and received that award, which greatly delighted Morris.

Ivan Morris was also a prolific translator of modern Japanese works including novels. He was a relatively close friend of Yukio Mishima, novelist and poet, whose belief that 'to know and not to do is not to know' was to make him so striking an exemplar of that Japanese nostalgia for heroic failure, a subject about which Morris himself wrote.

Goodlooking and convivial, Ivan Morris was a charming friend as well as scholar, and Yaki too was delightful company. As well as possessing beauty and a sharp wit, she would produce inimitable malapropisms in her otherwise fluent English. One of the best of these was to speak of the ghettos (grottoes) at The Chantry, where the Morrises stayed more than once. I do not, however, share (as did Violet) Ivan Morris's taste for puzzles, of which he published his own collection, divided into *Brief Diversions*, *Hard Nuts*, *Herculean*.

In the event I was given little time by the British Council's programme to make use of private introductions, though as things turned out came across most of the people recommended by Mayalls and Morrises; with a great many more too.

One of the Mayalls' Japanese friends (who was to turn up years later staying with them in Wiltshire and come over to see us) was Kenichi Yoshida, author and critic of some standing, son of a former Ambassador at the Court of St James's. The elder Yoshida had subsequently become Prime Minister of Japan, pursuing a policy that was anti-war and pro-British. His son had been up at Cambridge.

The Council had already arranged that Kenichi Yoshida should interview me (in English) for the Tokyo Radio on the subject of *The Craft of the Novel*, an ordeal for which novelists must always be prepared. This confrontation was to take place at 10.30 a.m., whether 'live' or not I am uncertain.

When I arrived in the studio Yoshida was drinking a large glass of what I supposed, from its colour and the fact that the glass had a removable base like a *café filtre*, to be strong tea. He looked like a somewhat battered version of T. S. Eliot transformed into a Japanese man of letters; an impression renewed with equal force when we met again long after this in England.

Yoshida held up the glass and asked me to join him in another. At first I accepted this offer, then withdrew when the beverage turned out to be one of those fine old nut-brown pegs of whisky (no doubt Japanese whisky) measured at a strength that would have knocked one out early for what was to be a day full of engagements. This morning pick-me-up, or perhaps an earlier glass, had already left a perceptible mark on Yoshida's manner. He gave a lively performance, during our duologue pausing in the middle to enquire: 'Well—how do you think it's all going?'

I was told later that Yoshida had a wide reputation for high-spirited toping, being at times deferentially referred to in Tokyo gossip columns as the 'celebrated writer and drunkard', respect thereby paid to his prestige in both spheres.

Uninhibited newspaper references to the foibles of the eminent were rarer in those days than they have since become. As Inez Holden predicted in her novel of the future *Born Old : Died Young*: 'No editors would print the dull paragraphs of 1932 . . . Gossip writers now referred frankly to sobriety, drunkenness, love affairs, gold-digging, lion-hunting, black-mailing and so on.'

When told of such paragraphs proclaiming Yoshida's fame as a tippler I was reminded of a somewhat similar example of taking people as they come retailed by a brother officer during the war who had served in what was then called the Gold Coast. He said that he had read in a local paper the obituary of a popular African clergyman, in which, after listing the many good qualities of the Revd So-and-so, the obituarist added that devotion to religious duties was performed in the face of being 'all his life martyr to gonorrhoea'.

3

I did not, as I should have liked, meet Yukio Mishima (I rather think he was away at the time), that extravagant combination of writer and man of action less common in England than other countries. Mishima was, however, the subject of a television interview by our elder son Tristram, who was in Japan undertaking a series of such programmes some years after I went there.

Watching Tristram's film I was once or twice struck by an odd resemblance that would sometimes cross Mishima's features to those of John Betjeman, his manner too occasionally recalling Betjeman's, though as poets it would be hard to find less similarity, except perhaps a common nostalgia for the past. Possibly all Japanese men of letters possess some sort of visual equivalent in Great Britain.

If one of my Oxford contemporaries in the literary field had to be chosen to illustrate Mishima's theory that 'to know and not to act is not to know' a remote parallel might be seen—the approximation pretty far-fetched—in Robert Byron (utterly different from Mishima in personal appearance), though I think Byron would never have taken his own life.

Mishima's crazy coup d'état (more truly coup de théâtre) in 1970 was staged with the object of bringing back the absolute rule of the Emperor and other traditions of Old Japan. This melodramatic gesture, doomed to disaster from the start, ended on Mishima's part with *seppuku*, ritual suicide; his salute to death as final work of art. I think Ivan Morris felt his Japanese friend's loss deeply.

4

At the British Council's Book Exhibition in Tokyo I was presented to the Emperor's sister-in-law, Her Imperial Highness Princess Chichibu, a lady of great charm and beauty, who spoke fluent English. I mentioned that when, as Crown Prince, the Emperor had visited Eton in 1920 I had been among the crowd of boys in School Yard instructed to shout *Banzai!* (alas, without subsequent effect of keeping Japan out of the second war as ally of the Axis Powers). The Princess laughed, and assured me that she would tell the Emperor, who, she said, loved such memories. He may well have felt that those were happy days.

In the suite of the Princess, or possibly cruising round on his own, was Admiral Katsunoshin Yamanshi, in his middle eighties, straight out of a drawing by Hokusai. Commissioned as midshipman when Queen Victoria was still on the throne, the Admiral told me that he had served as liaison officer when the British Fleet was in the Far East in 1900. He was clearly very vigorous still, beaming and nodding when I asked whether he had known Violet's cousin Admiral Sir William Pakenham, who—as I suddenly recalled—had been naval attaché at Tokyo during the Russo-Japanese War of 1904–5. Admiral Yamanshi said he well remembered Captain Pakenham.

Willie Pakenham (who died the year before Violet and I married, so he and I never met) does indeed seem to have made a strong impression during his time in Japan. He was undoubtedly model for the British naval officer in Claude Farrère's novel about the Russo-Japanese War *La*

Bataille (1909), an enjoyable book in its genre, later adapted into a very tolerable movie (Charles Boyer, John Loder, Merle Oberon).

Claude Farrère (a novelist first recommended to me by Constant Lambert) was a French naval officer who wrote books in his spare time. The French authorities, impressed by Kipling's work as a stimulus to patriotic sentiment, are said eventually to have seconded Farrère to authorship as a naval duty.

So far as Farrère's stories are to be looked on as propaganda they are never in the least clamorous. If he speaks with respect of bravery and honour he can be satirical too (as indeed could Kipling) about life in the Services; Farrère not always restricting his stories to the French navy. In fact *La Bataille* is primarily a tribute to British seamanship in war, albeit manifested through an adulterous connexion.

The character for whom Willie Pakenham was prototype in Farrère's novel, Captain Fergan RN (one of those rather unconvincing surnames French novelists are apt to bestow on their British characters), sent by the Admiralty to act as observer in the war with Russia at sea, has already seduced 'la marquise Yorisaka' when the story opens. Aristocratic, beautiful, imbued with French culture, dressed by Paquin, the Marquise is paradigm of the Westernized Japanese lady of the moment. Her husband, a naval officer, is equally drawn towards Europe; an attitude by no means universally approved by his compatriots, especially those in the navy.

Yorisaka is not only a Westerner in taste, he is also Fergan's friend and 'opposite number' in official duties. He returns to his house unexpectedly one afternoon, and enters the drawing-room to find his wife playing the piano while Fergan stands beside her. She is singing a love song written by Pierre Louÿs to music by Debussy. Fergan has just kissed her neck. The husband appears to have noticed nothing.

The war takes a new turn. Yorisaka is ordered to sea. Fergan as British naval observer is posted to the warship Yorisaka commands; foremost vessel in the squadron engaged in an operation leading up to the battle of Tsushima (invoked by Apollinaire in very different context), where the Russian fleet was so heavily defeated by the Japanese.

A Russian shell sweeps the decks, killing most of the officers and mortally wounding Yorisaka, who has hitherto been issuing gunnery orders personally with devastating effect on the enemy. When he expires no Japanese officer will remain alive sufficiently equipped in grasp of range-finding to carry on.

The dying Yorisaka begs Fergan, as the only man capable of continuing the fight, to take command. Fergan protests that as a neutral observer and British naval officer he cannot possibly do that. In answer the wronged husband with his last breath repeats the words of the Pierre Louÿs love song his wife had been singing to the Debussy setting while Fergan stood beside her. Fergan sees that honour permits no refusal. He takes command, is himself killed, but Japanese victory is assured.

Willie Pakenham, who had a wide reputation for dash and elegance, though well disposed to the opposite sex, never married. There is a persistent tradition of a love affair with a Japanese lady, and he was certainly present at the battle of Tsushima. Pakenham is indeed on record as having been sitting on deck watching the battle through field-glasses when a shell burst nearby, causing casualties that spattered his uniform with blood. He at once retired below. It was assumed that for the moment he had seen sufficient of the battle. Some minutes later, however, Pakenham reappeared wearing a pair of spotless white drill trousers.

The white ducks were possibly his only spare garments, since the weather conditions at Tsushima as described by Farrère (unlikely to be inaccurate on that point) suggest anything but a torrid climate.

5

One afternoon, escaping from British Council functions, I set out for the principle museum and art gallery of Tokyo, where in addition to many treasures, a special show had been mounted; I think a selection of the Impressionists, a school on which the Japanese are very keen. The gallery was twenty minutes or more in a taxi from my hotel. Tokyo taxi-drivers are equipped with a Japanese/English phrase-book which covered most eventualities. They did not expect to be tipped. By some miracle that practice had survived the American occupation (Americans being probably the most irrepressible tippers in the world), and if given more than the registered fare handed the surplus back.

On this occasion I first truly understood all that had been repeatedly asserted about Japanese intoxication with Western culture. As the taxi approached the art gallery it was soon apparent that vast crowds were being drawn there by this special exhibition. If the building had been the British Museum, one queue would have stretched to New Oxford Street, another to Tottenham Court Road, a third to Southampton Row; while columns of students bearing banners, in military formation and para-military dress, approached over the horizon from Euston Road.

Deciding to give up any attempt to obtain entry with so much competition, I indicated to the taxi-driver from the phrase-book that I wanted to return to the hotel. I was rather apprehensive as to the consequence of this abandonment of objective, since I feared its undeniable loss of face on my own part might be held to include the taxi-driver too, causing him deep distress, perhaps even inducing thoughts of suicide.

This was no empty fear. Someone had told me only a day or two before that his taxi-driver, unable to find a Tokyo address and appalled at having to make this admission of failure—almost heroic failure after their combined strenuous efforts in the search—had drawn up by the kerb, then buried his face in his hands. This time, however, all passed off without drama, and I was delivered back to my base.

Before going to Japan I had not taken in what could be implied by belonging to the male sex. In Japan—anyway at that period—it was impossible to have a dish set in front of one by a waitress, ascend in a lift worked by a lift-girl, without being made aware of male status as such. At the same time, if apparently submissive (no doubt extremely tough beneath the surface), Japanese women seemed unselfconsciously at ease with men. One had that sense far more than in the West, submission not implying the least sense of inferiority, if anything awareness of power. These comments may, however, be altogether out of date.

At several academic functions attended it was literally impossible—short of picking them up and putting them through the door—to persuade distinguished female professors to pass over the threshold first. Among such learned ladies one could not help feeling moved that some had been persecuted during the war years for their devotion to Jane Austen. One would like to read Jane Austen's own phrases describing that harassment coming about.

At one of the university 'quizzes' during which I was on the platform replying to questions a Japanese professor asked: 'What do you think of Shakespeare?'

Off the cuff that was a tall order, not least in front of quite a large assemblage of people. Fortunately, on my setting out for the East, Violet had advised that I should take with me her own three-volume pocket edition of Shakespeare's Works. This brilliant suggestion brought a great piece of luck. I had cast my eye over a page or two of *Richard III* the previous evening before going to sleep.

'Well as a matter of fact I was reading *Richard III* last night, and it struck me that particular play was etc., etc.'

6

Moving on from Tokyo to Kyoto, I was shown round that attractive city by Peter Martin of the British Council and his American wife. This is not a guide-book, but the classical simplicity of the Katsur Imperial Villa, built at the end of the 16th and beginning of the 17th centuries for a Prince of the Imperial House (who was also much concerned for the preservation of the Murasaki manuscripts of Genji), cannot pass unmentioned.

Apostles of Zen (memories of Amherst) would deplore the dualism of considering villa and gardens separately (the two being a single concept in that school of enlightenment), but among the fine painted screens of the former I suddenly noticed a familiar smell that seemed to bring back England; an old friend; talk about books. Then I recognized why this Proustian trick of memory had come about. The Katsura Imperial Villa smelt like a 17th-century Norfolk country house where we had often stayed, in fact Wyndham Ketton-Cremer's home Felbrigg (*Infants*).

Japanese architects and landscapists like playing tricks with perspective (again related to the intricacies of Zen) so that some of the passages of the Villa are narrowed at one end with strange visual effects. In the matchlessly kept gardens scenic illusion is even more striking, for instance the training of exterior foliage round the back windows of a tea-house on ground level causing an impression of looking out on to a steep mountain side descent immediately below.

On the last night of my stay in Kyoto the Martins, whose easygoing hospitality greatly contributed to the Kyoto visit, gave a dinner-party.

I found myself rather too aware of their conviviality on boarding the plane for Tokyo the next morning, but consoled myself with the thought that I could sleep at the hotel until about half-past four, when I was seeing a performance at the Kabuki Theatre.

After being airborne for some little time the Japanese businessman beside me began to grow restive. He could speak no English, but clearly felt powerfully that fascination with the oddness of foreigners that is endemic among the Japanese. He began shyly to finger the camera that I was carrying, seeming to indicate that I should look out of the window (I was next to it) for some subject worth photographing.

He was right. Quite suddenly from out of the opaque grey-blue mist of cloud—indeed as if a mountain were actually standing on a cloud—the snowy apex of Fuji came into view. This was the sight my neighbour was determined I should not miss. It was truly magnificent. All at once I felt my eyes fill with tears.

As already mentioned I was suffering from a hangover. I do not deny that for a moment. The condition may well have had something to do with such a display of emotion. Nonetheless I had been quite unprepared for this vision of the Holy Mountain (the slopes for ever traversed by pilgrims), still less selfconsciously expecting to wallow in an aesthetic experience. Fuji was an utter surprise. To the satisfaction of the Japanese businessman I quickly took a photograph through the glass of the aircraft window.

By the time Tokyo Airport was reached I was looking forward more than ever to that afternoon's sleep. The Kabuki Theatre was to be followed by a visit with Frederick Tomlin to Shiboya (former Red Light district) for a glimpse of Japanese night-life, which fortunately begins at an early hour in the evening. The following morning I was to set out for Manila, The Philippines being included in the British Council's Far East scheme of things.

Repose, however, was not to be. Waiting at the airport was Mr Sunio Saito, Heinemann's smartly turned out representative in Japan. This courteous attention from one's publisher was not to be ignored. Saito, who spoke excellent English, wanted me to lunch with him. There seemed no way out.

We started luncheon with a glass of beer each, which was acceptable. Saito then explained that, since vineyards had only recently been established in the country, he was anxious that I should try a bottle of Japanese wine. I am always glad to improve my knowledge of exotic vintages—a hobby only partially shared by Violet—and although I should have preferred some other moment to be introduced to the Japanese grape, I agreed to Saito's proposal. The wine turned out to be of claret type.

I can unhesitatingly confirm that Japanese red wine is better than Guatemalan (to be sampled on a visit to Central America some years later), beyond that I should not be prepared to make a considered judgment on a single bottle. That particular bottle might have been said to glory in its own lack of pretension. Since then many years have passed, and I don't doubt that Japanese claret has made great strides.

My host told me that when younger he wanted to be a journalist. Instead he had earned a living teaching Judo to US troops during the occupation. He had found that very tolerable. He said he was 'not quite an atheist', and Judo, with its appeal to the will, had become something of a religion with him. I hoped that hospitality to a Heinemann author would not entail a free lesson in elementary Judo, which politeness might make impossible to refuse. I was not really up to it that afternoon. Happily no such offer was made.

We did not manage to finish the whole bottle between us, but on top of the beer and the Martins' brandy my share was sufficient to bring immediate sleep for an hour or more on return to the hotel.

Kabuki performances continue for eight hours. I proposed to watch only about half that, emerging at eight o'clock to meet Tomlin, who was dining with me. The plays, mainly traditional though from time to time a new piece will be introduced, are part of Japanese national life, Kabuki's place to be compared with that of opera in Italy. An all male cast undertakes female roles too, doing that with an astonishing skill and delicacy that never in the least gives the impression of a lot of men in drag; perhaps what Shakespeare's transvest boy-actors were like.

Indeed all Kabuki acting is finished to a degree. One could easily understand how the stylization, the classical severity, takes a strong hold on the imagination the more familiar the plays become. The actors are applauded not only with the normal hand clappings of a Western audience, also with shouts—appreciative, more rarely the reverse—from *omuko-san* ('honourable giver of cries from the gallery'), members of an organization put on the free-list by the management from their highly specialized knowledge of Kabuki techniques.

That evening Tomlin and I visited the Shiboya together. The lanes of this area of pleasure are closed to traffic giving the quarter an air of mystery and melancholy; like the shuttered geisha-houses that had been pointed out to me. That is not seldom the atmosphere in Japan. By no means all bars would admit foreigners, an attitude very reasonable even if opposed to some contemporary social teachings. We looked in on a few of these *boîtes*, but embarked on nothing at all highly spiced. Then, Tomlin admitting to work still to do, my start in the morning comparatively early, the day having been long, I turned in.

7

After splitting a final flask of *saké* with Frederick Tomlin at the airport I stepped into an Air France Caravelle en route for Manila. *Saké*, in spite of its flavour of warm sherry and water, is a taste easy to acquire. You can drink it at any moment of the day; quiet intoxication without too disturbing a kick. Incidentally *saké* is *san*, honourable, which beer is not.

The Caravelle provided delectable food and drink, opening with *pernod*; one might have been in France. At Manila I was met by a young secretary of embassy (there being no British Council in The Philippines), who announced that it was St George's Day, accordingly I should be expected to attend the annual ball given by the British community at the Polo Club. That meant a dinner jacket. Unfortunately, the climate by now being pretty hot, I did not possess a white one.

Once a picturesque Spanish town of the colonial period, a typical port of call for Conradian schooners, Manila has now only about one church of historic interest left. The place was occupied by the Japanese (greatly detested by Filipinos) during the second war, then badly knocked about when the Japanese forces were ejected. The built-up areas tended to look like the untidier parts of Southern California, though one could see where once might have been the relics of a Spanish past. After dark the sombrely lit boulevards were discreetly illuminated with the electric signs of louche nightspots.

The St George's Day Ball, an essentially Somerset Maugham occasion, immediately revealed the beauty of Filipino ladies, who, so I discovered, often look in their twenties when fifteen years or more older than that. They have a national dress they wear in the evening, slightly puffed out shoulders, modification of Nineties leg-of-mutton sleeves, the ensemble very becoming. The men wear white silk shirts with ruffles (no jacket), a style acceptable in the Tropics, though not adapted to London grime.

Tables were arranged round the dance-floor with a high table at the top for members of the Government and their wives, Ambassadors and Ambassadresses. Official wives included several superb Asian or possibly African ladies with faces of exotic and baleful beauty. Their unsmiling countenances watching the formal steps of The Lancers or Sir Roger de Coverley suggested that ritual dances were being performed by the British community prior to mass sacrifice. This impression was not lessened by a speech quoting The Sceptr'd Isle from *Richard* II. I did not leave until 3.0 a.m.; in the light of the previous forty-eight hours feeling that once more I had done my duty by my country.

At the Ball were Ralph and Telly Zulueta da Costa, prominent in the social and intellectual life of Manila, where they also undertook many good works. The Zuluetas were very hospitable to me. How can one make these acknowledgments without their sounding like clichés? But on a trip such as this one received many such kindnesses and was grateful for them.

Mrs Zulueta, a lady of great beauty, took a party to spend the day at Cieleto Lando (Little Heaven), a holiday island with a good restaurant, while her husband remained at home as he wanted personally to prepare the sucking pig to be roasted whole for their dinner-party that night: a Philippine feast in which paella of lobster, fried bananas, coconut pudding, all played a part. The Philippines produce by far the best soft drink (made from limes or kindred fruit) that I have ever tasted.

A group of young Filipino poets and writers who entertained me to dinner one night in a bamboo-faced room of a Chinese restaurant were as remarkably well up in the writing of the West. Such contacts bring home the luck of European writers, anyway those not too far East and constrained by Communist governments. Books are incomparably easier to obtain in Manila than in the states of Eastern Europe, but even in The Philippines Western books are one of the luxuries of life that require a certain amount of trouble to obtain simply on account of distance.

The last night of my stay I dined with (Sir) John Addis, an authority on Chinese art and agreeably familiar with my own works. Addis, who spoke with some nostalgia of the Duff Cooper régime in Paris when he had been of the Embassy staff, was subsequently aptly posted as Ambassador to Peking. The Zuluetas were among the guests at this dinner-party, and a lively couple from the Embassy, the O'Bryan-Teares ('the first half of the name Spanish, the second Manx'), with all of whom I was swept on to La Guardarama, a very dark night-club where a torch-singer flatteringly sang a song of personal welcome to me. The party ended about half-past two.

It was perhaps not surprising that Manila Airport at eight o'clock the following morning seemed a lonely and depressing spot. That was no doubt in some degree consequence of the previous night's festivities, though not entirely. The officially cushioned period of the trip was now over. The next port of call was Saigon, where I should have to look after myself. This was the eve of the Vietnamese War—or rather wars—and the country was already in a fairly ominous condition that had communicated itself to neighbouring states. I felt rather apprehensive as to ways and means of travel.

Then a charming thing happened. Mrs Zulueta, before she took her children to school, came to see me off. It was a delightful final gesture. I left greatly cheered, and with the warmest feeling for The Philippines and their lovely ladies.

8

The object of this journey to Saigon was to see Angkor Wat in Cambodia (a euphonious name I shall continue to use), the country between Vietnam and Thailand. The excursion to Angkor, for which I had obtained the required passport visa from the Royal Cambodian Embassy in Tokyo, was reported to be best made from Bangkok, but, on account of trouble already well under way between North and South Vietnam, there might be difficulties in doing the trip *allez et retour* across the Thailand/Cambodia frontier. Accordingly I had decided to fly from Saigon to Phnom Penh, the Cambodian capital, whence Angkor was to be easily reached. A few days could be spent among the temples before returning to London via Bangkok; a city for which twenty-four hours would suffice.

Angkor Wat has often been described. One of the authentic Lost Worlds of Science Fiction, submerged for half a millenium in the creeping oblivion of the jungle, the temples were stumbled upon by a mid-19th century French botanist. Under the French colonial empire (whatever its faults a paradise in the light of what was to come to Indo-China after the French had moved out) much clearing of the six hundred temples had taken place. The Cambodian government still encouraged archaeologists at Angkor. Excavation was at its highest peak when the Communist Khmer Rouge, and their equally bloodthirsty Communist antagonists, were soon to murder the curators, and by the very latest modern equipment devastate one of the Wonders of the World.

Cambodia was at this time governed by the despotic though relatively benevolent Prince Norodom Sihanouk, a near-Communist hereditary ruler of unpredictable temper. At the moment of writing (1982) Sihanouk, although excluded from his Marxian throne, has not only managed to survive in Chinese exile—in itself something of an achievement—but is still from time to time spoken of as a potential force to grapple with the tribulations of his native country.

At the moment of my projected Cambodian trip Sihanouk's predominantly anti-American reactions were said to be easily aggravated by the moods of his French mistress and diets ordained by his doctor, also French.

The wonders of Angkor have now been long battered by the guns of warring Communist factions; vandalized by their troops from sheer love of destruction; pillaged by looters for gain; the last detaching bas reliefs from temple walls and decapitating statues for sale to rapacious dealers in works of art. All that had not yet come to pass.

9

I had always supposed there would be something heavy, brooding, menacing, about the Far East, an atmosphere of which one becomes aware quite strongly in Istanbul (certainly a city which has seen plenty of unpleasant events to account for that), and imagined such an ambience would continue, perhaps increase, after crossing the Bosphorus into Asia.

The Turks themselves as a race may be partly responsible for this sense of melancholy oppression that descends, even apart from Byzantium's bloody pre-Turkish history. In any case Islam leaves an indelible mark even where the Muslim has only passed as in Sicily or Southern Spain. Nonetheless Asia on the whole surprised me by a kind of lightness and buoyancy altogether unexpected. I did not in the least want to spend the rest of my life there; I could now easily understand the hold that 'The East' might exert.

In this respect Vietnam lying below brought one up short. As the plane dropped to a lower altitude on approaching the coastline a flat ochre-coloured landscape of paddy fields could be seen bordering the delta of the Mekong river. Something about this country was infinitely threatening. A little of the apprehension felt earlier that morning now returned, I could not say why. We touched down.

In the customs hall a bearded Englishman approached. He said his name was Leonard Downes, British Council representative in Saigon, and he had come to meet me. That was kind because I was no longer a Council responsibility. He had a car.

Downes drove me to my hotel (later I think blown up), run by a French-woman and turning out to be reasonably comfortable. The cooking was French but decidedly odd, an item on the menu called *poussin* being anatomically less like *poussin* than possible to imagine. Downes asked me to dine with himself and his family that evening, saying he would pick me up.

On the way to the Downes house I asked why there were so many police about the streets. It was almost as if they were lining the way for a procession.

'Tomorrow is the First of May. The results of the university examinations will be published. If there is a single failure there will be student riots.'

'I see.'

Saigon had always been Constant Lambert's dream city (probably induced by Farrère's *Les Civilisés* which is placed there), and it was through Lambert that I first heard Saigon's name as well as Farrère's.

'Oh, God,' he used to say. 'What cosmic gloom. I wish one was in Saigon. That's the place I should like to be at the moment.'

This first sight of Lambert's Promised Land of oriental radiance was not disappointing. One descended into a pageant of tiny ladies all apparently dazzlingly beautiful, all wearing hats like large shallow saucers, black (occasionally white) divided silk skirts or trousers. Uniformity of dress often inclines to raise the apparent standard of looks, something not always sufficiently appreciated. In due course one found that although in principle a goodlooking race, not every Vietnamese woman was necessarily the goddess of Indo-Chinese elegance they all seemed at first sight. Even so there was plenty to captivate Lambert's romantic imagination.

The sense of danger inspired earlier, diminished in this musical comedy setting, still lay beneath the surface. The two main boulevards might easily have passed architecturally for streets of a French provincial town in the Midi. As soon as one left them all touch with France immediately vanished. I discovered that in the afternoon.

When I had eaten lunch I thought I would take a look round. As soon as one abandoned the boulevards and entered a labyrinth of narrow lanes and alleyways the throng enormously multiplied. Even on the boulevards people were preparing meals on the pavement and sitting about selling things, activities greatly extended in the areas beyond. Within about two minutes of leaving *centre ville* I was lost.

I enquired in French from a middle-aged passer-by wearing a city suit, collar and tie, who looked conventional enough. He only barked back at me furiously in an unknown tongue as if being importuned, and hurried on. After a few turnings I struck the right road; otherwise should have had to await the arrival of the US Expeditionary Force.

Downes took me the following morning to see the British Council's premises. He said his real subject was Romance languages. A vacancy had turned up at Saigon so he had not much choice except to go there. When we reached the Council's offices the flight of steps leading up to them was cluttered with members of the local population sitting or lying supine. We stepped over the recumbent ones.

'I must apologize for these people,' said Downes. 'The other day when the town was being bombarded they were dreadfully frightened, so I allowed a few of them to come into our place. They've been very grateful ever since—do anything for us in the way of odd jobs.'

'Is Saigon often shelled?'

'Oh, yes, it is from time to time. Not frequently though.'

Downes took bombardment with the most creditable *sang froid*. I was unaware that the Viet Cong forces were so near. It was not the first time that being a British Council representative had been revealed as a potentially risky business. Before the Martins had come to Japan their experiences in Malaysia had often been far from tranquil.

The British Council has sometimes been attacked as a medium for giving readings to Lapps of Gerard Manley Hopkins or demonstrations of Cornish folk-dancing to Patagonians, and it was true the higher up officials I reported to in London after this trip did not strike me as particularly inspiring. The people on the spot, on the other hand, gave the impression of doing a first-rate job. One heard that everywhere I went; the same later in the Indian subcontinent.

The importance of 'cultural' organizations is better understood by countries other than our own. In Tokyo, for example, the equivalent institutions of France and the Soviet Union were grandly housed in a fashionable area. I believe the British Council's premises were moved not long after my visit. At the time I was in Japan, as if ostentatiously to disregard such snobbish considerations, the Council's offices were not only remotely placed, but situated in the midst of a quarter given over to the *Eta*, the Japanese 'untouchables'.

The existence of this last section of the community, numbering probably about two million, is kept rather quiet by the Japanese authorities. A parallel to having the British Council among the *Eta* is not easy to draw in London, that might be faintly suggested by the American Embassy locating its library, Cultural Attaché and staff in one of the toughest and most run-down streets of the East End; though these Japanese outcasts are depressed rather than tough.

10

When I set off for Saigon Airport the following morning the town was fuller than ever of police. No violence was to be seen, so presumably all students had passed their exams. The next staging point was the Cambodian capital of Phomn Penh; thence to Angkor. The flight (Royal Cambodian Airways) went on to Bangkok. I was one of only two or three passengers for Cambodia.

On alighting at Phomn Penh Airport one passed through a narrow passage on one side of which behind a counter sat a row of pistol-toting Security Officials on high stools. I handed the first of these my passport open at the Cambodian visa. He flipped back to the front of the passport, read what turned out to be those fatal words: *Profession*: author and journalist. Speaking reasonably good American-English he announced that I must re-embark in the plane. At that moment no foreign journalists were allowed into the country.

This was something quite unenvisaged. I pointed out that the Royal Cambodian Embassy had read that description of myself less than a week before, and seen no objection to granting a visa. I explained that my journalism was not political but literary; that I did not write travel books but novels about love. It was no good. The Cambodian Security man was unmoved. Novel writing seemed to disturb him as much as journalism, if not more.

After prolonged argument there was no alternative but return to the aircraft. I did my best to conceal the rage and disappointment I felt at being done out of Angkor by a little Cambodian jack-in-office dressed like a golf-caddy. When I was once more settled in my seat, the plane about to take off, the Captain's voice came on with an announcement:

'We are sorry for the delay but police enquiries were being made into one of the passengers.'

I must have smiled.

At some subsequent point in the journey to Bangkok, probably while hanging about in the customs shed there after arrival, an elderly man of indeterminate nationality, who had been on the plane, accompanied by a young girl of Mediterranean good looks, came up to me:

'You're English, aren't you?'

'Yes.'

'I thought you must be because you laughed when they made that announcement about your not being allowed to land at Phomn Penh. Any other nation would have been sore.'

I was relieved that inner fury had not been too apparent. The elderly man settled down to tell me his life story. He was Greek by origin, had emigrated to the US as a young man, done pretty well there. Recently he had returned to Greece with the object of finding a bride. He had achieved that. They were on their honeymoon.

'I married this young lady. Now I'm giving her a just *wonderful* time.'

The girl was decidedly pretty. There must have been at least forty years between them, perhaps fifty. She was wandering about looking at the windows of the airport shops, closed because of the First of May holiday. It had to be admitted that her demeanour did not transmit unqualified conviction that she was having a just wonderful time; but then—as everyone is given an opportunity to learn sooner or later in life—wonderful times are always apt to be relative.

Arrival in Bangkok being unexpected, I had no Thai money to engage a porter. I managed to find a taxi without too much difficulty, and drove to the hotel, where a room had been booked for several days ahead. Bangkok was a hot ugly distended modern city, with a few palaces and temples, mostly of the 18th century. The traffic made the Japanese seem comparatively careful drivers. On the way from the airport I saw only one taxi upside-down by the highway.

At first it was touch and go whether the hotel could offer a vacant room. After a long and nerve racking delay accommodation was found. When I was installed there I called up the British Council as a matter of principle, though I had been told that the Thais are so unintellectual that selling culture to them is an all but impossible task. It also occurred to me that the British Embassy might be interested to hear that the Cambodian frontier had been closed to journalists. That proved a misjudgment. To say that the British Embassy was not in the least interested in that fact would be greatly to understate their indifference.

After dinner (Thai food very tolerable) I retired to bed early. I must have been asleep for two or three hours when the telephone bell rang. It was Pryce-Jones. He too had just arrived in Bangkok from goodness knows where, and staying at another hotel. He had learnt of my own presence through the British Council (who later arranged for me to picnic with their accounting staff on the *klongs* or canals).

Pryce-Jones and I explored some of the Bangkok restaurants together, his company greatly cheering the two or three days spent there. Thai temples and palaces have a temporary look, as if put up as huge kiosks at a festival or fair. The bright colours, crimson, yellow, sage green, all set against dead white, give an oddly Scandinavian impression. One could imagine the buildings in Norway.

I flew home by Japanese Air Lines. Once more the food was good, though not up to Air France. There were many presents including a pack of cards. The pretty air hostess, very young and gentle, suggested a game. Cards are not my forte. I taught her snap. In a very short time she was much better at the game than myself. She told me the metal clasp on her *obi* was her family crest.

Owing to the time-change flying west I was eating dinner (smoked salmon, roast beef, white bordeaux) when we approached London at what was breakfast time in England.

The 'magic circle' of Conrad's melancholy hero Heyst in *Victory* 'just touched Manila, and he had been seen there. It just touched Saigon, and he had likewise been seen there once.' There was no reason to suppose that Heyst had sailed to Japan, otherwise one now knew something of his beat.

VIII

Men of Letters

When housekeeping was still difficult after the second war we used to lunch fairly often at The Chester Arms, which stood nearly opposite our house. The pub was run by a very nice family, a handsome widow and her two pretty daughters. We once took an American to lunch there. Could he have been an American officer? I can't remember. When I remarked that it was lucky to find such people in the local, he replied: 'I've often heard that said over here. I don't understand it. In the US we go where it suits, and don't bother about people.'

Possibly because the staff was prepossessing, also no doubt because the place was comparatively remote from frequented scenes, an occasional acquaintance might choose The Chester for lunching someone not his wife. One would look the other way, or give a myopic nod before returning to rationing and bomb damage.

Among those who appeared there from time to time with a guest evidently not his wife was Rupert Hart-Davis. He was unique among these couples with a faintly clandestine air in boldly underlining his presence within the pub by parking outside the entrance a publisher's van on the side of which was inscribed in large letters the words: RUPERT HART-DAVIS.

In those days I hardly knew him; certainly did not know him enough to have the faintest sense of unease at inadvertently happening on a friend's equivocal situation—if it were an equivocal situation—far less did I have any notion of the story behind the Hart-Davis luncheons *à deux*. I can't remember when Hart-Davis and I first met. Not at Eton, where, two years younger than myself, he was latterly absent for long periods owing to ill health. I did not even know him by sight. He went up to Balliol the term after I came down (and remained from choice only two terms in residence). I never saw him perform as an actor, earliest of his incarnations. We may have run across each other in pre-war days, when (as he records in *Who's Who*) he was working as office-boy, like myself, in a publishing firm.

In the war he served with The Coldstream (adjutant to a Guards battalion can have been no rest-cure, though pleasant for others to have so understanding an officer in that unavoidably brusque role); when demobilized founding the small lively publishing house advertized on the side of the van. By the time his biography of Hugh Walpole came out in 1952 I seem to have known Hart-Davis scarcely less than I do now; now perhaps scarcely more than then. I say that on account of the hitherto unguessed tracts of Hart-Davis's life that his own books have from time to time revealed.

To bury one's friends is notoriously an easier undertaking than to praise them: the latter, anyway in print, a delicate even potentially embarrassing business. Nonetheless I am prepared to say that the virtues of *Hugh Walpole* as a biography seem peculiarly to exemplify Hart-Davis's individual mixture of tact, humour, instinct for dealing with a tricky subject in a no-nonsense style—a style apparently simple to the point of heartiness, while concealing a good deal of undercover subtlety.

I never met Hugh Walpole, though he once flicked towards my first novel a scrap of implied praise. Hart-Davis liked him as a man, even found his works 'easy reading' (which I have never done except some bits of *Mr Perrin and Mr Traill*), but had few illusions as to Walpole's standing as a writer. At a period when plain speaking was far less allowable than today he dealt openly with an exacting brand of homosexuality which drew Walpole towards middle-aged married men. Sympathy on the biographer's part was never confused with commendation of books by Walpole that did not deserve commendation.

Hart-Davis's offices were in Soho Square. Someone said it had the atmosphere of a schooner, the master bawling down the hatchway: 'Below, there . . .' The veteran courtier Sir Alan Lascelles (1887–1981)—always for some reason known as Tommy Lascelles—an old friend of Hart-Davis and key-figure in the dining-club to which we all three belonged, was nearer the mark in observing almost to himself: 'Rupert's more like a Life Guards officer than a publisher.'

The firm, if not run literally singlehanded, was not far short of that, and if Hart-Davis did not normally undertake the packaging of books, I should by no means be prepared to guarantee that he never formed a one-man packing department in moments of crisis, which must have been fairly recurrent.

In addition to seeing authors, reading MSS, sitting on bibliographical committees, acting as secretary (anyway moving spirit) to several dining clubs, Hart-Davis was occupied with editing such works as the Collected Letters of George Moore, Max Beerbohm, above all Oscar Wilde; and incidentally correcting the proofs of my own books with precision and severity.

The Letters of Oscar Wilde (1962) constitute an achievement altogether unusual in the field of editorship. Hart-Davis admits to a passion for fossicking out information to provide the exhaustive notes which make the *Wilde Letters* an unmatched repository of biographical material about people Wilde came across, or were connected even in a minor manner with him. Here is a kind of encyclopaedia of the Nineties, as I have found myself half-a-dozen times, always worth consulting for obscure individuals impossible to run to earth elsewhere.

Hart-Davis's own personality, powerful, buoyant, at the same time screened rather than revealed in public appearances, is lighted up more clearly by *The Lyttelton/Hart-Davis Letters*, three volumes of which cover the years 1955–1958, a fourth being promised. Even more is disclosed in *The Arms of Time* (1979).

The Lyttelton/Hart-Davis Letters had their origin towards the close of a dinner-party which included both Rupert Hart-Davis's and George Lyttelton (1883–1962), a retired Eton housemaster. By then seventy-two and living in Suffolk, Lyttelton complained that no one any longer wrote discursive letters to cheer the boredom and loneliness of later years. Accordingly Hart-Davis, then aged forty-eight, characteristically promised that he would write Lyttelton a letter once a week.

George Lyttelton, notable athlete when a boy at Eton, had returned as assistant master. Hart-Davis was up to him for 'English Extra Studies', a not particularly onerous aspect of the work programme as a specialist. Lyttelton's reputation for teaching English in an inspiring manner is to some degree supported by the careers of pupils: Aldous Huxley, J. B. S. Haldane, George Orwell, Cyril Connolly, Peter Fleming, John Bayley, forming a literary *macédoine* to which other names could be added.

As it fell out I had no dealings with Lyttelton at school, knowing him only by sight. He looked young for his age, a tall apparently genial beak, well regarded by the boys. We met only in his last years at the dining-club mentioned, when he was always an agreeable neighbour at table.

Apropos of the *Letters*, a story comes to mind told me years ago by Sacheverell Sitwell. Sitwell said that when he was at Eton a boy threw a lighted firework (something Jocelyn Brooke would have enjoyed) into the aisle during a service in chapel. The Lower Master, F. H. Rawlins (runner-up for the Headmastership when Lyttelton's Uncle Edward was appointed in 1905), rose at once from his stall. Above the echoing crepitations and showers of sparks exploding between the rows of boys facing each other from their respectively *decani* and *cantoris* knifeboards, he pronounced anathema:

'The boy who has done this thing has disgraced himself as an Etonian, as a gentleman, as a Christian, and as a man.'

The Lower Master went on to foretell that a disastrous future would be the lot of the instigator of so sacrilegious an act. I don't know whether the delinquent was incriminated at the time by the school authorities, but these calamitous predictions were in some degree fulfilled in due course, because when the firework thrower grew up he was sentenced to a term of imprisonment for sending fraudulent betting telegrams. That, however, is by the way. I quote the anecdote for Sachie Sitwell's comment: 'The Lower Master's descending order of values was so good.'

More than one reviewer of *The Lyttelton/Hart-Davis Letters* complained that a somewhat similar scale of absolutes was adhered to by the correspondents. That was a little unjust. Since Lyttelton's working life had been spent at Eton it was not surprising that much of his interests in individuals and happenings is connected with the school. If a few of these may seem cabalistic Lyttelton must also be credited with the illuminating item of noncollegiate lore that 'the hero of *The Ballad of Reading Gaol* had cut the throat of the Eton postmistress who had jilted him.'

In exchange of views about books and writers, notwithstanding that these were Lyttelton's old pupils, both correspondents find Orwell overrated and have little enthusiasm for Connolly; Lyttelton is disturbed by what the French were then calling *les jeunes gens furieux*. These barterings of literary taste can be amusing, but as I am speaking here of Hart-Davis, rather than the *Letters* as such, a more striking aspect is the 'plot' which develops on his side of the correspondence.

At the very beginning, the reader's attention is caught by a mysterious reference to a cottage in Yorkshire to which—so Hart-Davis tells Lyttelton —he retires from time to time to work undisturbed at his editing, while at the same time taking the sort of holiday he likes in the Yorkshire dales. He hints that there is more than this; a secret that will some day be revealed.

One cannot help wondering how far Lyttelton's curiosity was aroused. He came of a generation—and profession—rigorously schooled in not probing too closely into the personal lives of friends and acquaintances, a 19th century doctrine perhaps not always put into practice, but to which respect was paid anyway in theory.

There is possibly more to be said for this social attitude than might at first sight appear. The taste for holding everything up to the light for examination (like widespread pornography another of the byproducts of contemporary preoccupation with equality, emotional and sexual equality becoming thereby also a requirement) may not necessarily ameliorate life. That is *en passant*. The question is whether Lyttelton ever allowed his mind to dwell on the possibility that something more than the beauty and peace of the Dales added charm to his friend's periodical retirements there.

Lyttelton's own personality, although growing clearer (especially the melancholy) as he gets into his letter-writing stride, is never, like Hart-Davis's, rounded off into what amounts to a lightly drawn self-portrait, one which almost makes the *Letters* into a story; a novel of letters such as (the very different) *Les Liaisons Dangereuses*. We appreciate that on Lyttelton's side no remotely comparable disclosure is easy of belief, but at the same time (if only as father of Humphrey Lyttelton the musician) he might have allowed himself to be a little less buttoned up.

Such an attitude adds, however, to the dramatic impact when the disclosure comes. Hart-Davis chooses his timing carefully. When the revelations are made Lyttelton shows all the best qualities of the 19th century viewpoint in receiving them without a tremor of surprise.

In his acting days Hart-Davis had been very briefly married to a fellow mime (to use Beerbohm's term), and, though remaining friends, they quickly parted. After a while he had married again, a wife who was partly American, settled down in Oxfordshire, become father of a family, gone into the army when the second war came.

After the war, so Hart-Davis tells Lyttelton, his second wife indicated that not only did she prefer to bear no more children, but wished to bring physical relations between herself and her husband to an end. This was not combined with an immediate desire in other respects to break up the household; at least not until the children had grown up.

Hart-Davis explains to Lyttelton that by temperament he had no taste for casual affairs (a subject upon which it might have been interesting to hear Lyttelton's own views, even if from observation rather than experience). Hart-Davis goes on to relate how, not long after this domestic disjunction, he himself fell in love. His feelings were returned. He told his wife, who accepted the contingency, and a place was found in the Hart-Davis office for this new attachment; which was why Violet and I used to see the two of them lunching together at The Chester.

In short—to speak with his accustomed plain language—for many years Hart-Davis had two wives; one at home in their house in Oxfordshire; the other in Soho Square and in the Yorkshire cottage. The really remarkable thing is that he seems to have run this conjugal troika in a manner acceptable to both parties concerned; something that not every man could have brought off.

In due course, when the children grew up, Hart-Davis parted from his second wife; then retired to an Old Rectory in the Dales, the country long associated with the other side of his life. Unhappily there were only a few years to be enjoyed before the sudden and tragic death of Ruth Hart-Davis, as she had by then become.

2

During these happy Hart-Davis years we were in the North in 1966, and stayed with them at Marske-in-Swaledale, a very attractive spot looking across a kind of gully or coomb with a Georgian manor house among trees on the opposite slope. The other guest was Tommy Lascelles, then close on eighty, who was to live on to ninety-four.

I had first heard from Lascelles seven or eight years earlier in connexion with election to the already mentioned dining-club. His writing paper heading 'St James's Palace. SW. 1.' had been crossed out, 'Kensington Palace, W. 8.' scrawled in. This had something stylish about it, but like all his generation (no doubt a habit developed during the paper shortage of the first war) Lascelles liked economizing in stationery. I once received a letter from him with my own name and address pasted over a re-stamped reply-paid Football Pools envelope; a postscript saying: 'I don't do Pools myself. But one of our former cooks did, & they still send these lovely envelopes, which I can't bear to throw away.'

Lascelles had been assistant private secretary to the Duke of Windsor when Prince of Wales, and later as King Edward VIII; assistant private secretary to King George V; Private Secretary to King George VI; Private Secretary, though only for a short time, to Queen Elizabeth II. I found that in fact it had been Lascelles who had accompanied the royal party at the Victory Day Service in St Paul's in 1945, the courtier who is called Colonel Budd in *The Military Philosophers*.

'I like that name,' said Lascelles, when I drew attention to this. 'I'm glad to figure there.'

Although a man of exceptional influence in public affairs he possessed a genuine detestation for being in the limelight, even to an extent of what was necessary professionally. On retirement he refused the peerage which would have come his way as a matter of course. His great love was music. He was well read, especially in the works of Kipling, a field in which Violet could give him a game, and from time to time they would exchange erudite letters about Kipling characters.

Tommy Lascelles told me that he had danced with Kipling's daughter Elsie Bambridge at Bateman's in 1913. After that he had never seen her. In general as a survivor of the first war (in which he had won an MC) he was a great repository of information about contemporaries. This was likely to be filtered through the language of that generation. On the other hand he was utterly unpompous about his duties in various royal households, making no bones whatever on the subject of the deep disapproval he felt for the Duke of Windsor's selfishness, conceit, triviality, irresponsibility.

While on the subject of monarchs and courts, I myself attended an investiture at Buckingham Palace in 1956 to receive a CBE. When the Queen was hanging a decoration on the man in front of me in the queue of recipients she asked what he did.

'I kill mosquitoes, ma'am.'

'Oh, *good*,' said Her Majesty.

3

If George Lyttelton had lived on into his nineties (perhaps achieved the century that must have been his as a cricketer) he would not only have seen his old friend Hart-Davis married happily again for the fourth time, but would once more have been required to show imperturbability—it is hard to think an inward effort would not have been needed—when he read *The Arms of Time* (1979), Hart-Davis's memoir of his mother.

In my own experience it is rare to find exceptional people without exceptional antecedents of one kind or another. Even if the unusual nature of those antecedents may not be immediately obvious on the surface of things they are apt to become plain on closer investigation. I certainly do not affirm that no extraordinary individual is ever thrown up by unquestionably humdrum forebears, but almost always contributory influences are to be traced; the more obscure echelons of life often producing every bit as strange an ancestry as the showy ones.

Even on the face of things the origins of Rupert Hart-Davis are singular enough; with plenty of collateral idiosyncrasy to flavour the dish. His mother was born Sybil Cooper, sister of Alfred Duff Cooper (created 1st Viscount Norwich 1952), so that Lady Diana Cooper became his aunt; he Lady Diana's publisher. On the maternal side Sybil Cooper was descended from King William IV through his mistress Mrs Jordan, a celebrated actress in her day. It is not, I think, altogether illusory to see in this blood cause for Hart-Davis's own inclination towards the Stage, with traces in him of the Sailor King's Hanoverian bluffness.

The next two or three generations of left-handed royal descendants in the Jordan line, a fairly numerous brood, tended to make aristocratic marriages and to behave in a rackety manner. For instance Hart-Davis's maternal grandmother (née Lady Agnes Duff), having run away from her husband and been ostracized by her family, found herself in considerable financial straits when the lover to whom she was by then married almost immediately died. Lady Agnes, trying to earn a living as a hospital nurse was seen (allegedly scrubbing the floor) by the subsequently eminent surgeon (Sir) Alfred Cooper, who not long after married her. One of their daughters was Sybil Cooper, Hart-Davis's mother.

Sibbie Cooper was a beauty. At the age of seventeen, staying in a house-party in Hampshire, she was seduced by a fellow guest Richard Hart-Davis, a stockbroker. He also possessed unusual talent as a musician, but no interest whatever in the other arts. As it happened Sibbie Cooper was devoted to books and pictures, but entirely unmusical. They were married, settled down to an unhappy life together, though the marriage was never dissolved.

Before she died, at the age of forty, Sibbie Hart-Davis took a long succession of lovers. Her son states in the memoir that he is fairly certain Richard Hart-Davis was not his father. Attendant circumstances, a shared physical appearance, suggest the true paternal relationship belonged to a Yorkshire landowner (perhaps accounting for the lifelong pull towards Yorkshire) named Gervase Becket, a banker and MP.

Sibbie Hart-Davis was one of that group of young people touched on earlier in connexion with the monuments at Mells; sparkling and gifted, but on the whole with tragic destinies. Their mélange of semi-smart semi-bohemian life, never quite the same before or since, often associated with the Twenties, takes its most characteristic form in people like her; ducal castles at one end of the scale, the studios of Fitzroy Street and Chelsea at the other.

Rupert Hart-Davis was by no means the only child to be drawn by Augustus John, but he must surely have been the only small boy for whom Wyndham Lewis preserved cigarette-cards. Incidentally, it is a remarkable coincidence that both Hart-Davis's mother, and his second mother-in-law (an American), had affairs with Lewis.

Sibbie Hart-Davis adored her son. Throughout the whole of his school-days they wrote to each other every day. We have his word for this in *The Arms of Time*. A stifling connexion with his mother; an uncomfortable paternity; parents mutually at odds; poorish health; the silver spoon was not altogether missing certainly, but that too might have been a positive disadvantage in a homelife that was always irregular, sometimes down-right disorderly.

It is a fairly ominous picture. Yet this is a man who became adjutant of a Guards battalion, founded a vigorous publishing firm, wrote an accomplished biography, is perhaps our foremost editor of writers' Letters.

There is a temptation to shout that all very loud and clear to any passing psychoanalyst. In short, had Rupert Hart-Davis made a mess of his life oceans of self-pity would have been available for a hard-luck story based on the doctrine that nothing is ever anybody's own fault. This time the theory seems to have been turned neatly upsidedown.

4

But to return for a moment to life at Chester Gate where this chapter began, one of the regulars at The Chester Arms was our butcher Mr Cutts, a man of great ironic humour. In earlier life he had kept a butcher's shop in a tough part of London (whether Shoreditch or a quarter like the New Cut I can't remember), where pease pudding was a popular item. If the pease pudding was thought not to be up to scratch (connoisseurs were very particular) buyers were accustomed to return in the evening and plaster the shop-window with below-standard puddings. In winter Mr Cutts would heat the poker of the saloon bar fire red-hot, then mull his beer by plunging it into the mug.

Another customer, though a less habitual one, was (Sir) Seretse Khama, later President of Botswana, a Balliol man. At that period he looked rather gloomy, having been exiled from his country, where later he returned and was knighted.

The story of The Chester ends a little sadly. The handsome widow married again, an ex-policeman rather younger than herself. She was very anxious to carry a white prayer-book at their wedding. As it happened I possessed one that had belonged to my mother. It was bound in vellum, her name *Maud* engraved on the corner in my father's handwriting. I leant it for the ceremony, the true owner's name covered by a white satin marker. We did not go to the Albany Street church (where Orwell's funeral also took place), but attended the festivities after in the pub.

Alas, the marriage was not a success. Within a year, on my way home one evening, I met the disconsolate bridegroom lugging two huge suit-cases down through the Park. His face showed that he was leaving for good.

5

Late in 1953, after we had moved to the country and I had begun work on *Punch*, a press-cutting agency sent a short extract from one of the weeklies (probably *The New Statesman*), either a review of someone else's book in which my own name had been mentioned or a piece about writing in general the context of which I don't remember. The remark about myself was well disposed, but not in the least fulsome. It was signed 'Kingsley Amis'.

The name was unfamiliar. The style seemed so assured that I suspected a *nom de guerre* masking an experienced contributor, possibly even a vehicle for several persons to write anonymously. The second half might be intended to suggest friends (*amis*) of Kingsley Martin (name of the then editor of *The New Statesman*), on the analogy of the art historian Berenson's invented—subsequently liquidated—Amigo di Sandro, imaginary painter in the manner of Botticelli.

On the other hand the tone of the cutting did not sound at all like a declared friend of Kingsley Martin; equally far from the Victorian writers Charles and Henry Kingsley. Perhaps the pseudonym was used satirically. Something about the phrasing aroused my curiosity. I addressed a letter to the paper for forwarding, asking 'Kingsley Amis' if he would lunch with me one day when I was in London.

In due course a reply arrived from Swansea, again signed Kingsley Amis—evidently a perfectly genuine name—saying the signatory could not be in London for a month or two, but when next there would be happy to accept the invitation. The letter gave nothing away. It did not, for example, hint that one of the reasons for being in London during the New Year would be to keep an eye on the publication of a first novel.

Although the date on the title-page of *Lucky Jim* says 1953, review copies did not reach the shelves of the *Punch* office until January of the following year. On glancing through Amis's novel I saw at once that I had guessed right in marking down from a dozen lines of journalism a new and notable writer. I take some credit for this. As already observed, *Punch* short notices did not leave much room for manoeuvre, but, dealing with *Lucky Jim* myself, I managed to include a statement that the author was 'the first promising young novelist who has appeared for a long time.'

We did not meet until March, when Amis—who had asked that he might bring his wife with him—lunched with me at The Ivy. In appearance, as I have said, Scott Fitzgerald and Kingsley Amis had a look in common, though naturally Amis was younger and less battered. I don't think I noticed that similarity until a long time after. Amis's wife (the first) Hilary—more usually Hilly—was a lively blonde, hair very yellow, looking about eighteen. She made me laugh by asking for sherry-and-tomato juice as an aperitif; then being indignant at my thinking that drink funny.

I don't remember much of the occasion except that Amis, revealed as having been up at St John's College, Oxford, was now a don (EngLit) at the National University of Wales. From the first I greatly liked both of them. Probably conversation started off about the reception of *Lucky Jim* at the hands of reviewers, a mixture of ecstatic praise and shocked horror. No doubt also as a matter of routine I suggested in the course of luncheon that Amis, after return to Swansea, should write something for *Punch*. I think he never did.

Amis's emphatic personality was at once apparent, although on this first encounter I did not grasp how public a form that would soon take, indeed to some extent had already taken. The first hundred pages of *Lucky Jim* move with unsurpassed gaiety and force, effortlessly introducing—with the author's own *persona*, to remain an essential part of his stock-in-trade—an entirely individual style.

I had laughed a lot over the book (as I do today), not in the least—like many readers by no means all of them stupid and humourless—appalled by what seemed to some an unforgivable attack on (the phrase must be forgiven, no other quite covering the nature of the complaint) civilized cultural values.

Rupert Hart-Davis's correspondent George Lyttelton had been one of those outraged by *Lucky Jim*, a state of mind not improved by his friend, Eton contemporary, fellow athlete, Sir Lawrence Jones, who had himself written cranky but readable memoirs, and was regarded by Lyttelton as an amiable bore, finding *Lucky Jim* exceedingly funny. Even Wyndham Ketton-Cremer, admittedly prim but a capable critic, while agreeing that he had been amused quite often, was unable to forgive some of Jim Dixon's reflections on the arts.

For my own part, so far from being taken aback by the more abrasive overtones of the novel, I had scarcely noticed them, apart from their being the angle from which the narrative was launched. After all every novel is written from a given point of view, which, as such, has to be accepted. To object would be like hissing the villain in a melodrama; though true that action is said to denote enjoyment of the play.

Nevertheless I found that in certain quarters *Lucky Jim* was looked on quite simply as a shower of brickbats hurled by a half-educated hooligan at the holiest and most fragile shrines of art and letters, not to mention music. That such altars could be so easily demolished was an odd point of view, though one quite widely held at the time.

There were also those who, so far from decrying Amis as an iconoclast, hailed him as foremost representative of a young (he was just in his thirties) and rebellious generation, 'angry' and anxious to remake the world without delay in a manner to omit its many unsatisfactory elements. The people who thought that turned out to be just as much at sea as those who were scandalized by the novel.

Amis himself was of note because his gift was a new and unusual one, not because the content might at times be possible to assimilate with 'angry' concepts; so far as those existed outside the feature pages of the press and in the media. Certain other young writers were happy enough to see themselves in such terms when pointed out to them, and it was Amis's misfortune to be lumped with one or two of these lacking a particle of his talent; which included an ability (not given to all able writers) to adapt their views for popular journalism without deterioration of style.

I do not by any means subscribe to every statement uttered by Jim Dixon (nor to many of the literary judgments of his creator), but *Lucky Jim* seems to me to represent something not far distant from the precise reverse of the attitudes so deprecated. Far from being a professionally philistine book it is one that could only come from a writer who had thought a great deal about the arts—notably the art of writing—and a novelist who himself possessed more than a touch of Swiftean horror (later illustrated by *Jake's Thing*) at the goings-on of human beings, particularly their sexual antics. At this early stage sex remained fairly muted compared with the place it was subsequently to take in Amis's novels. So also did death.

The Ivy luncheon led in due course to an exchange of visits: the

Amises coming to Somerset: ourselves to Swansea. They lived in the Uplands quarter of that town, a district of some charm; this first sight of Swansea bringing back memories of Welsh troops during the war, and the passionate antipathies between 'Swansea people' and 'Cardiff people'.

Among those who never accommodated themselves to Amis's writing (although someone as unexpected as Edith Sitwell had written a fan letter about *Lucky Jim*) was Evelyn Waugh. At the same time Waugh had a kind of obsession about 'Little Kingsley', whose surname he always pronounced as Ames.

This factious misnaming of people of whom he disapproved was a tease going back to Waugh's Oxford days. He would, for instance, always refer to Dylan Thomas as Dilwyn Thomas. Waugh himself had often been victim of such misnomers himself in earlier days, not only those rhyming his surname with 'buff', or supposing his first name feminine (like the *TLS* reviewer of his first book), but also straight misprints, as when the announcement in *The Times* of his second child's birth in 1939 designated the father as Emlyn Waugh.

During the Swansea visit the three Amis children were in some skilful manner relegated so that the Uplands house was entirely free from them throughout our stay. Since Waugh was very keen on the doctrine that children should neither be seen nor heard, Violet mentioned to him the adroitness of the Amises in having so resourcefully disposed of their family. The story fell very flat. In fact thoroughly annoyed Waugh.

Swansea left, I think, a discernible mark on Amis as a writer. Certainly his second novel *That Uncertain Feeling* shows him adept at recording South Wales behaviour and diction. The sense the book gives of understanding the South Welsh (without so far as I know possessing a drop of Welsh blood) is also evident in Amis's poems.

When Amis left Swansea to become a don at Peterhouse (where he remained only very briefly) we also stayed with the Amises at Cambridge. Not long before he had shown round the University a young Russian poet Yevgeny Yevtushenko, then doing a well advertized tour of Great Britain. Yevtushenko was regarded as a shining example of the comparative outspokenness allowed in the supposedly inhibited intellectual climate of the Soviet Union. Amis gave some account of acting as guide to Yevtushenko, and their meeting remained in my mind, leading to a droll incident many years later.

6

When we first met I did not know that Amis belonged to that comparatively small group of novelists equally at ease with poetry; indeed thought of himself principally as a poet. Celebrity as a novelist has undoubtedly tended to obscure that role (just as Roy Fuller's as poet has to some extent veiled Fuller's novels), although giving a glance at dates one sees indications that *Lucky Jim*'s success actually stimulated Amis's poetry.

A critical misapprehension about one group of poems is worth a moment's pause on account of the general principle involved. A sequence in the Amis *Collected Poems* (1979) is called *The Evans Country*. These verses adumbrate the experiences of a Glamorganshire Don Juan, a South Welshman depicted as more dexterous than edifying in his chosen pursuit.

A reviewer of the *Collected Poems* (a competent poet himself, now deceased) remarked that Amis had a peculiar hatred of the South Welsh. This comment—trivial in the context of a favourable review—is perfect example of a critic being unable to distinguish between realistic observation (if you prefer, knockabout banter) on the subject of an individual or a community, and a malicious attack.

Having chanced to see Amis living in South Wales I happen to be in a position to state unequivocally that no one could get on better with the South Welsh, nor show less of a tendency to dislike them. Quite the contrary. The fact that Evans and his seductions come most creditably alive in the poems does not indicate like or dislike. To suggest the reverse is to lapse into the principle (one no doubt dating back to the birth of half baked literary criticism, but peculiarly prevalent today) that a novel about an adulterous stockbroker represents an attack on the City's morals, a limerick celebrating a pederastic bus-conductor must be intended to undermine London Transport. One of the basic human rights is to make fun of other people whoever they are. That now seems threatened on all sides.

7

Speaking of limericks, Amis—like Constant Lambert—is something of a master in that art-form. So too is Robert Conquest, another poet, whom I met through Amis. This was about the moment when I was writing the latter volumes of *Dance*, on the subject of which Conquest from time to time gave me valuable advice.

Robert Conquest, during the years that followed coming out of the army, played a main part in launching the new approach to poetry that is sometimes known as The Movement, with which Amis was also associated, Philip Larkin the monitor. Conquest is probably better known for *The Great Terror* (1968), that scholarly and judicial work recording the fearful post-Revolution developments in Russia under Stalin.

In attempting a thumbnail sketch of Alick Dru earlier in these memoirs I suggested that transplantation of nationality can add force and subtlety by imparting faculties to an individual which do not seem to be home-grown in the country of birth and upbringing. It would not be difficult to find instances in history. In the case of Dru one saw certain French characteristics, pre-eminently in his methods of thinking and reasoning, processes taking place in an otherwise entirely English system of under-standing.

Bob Conquest, wholly unlike Dru in almost every other respect, has sometimes given hints of a similar variation in species brought about by regrafting of the plant, more specifically by change of soil. In both cases the mother was English, and the father came to live in England: Dru's father French; Conquest's of a family settled in Virginia since the 17th century, having emigrated to America from Houghton Conquest in Bedfordshire. Both were educated in England, but Conquest (Winchester, Magdalen Oxford), unlike Dru in early familiarity with France, did not set eyes on the US until his early thirties.

Nonetheless one sees in Conquest an English point of view, English individuality, linked with characteristically American forms of energy and resilience. He has also the American capacity for taking enormous pains in relation to any enterprise in hand; particularly in the concerns of friendship.

This inner Americanism in Conquest seems to me also observable when, as a poet, he passes effortlessly into transatlantic themes, and he is of the few—as one gets older one realizes how few there are—to take an interest in extraneous things (e.g. Roman Britain) for their own sake.

8

Quite early on during my time at *Punch* (certainly well before 1957, when his first novel *The Mystic Masseur* appeared) I met V. S. Naipaul. We had a drink together at El Vino's in Fleet Street. He had been suggested as a potential *Punch* contributor, though like Amis never became that.

Naipaul, then about twenty-three or twenty-four, was already mature, and married to his English wife Pat. An Indian of Brahmin family from the borders of Nepal (with which land his name records association), he was third generation in Trinidad, furthest south of The Antilles, only a mile or two off the coast of Venezuela.

From his Trinidad school he won a scholarship to Oxford, where he was in residence at University College for four years. Naipaul had not greatly enjoyed his time at Oxford. He was now trying to earn a living by writing; when that did not work, what he called 'going underground'.

Vidia Naipaul's early novels naturally rely on a Trinidadian background, but from the very first he had none of the marks of a 'regional' writer. Quite the contrary. Then and later he always liked to emphasize his own rootlessness, the condition of being a man without a country.

In one sense Naipaul seems to me an 'English' writer, even in preference to being a 'British' writer, possessing none of those tricks of language or style that have to be covered by the more inclusive national epithet. Still less could Naipaul be called 'American', in spite of coming from so near the South American continent.

There is, however, a directness, a naturalism (can one ever get away from that tricky label?), ability to stick to the point (all increasing in Naipaul's writing as he developed), that English writers, as such, do not always find easy; one eye always swivelling in the direction of fantasy.

In the fantasy area Naipaul's very funny first novel *The Mystic Masseur*, notwithstanding the Trinidad setting essentially English in humour, just skirts the allowable unrealities of comedy without ever becoming farce;

even when the Trinidadian Indian hero Ganesh Ramsumair ends up as a Scotchman—G. Ramsay Muir, MBE. I once suggested that in the very unlikely event of its author ever wishing to undertake a similar metamorphosis, Naipaul might become a Welsh writer, Nye Powell.

Ganesh, having decided early in life that the only options open to him for taking things easy are either to be a masseur or a mystic, embarks with dazzling success on a career combining both vocations; eventually standing as candidate in the Island's elections on the acrostic ticket: *Ganesh is Able, Nice, Energetic, Sincere, HOLY*.

On my own first reading of *The Mystic Masseur* I did not appreciate some of the inherently serious comments interpolated in an apparently lighthearted manner; which is just what good writing should achieve if that is the aim. Nor did I sufficiently grasp Naipaul's deeply rooted melancholy; though perhaps melancholy should be taken for granted in any writer with a true gift for comedy.

I make this first point because when Naipaul's sixth novel *The Mimic Men* (1967) appeared I thought (after one reading) that the hero, a young local politician in exile from the Caribbean, showed over much sensibility, too wide a literary imagination, to be the sort of man who would have chosen politics for a career. He was represented as subtly aware of such things as the individual characteristics of the people round him, conscious of the atmosphere of London, its beauties and its squalors; the average politician of any country likely to see his surroundings in terms of political ambition rather than aesthetic reflection.

I mentioned this to Naipaul. He had an interesting answer to such objections. He explained that for a bright young man born on a Caribbean island politics (were he not a cricketer) offer pretty well the sole route to substantial advancement.

What had been adumbrated in a frivolous manner in *The Mystic Masseur* was illustrated in a different (if you like more serious) tone of voice in *The Mimic Men*, though there too always with lightness of touch. Naipaul himself did not invoke Ganesh in this connexion, but I now grasped the correlation of theme. In Europe—more especially in England —the intellectual might choose to take up politics, prefer to leave politics alone. In Trinidad that alternative was scarcely available.

In one sense Naipaul could hardly be less 'committed' (to use an old-fashioned term); in another his political interests, in the deeper meaning of the phrase, are intensely alive. *The Mimic Men* can be looked on as the bridge between the serio-comedy of the earlier and the severe satirical investigations of the more recent books; incidentally an extremely difficult personal transmutation for a writer to undertake.

The title of the novel announces Naipaul's searching and bitter individual observation of those countries of the world who possess only 'mimic' civilizations; countries pretending that—politically, socially, industrially—they are living as civilized people live, while unable to govern themselves without secret police and torture, or to produce by their own efforts the goods required for economic existence at the levels to which they aspire; incapable of even such civilization as attempts to survive in our disillusioned epoch.

Under much humour, understatement, irony, Naipaul's excoriation is pitiless; a stinging call to order for a world still partly bemused by 19th century sentimentalities and optimisms, to which it has added some of its own yet more futile. Perhaps not surprisingly Naipaul's strong potions have not always been appreciated locally.

Even *An Area of Darkness* (1964), Naipaul's absorbing book describing a visit to India, a country about which he feels profoundly on account of his own Indian origins, caused some offence in the subcontinent. Naipaul had greatly looked forward to the journey, and much of what he found was painful because his feelings were deeply involved. This intensely personal approach took the book outside the ordinary traveller's account of going to a hitherto unvisited country. Naipaul was not understood.

In the British edition of *An Area of Darkness* he speaks of 'my companion', in fact Pat Naipaul, who on that trip was providing support for her husband's work. For some inexplicable reason—possibly a late in the day atavistic puritanism—the American publisher jibbed at the phrase, and 'my wife' was substituted.

'*My wife* sounds too cosy,' Naipaul remarked to me on this subject.

That is perfectly true; one of those special sorts of difficulty in autobiographical writing that are often misunderstood by those to whom writing is not a profession. Indeed we are back with Jocelyn Brooke's epigraph from Sir Thomas Browne: 'Some Truths seem almost Falsehoods and some Falsehoods almost Truths.' The autobiographical writer, with problems enough as to what actually happened, has also to pick a way between right and wrong impressions given by the words themselves.

Phrases perfectly reasonable to describe a given experience can yet add to or subtract from accurately conveying the scene. This prescript applies most of all to the commonplaces of life. It is not what is startling, obscene, unpalatable, moving, that is difficult to handle without threatened flaws in language, but what is normal, humdrum, banal, elements seldom absent from human existence. Naipaul's instinct makes him extremely capable in dealing with such matters. He can also diagnose handwriting.

9

Notable events of 1968 were that Tristram married the painter Virginia Lucas, and her twin sister Julia became wife of our nephew Ferdie Mount.

I had just met the Lucas twins' father Archie Lucas (who was three or four years older than me and died in his early forties) in Sligger's rooms at Balliol (*Infants*), but never otherwise came across him at Oxford. Nor, as it happened, had I met their mother Nina Grenfell well known to me by sight in days of dances. Nina Lucas's father Field Marshal Lord Grenfell remarried in his sixties, and, apart from a distinguished military career in Egypt and elsewhere, had been the last officer in the British army to obtain his captaincy 'by purchase'.

Vidia Naipaul had bought a house in Stockwell Park Crescent, which, when the Naipauls moved to the country, Tristram and Virginia took over.

When Naipaul had contemplated buying this Stockwell house he had asked me to look over it with him before making a final decision. Together we examined the place, discussing advantages and disadvantages of living in that particular house, and in South London generally; this carried out in the very individual Naipauline manner, forceful, penetrating, unexpected.

One of the aspects upon which Naipaul felt vehemently was the possibility of neighbours making a noise. On the face of it the quiet respectability of the Crescent was reassuring. Naipaul, however, remained apprehensive. All angles must be studied.

'The house opposite is scheduled as an Old People's Home.'

'Does that matter?'

'*But will they make a noise?*'

I had a sudden vision of those scenes of riotous carousal on the part of intoxicated geriatrics that seem to have preoccupied the painters of the Netherlands: the Stockwell Kermesse, so dreaded by the younger parishioners for the deafening hubbub created by Bacchanalian pensioners. I also remembered a tradition I had come on when writing *Aubrey* that ten Morris dancers whose accumulated ages added up to more than a thousand had performed before King James I at Hereford races.

XI

The Writer and Society

When Europe had begun to recover a little from the second war the age of Writers' Conferences began. It is not easy to imagine Fielding or Smollett, Hardy or James, Kipling or Conrad, discussing such subjects as 'The Writer and Society' at such convocations; perhaps Dickens conceivably. In any case literary modes change. I was invited to one or two gatherings of this kind, but always returned a negative answer, since I dislike public speaking if that can be avoided without seeming uncivil.

Authors are rarely at their best discoursing about the lumber of authorship, and when they hold forth from the rostrum they are usually tedious. Even more compelling in keeping me away was the fact that the rise of the Writers' Conference developed at a moment when I was trying to get the earlier volumes of *Dance* under way; the ever haunting threat of ceasing to be a writer on account of producing no books.

This urgency had slightly abated when the Société Européenne de Culture issued an invitation to a meeting in Venice in 1958. Several of their members in London gave an assurance that those writers without a compulsive desire to speak would be perfectly acceptable in contributing a line or two to the Society's organ *Comprendre*. It was the year of the *Biennale*. The Venetian authorities had announced that they would co-operate in entertaining the guests of the Conference. In short the enchantments of Venice were too strong to be denied.

In the event the occasion was thoroughly enjoyable; incidentally providing a background (much adapted) for some of the scenes in *Temporary Kings* (1973).

I was put in an hotel on The Lido, agreeably cool for August in Venice. The sessions of the Conference took place on the island of San Giorgio, which is well provided with buildings for such meetings. These conclaves held morning and evening, by their nature prosy, were alleviated by social and cultural jaunts arranged by the Conference organization or the Venetian municipality. They included at least one banquet a day at which food was good and wine flowed. French, in practice often demotic variations on that language, was the medium ordained for speakers to address their audience, equipment for mechanical translation through earphones having not yet come into fashion.

The only compatriot I knew at all well who was present at the Conference was Alan Pryce-Jones, already invoked in these pages as fellow literary exhibit in the Far East. In Venice local opportunities for conviviality were much enhanced by the influence of Pryce-Jones, a man of unsurpassed social energy.

Among other rules laid down by him (one with which I readily fell in) was that in order to avoid a sense of guilt in accepting the hospitality of the Conference without doing anything in return, a just man—anyway a just writer—ought to sit in on either the morning or the afternoon session. To be present at both—unless irresistible to registered Conference addicts—was supererogatory. A bad conscience was thereby assuaged without too much strain on physical and mental endurance in the lecture-halls of San Giorgio.

Rencontres, so to speak off duty, with writers from other countries were greatly to be preferred to listening for hours to platitudinous speeches about the woes of a writer's life. Among friends made in Venice on this occasion with whom some sort of a contact was maintained for many years were Maria-Luisa Astaldi, biographer of Manzoni, editress of the Italian literary magazine *Ulisse*; and, with his American wife Jeanette, the Netherlands author and editor Adriaan van der Veen. There were several others too. If such functions have any point it is to form such acquaintanceships.

I feel fairly sure that Pryce-Jones must have been the intermediary to fling wide the portals (one uses the high-flown phrase advisedly) of the Palazzo Labia, a setting which was to provide in literary terms for *Temporary Kings* what is called in music and painting a *capriccio*; the painting sense being the one I have in mind.

The Labia Palace was then occupied by Charles Bestigui, a Latin American Old Etonian, whose considerable fortune was said to derive from large profits in guano, those valuable droppings of seabirds associated with the islands off Peru; about which the Baronet in Tennyson's *The Princess* had written pamphlets for which he is commended. So far as I know Charlie Bestigui had never written any pamphlets on the subject, but friends said he had made a lot of money out of the product itself.

I can't remember the precise circumstances of going to the Palazzo, but, arriving at the entrance from the canal (in Venice likely to be the main one), I left a pair of ancient and wet bathing pants in the outer hall. In the course of the visit Bestigui himself showed me the magnificent frescoes in the Palace executed by Gianbattista Tiepolo. On leaving by the street entrance I forgot to reclaim the bathing pants.

The following day a message was conveyed to my hotel to the effect that, if I presented myself at twelve o'clock the following morning in Harry's Bar, the bathing pants would be returned by Lady Diana Cooper.

I was overjoyed at this kindness (especially as I did not then know Lady Diana), fearing this venerable and favourite garment had passed out of my life for good. Diana Cooper's memoirs *The Rainbow Comes and Goes* (1958) refer to a bib worn by her in childhood inscribed with the stern words *Don't be Dainty*. Willingness to handle so unalluring a burden must have been an extension of that well learnt lesson.

But to return to the Palazzo Labia: the building, quite a fine one, dates from the 18th century, though the façade on the street side overlooking the church of San Geremia stands in one of the less enchanting quarters of Venice. The Palace is now used as assembly rooms, the interior somewhat disfigured by rows of small black chairs for meetings or lectures. In Bestigui days furniture and appointments were appropriately gorgeous.

Charles Bestigui himself, middle-aged but retaining an undiminished zest for entertaining, had that buttoned-up anxious air that some international playboys seem to develop when first youth is passed. He looked particularly worried while displaying the frescoes, which had been restored but remained splendid enough. They depict *The Meeting of Antony and Cleopatra: The Banquet of Antony and Cleopatra.*

These scenes are represented as if taking place in an area beyond the room in which the onlooker stands, each fresco placed between real doors, three marble steps below painted in perspective as if leading up into a magical land of Egypt. The first shows a courtyard or quay where Cleopatra has been waiting to greet Antony on disembarkation from the ship which has brought him to her realm: the second, a pillared hall in the foreground of which the Egyptian Queen—a glorious Venetian beauty—entertains (Antony still wearing his helmet no doubt to set himself off to best advantage) to dinner. One other guest is at the table. Attendants stand by.

Among this surrounding retinue—which includes a Beardsleyan dwarf and small dog disporting themselves on the steps—*The Banquet* offers one of the self-portraits Tiepolo would sometimes insert in his works. Clad in a robe the painter stands in the background watching the proceedings rather sardonically.

Another self-portrait (familiar to me only in reproduction) appears on the frescoed ceiling of the Residenz at Würzburg, this time with open neck and a cap, the face ill and worried. Behind appears his son Domenico (who followed the same profession) in a tie-wig. Tiepolo's features, to some extent his son's too, are distinctly Sitwellian in cast.

In the two Labia frescoes, more especially the scene at the dinner table, the suggestion of mutual sexual expectancy on the faces of Antony and Cleopatra is marvellously conveyed.

2

The Conference in Venice had been held in the shadow of writers being given a bad time in Eastern Europe generally since the war and Communist takeover; more specifically Soviet persecution of the poet and novelist Boris Pasternak.

After *Doctor Zhivago* found its way to publication in the West, an event followed by the Soviet authorities putting pressure on Pasternak to refuse the Nobel Prize, the régime must have felt some sort of counterblast was needed to dispel, at least by distracting attention reduce in volume, the poor impression this tyrannical course of action had created all over the world where books were still allowed to be read.

The only officially approved novelist in the Soviet Union possessing anything to be called an international reputation was Mikhail Sholokhov, whose name was known to English-speaking readers from *And Quiet*

Flows the Don (1933), a novel which had received a certain amount of acclaim on publication in the West. Sholokhov, Cossack by origin, had accordingly been dispatched in the spring of 1958 on a promotional tour through Europe beginning in London.

The Russian Civil War of 1918–22 which followed the Revolution had been theme of *Doctor Zhivago*, a novel somewhat diffuse and lacking in form, though one that could have been written only by a man of high courage and literary distinction. The Civil War was also the background of a trilogy by Sholokhov, of which *And Quiet Flows the Don* was the first volume.

In Russian, Sholokhov's book was simply entitled *Quiet Don*, but the London publisher rightly judged that a direct translation would immediately suggest to English ears a novel, probably satirical in character, with a setting of university life.

Almost from the start when Sholokhov's first volume of trilogy appeared in the West odd rumours were in circulation. It was suggested that *Quiet Don*, anyway most of it, had been lifted from the memoirs of another Cossack writer somewhat older than Sholokhov, killed fighting in the army of the Whites rather than the Bolsheviks during the Civil War. This imputation—certainly never authenticated—was raised again many years later in 1974 by Alexander Solzhenitsyn.

Solzhenitsyn identified the author he regarded as the genuine one as Fyodor Krykov, a Cossack officer who had already produced several books about the Don country before his own death. The fact that Sholokhov's name has never been associated with any other work so competently written as *Quiet Don* has sometimes been advanced as an argument in support of Solzhenitsyn's diagnostic attack.

When he arrived in London the British Council arranged a dinner party for Sholokhov at the Savoy Hotel. At this C. P. Snow, novelist, scientist, subsequently Life Peer, was to act as host. Snow, it appeared, was a personal friend of Sholokhov, and accustomed with his novelist wife, Pamela Hansford Johnson, to stay from time to time at the Sholokhov country house in South Russia. I had just met both the Snows, but knew neither at all well.

I was invited to the Savoy dinner party, also to a luncheon given the following day at the Soviet Union's Embassy in Kensington Palace Gardens.

On my appearance at The Savoy the British Council lady overseeing arrangements for dinner received me with the words: 'I'm afraid we've had to put you next to the Secret Police man. He doesn't speak very good English, and is in any case not specially easy to get on with. We are sorry about this, but there seemed no other way of arranging the places round the table. I thought we ought to warn you, and hope you will forgive us.'

I replied that so far from forgiveness being required I welcomed the assignment. The mere hint of bad English put me on my mettle, apart from this promising contact with the KGB (which I think that department of Soviet administration had already begun to be called). Wartime duties in Military Liaison had developed in me, an incompetent speaker of foreign languages, a certain mastery of broken English. I would sometimes bring Allied officers to the house after telling Violet they spoke fluent English to find she was scarcely able to understand a word they said. The Secret Police man would be a challenge. The more the Beria.

When Sholokhov entered the room accompanied by the Soviet Ambassador and various members of his staff I was reminded of old Hinks's comment quoted earlier: 'The man *looks* rude.' That was just the impression made by Sholokhov. He looked rude before he opened his mouth. Stocky, unsmiling, with a small fair toothbrush moustache, he had the bearing of a morose taxi-driver dissatisfied with his tip. His air did not at all belie frequent former outbursts against fellow writers, Russian or foreign, who had not seen eye to eye with Soviet methods.

Sholokhov offered no English, but conversation with him was not totally reduced to use of an interpreter at this party because the Oxford philosopher Isaiah Berlin was to sit on one side at dinner. Berlin was not only a Russian speaker, who had left Russia at the age of ten, but a conversationalist to be relied upon not to dry up whatever the lack of response in a neighbour. On Sholokhov's other side was a compatriot, probably the Ambassador.

My own next door neighbour the KGB man (possibly the British Council lady was on my other side to allow full concentration of my energies), as wonted in his profession, looked a little different from the rest of the Embassy staff, all of whom possessed that superficial uniformity imposed by diplomatic life that can make nationality barely distinguishable. The KGB man, probably in his middle to late forties, wore a dark silky mandarin moustache that curled down into the corners of his mouth like an 1880 officer of the Brigade of Guards. His manner, if not particularly genial, was perfectly correct; his English wholly intelligible, indeed much better than I had been led to expect.

By about halfway through dinner the KGB man and I were on sufficiently matey terms for him to have confided to me that he was by race Armenian, and, although no longer in the first flush of youth, only comparatively recently married. He was rather arch about this middle-aged marriage, even blushing slightly, and very proud of his two little daughters aged about two and three. The name of the elder daughter escapes me, some very usual one like Catherine or Natasha, but the younger—he strongly emphasized this—was Marië—not Maria but Marië—the Armenian version of Mary. By the end of dinner we were really getting on splendidly.

Toasts were drunk. Snow made a speech. He drew attention to the fact that 1905 had been a Vintage Year for writers, having produced Sholokhov, Powell, and Snow himself. This tribute was translated sentence by sentence. Sholokhov, whose sullen features had not for a moment relaxed under what I don't doubt had been a cascade of wit from Berlin, showed no particular pleasure on learning of this auspicious nativity. One of the Russians, not Sholokhov, replied for the guests. He was not the KGB man, who might have been worth hearing.

Eventually came that always gruelling routine on such occasions as this of being led up to the guest of honour for a word of two; in this case promising to be even less enjoyable than usual on account of Sholokhov's demeanour and the fact that that conversation had to be conducted through an interpreter.

When my turn came I took the Cossack bull by its Communist horns in going straight to the quintessence of Sholokhov's image by saying to the interpreter, a mild bespectacled young man evidently Jewish, that I understood Cossacks were not in themselves a separate race, but in the first instance had been a nomadic tribe of horsemen, principally Turkish in origin. I would like to hear Sholokhov's comments on that subject. My knowledge of Cossack origins, such as it was, rested on vague memories of a lecture given during the wartime Politico-Military course attended at Cambridge.

Sholokhov listened impatiently while a translation of this not very sparkling item of small talk was being rendered intelligible to him by the young man in spectacles. Then he spat out a word or two. His last angry sentence, uttered with much vehemence, for some reason made the interpreter smile; perhaps because Sholokhov had seemed to aim the words at himself rather than me:

'Mr Sholokhov says Turks—anyone—can be Cossacks. All peoples. Everybody can be Cossack except Jews. Jewish peoples cannot be Cossack.'

I did not prolong this dialogue, and in due course the party broke up.

The following morning on waking up and thinking over the dinner I had one of the worst attacks of *l'esprit de l'escalier* (from which I am a congenital sufferer) that I have ever experienced. Why had I not countered Sholokhov's disclaimer that Jews were not allowed to be Cossacks with the words:

'*What about Babel?*'

That unmindfulness was all the more inexcusable because I actually possessed a copy of *Cavalerie Rouge*, a French translation of Babel's best known collected short stories.

Babel, a Jew if ever there was one, had fought in a Cossack detachment of Bolshevik cavalry under Budenny, former Tsarist NCO who became a Marshal of the USSR. Later Babel's too realistic writing had given offence to the Marshal, whose thickheadedness was famous throughout Russia, and had probably saved his life as one of the few Old Bolsheviks not executed by Stalin. Budenny complained to Stalin about Babel. The writer had been liquidated in his early forties.

It would have been the perfect answer to Sholokhov; not only correction of an inaccuracy on the subject of his own special period the Russian Civil War, but a reminder of the fellow writers whose persecution Sholokhov himself had always applauded. I might even have caused the interpreter to laugh again—had he dared—but, alas, the question was never put.

That was the day of luncheon at the Soviet Embassy. I had for some reason, now forgotten, to visit that morning the Reading Room of the British Museum. Passing through one of the small Bloomsbury streets leading to the front of the Museum I paused to look in the window of an arty-crafty shop displaying all sorts of odds and ends. These included a couple of small dolls about six inches high and probably handmade: two little blonde girls, one wearing shorts, the other check trousers. I stepped in and bought these. Saying they need not be wrapped up, I slipped them into a breast pocket.

After leaving the British Museum I arrived a minute or two early for the invitation at Kensington Palace Gardens. When I was shown into the Embassy's long drawing-room the only other guests as over punctual as myself turned out to be the celebrated Negro singer Paul Robeson and his wife. As luck would have it they were sitting at the far end of the room talking to the only member of the Embassy staff present, the KGB man.

After introduction to Mr and Mrs Paul Robeson, and a moment or two's conversation, I produced the two little dolls from my pocket.

'I brought a small present for Natasha and Marië.'

The effect of making this trifling gift was absolutely galvanic. The KGB man sprang to his feet. He looked all at once greatly disturbed. Had he suddenly remembered something other than his children of which the dolls reminded him? Muttering a word or two that might or might not have been perfunctory thanks he literally snatched the dolls from me, turned away and walked fast—indeed almost ran—down the length of the long lofty room; disappearing from sight among the crowd of guests who were now beginning to flow in from a door some little way from where we were sitting.

The Robesons and I settled down again without him. I mentioned to Paul Robeson that I had been fortunate enough to see his Othello which he had played in London a long time before. I would have liked to discuss with him the Black WPA *Macbeth* watched in Los Angeles, but new introductions had begun to take place. In fact, Robeson's Othello had been interesting rather than impressive. He had seemed to tackle the role with a sense of grievance alien to Shakespeare's selfconfident Moor. The Black WPA players had been infinitely less tense.

By this time everyone had arrived; perhaps forty or fifty people, including all who had been at the previous night's Savoy dinner party. I did not set eyes on the KGB man again, though he must have been at the table somewhere, one would have expected.

When on some later occasion I ran across Isaiah Berlin I asked what sitting next to Sholokhov had been like.

'Hates everybody,' said Berlin. 'Touch of Muggeridge. A bad-tempered version of Muggeridge. Distinct touch of Muggeridge.'

3

All but twenty years passed after the Venice gathering before I attended another Writers' Conference. Then, in the spring of 1977, the Bulgarian Embassy sent a letter announcing an invitation from the Bulgarian Writers' Union to an international conference in Sofia. I excused myself on grounds mentioned earlier—the grip of writing-time's Old Man of the Sea if anything tightening as one grows older—and, as we were soon off to Italy for a fortnight, thought no more about the matter.

The Bulgarians, however, refused to take no for an answer, enquiring by telephone whether I would not reconsider the decision. I said we were going to Italy in three days' time, and I would think the matter over on return. At this reply the Embassy official asked if they might send down a representative right away to explain the attractions of this particular conference. They wanted me to come; they also wanted an early answer. June, the month of the Conference, would soon be here. It seemed discourteous to refuse this request.

A Bulgarian diplomat arrived. Over coffee I asked who were likely to be present from the United Kingdom. The answer was: C. P. Snow certainly; Iris Murdoch perhaps (when I rang her up she had heard nothing, and did not appear in the event); two or three other writers of varying note; Peter Elstob, secretary-general of the PEN club.

One of the names, known to me as that of a Communist writer, but perhaps not very familiar to many of the London literary world, made me laugh. In fact the Bulgarian diplomat and I both had a good laugh about him. Nevertheless the Bulgarian diplomat continued to insist I ought to come.

As an undergraduate I used to feel drawn to small capitals. I had visited Belgrade when merely a Serbian city; much later seen Bucharest. I did not know Sofia. The man from the Embassy, scenting indications of weakening, said it was written that God had asked the Virgin Mary whether there was any corner of the world she would specially like for her own. The Virgin had at once replied that she would like Bulgaria. No doubt in remembrance of her partiality the Virgin Mary still appears from time to time on the Bulgarian postage stamps.

This must have clinched matters. In short I agreed to go; but only on the understanding that I was neither expected to make a speech, nor sign any Resolutions; not even broadly-worded Resolutions, such as those which express pious sentiments about the establishment of World Peace. We laughed about these stipulations too, and I was assured that none-theless I should be welcome.

In one of the Lyttelton/Hart-Davis Letters the latter correspondent quotes those evocative lines of the Cavalier poet Sir John Denham:

> All on a weeping Monday
> With a fat Bulgarian sloven.

So far as I remember the poem describes a party of friends, who include the writer, going off for a rackety weekend in France, which was not a success. On the way to the airport the words came into my head (Denham being one of the people Aubrey records), I hoped not prophetically.

C. P. Snow, whom I had hardly seen since the Sholokhov jollifications, was the only person on the plane (a Bulgarian one) known to me. We sat next to each other for three and a half hours in rather cramped conditions, the aircraft being a Spartan model, Snow a big man. He told me that he quite often visited Bulgaria, and gave some account of what lay ahead.

Snow even more than most novelists conveyed the impression of having emerged from the pages of one of his own works. He was serious, not in the least afraid of being thought pompous, essentially good-natured and obliging. This acceptance of himself within his own literary terms of reference made him in some respects easier as a companion in circum-stances like these than certain writers with a lighter touch. He did not himself deal much in jokes, but had no objection to them.

We talked chiefly about books, a subject by no means all English writers find agreeable. I asked if he were a Dickensian. Snow replied that he was not; but if required to nominate the writer in English next in stature to Shakespeare he would find difficulty in thinking of any other than Dickens. That struck me as a sound appreciation; one that well defined my own feelings.

A battery of television cameras and microphones awaited us at Sofia Airport. We were allotted interpreters for the Conference. Far from being fat Bulgarian slovens they were slim and decidedly pretty. It was not in the least like Denham's Monday.

Bulgarian features might be compared with the language, in principle Slav but with Latin undertones; the second characteristic perhaps deriving in both from those two Roman legions said to have been left behind in Dacia from whom the Rumanians claim descent. Modern Bulgaria roughly covers what the Romans called Thrace; the distinction between Thrace and Dacia not always easy to determine.

On the drive to the hotel my own interpreter—who was to shepherd me through the whole of the Conference—turned out to speak really excellent English. When I told her my son had done a television programme on Beckett she asked whether Samuel or Thomas (it was the former), thereby setting a high standard of literary and historic grasp. She also charmed me by turning out to be an addict of one of my favourite books, Lermontov's *A Hero of Our Time*; while knowing in addition about J. D. Bourchier (*Messengers*), the Eton master who left because he could not keep order, and, becoming *Times* correspondent in the Balkans, still has a boulevard named after him in Sofia.

At the Moscow Park Hotel, a modern skyscraper on the outskirts of the capital, my bedroom was on the eighteenth floor. The old 19th century city of low houses, broad tree-lined streets, was some little way from the hotel. The architecture is of a kind once deemed uninspired, now exerting a certain nostalgic pull, like the Athens people used to grumble about fifty years ago, or for that matter Madrid; yet how greatly preferable to what the last two cities have since become. Sofia lacks that faint touch of Vienna observable in Bucharest, but, while not escaping the bleakness all Communist cities exude, is less actively dreary than those I have seen of the Soviet Union, and with a character of its own that suggests *The Prisoner of Zenda*. Now labelled *The Brothers*, the group of statuary showing Tsar Alexander II liberating Bulgaria from the Turks in 1878 remains in place, a reminder that independence is a bare century away.

4

Delegates to any Writers' Conference are a salutory monition as to what one must look like oneself. In this respect the Sofia delegates did not greatly differ in the aggregate from those assembled at Venice. Perhaps not surprisingly the meetings were more scrupulously attended, temptations to abscond being less than Venetian.

In Sofia apparatus for translating speeches into several languages had been installed by every seat, and it was no doubt my usual luck in such matters that I never found myself confronted by equipment that worked. That did not in the least disturb me. In a general way I am happy watching the behaviour of assorted collections of people brought together unmethodically; while speeches in unknown tongues do not unsettle the mind, and have some of the qualities of being in church or at the opera, when unexpected ideas about what one is writing can suddenly come to birth.

The second night in the hotel, feeling a trifle exhausted after the journey, introductions, spate of interviews by Bulgarian and other journalists, I retired to bed early. Sounds of revelry were coming from remote parts of the building (which appeared to include a certain amount of more or less governmental office accommodation as well as the bedrooms), whether carousing on the part of Conference delegates or locals I neither knew nor greatly cared. In spite of these I fell asleep at once.

Between two and three o'clock in the morning a great hammering reverberated on my bedroom door. This, I thought, must undoubtedly be the Secret Police. On his arrest Dostoevski had at least been aroused quietly from his slumbers. Assuming, so far as possible in pyjamas, the air of Bulldog Drummond, I opened the door. The man on the threshold, to all appearances a Bulgarian, must have seen, pyjamas or no, that I was English. He adapted to that language at once:

'Excuse me—you have a bottle-opener?'

'Alas, no.'

'Thank you, excuse me.'

He rambled off down the corridor to try some other likely number. I wondered how he chose probable bottle-opener owners; possibly a system of numerology connected with the numbers on the doors adding up to a magical combination. Continuing sounds of revelry in the distance suggested that at least some inmates of the hotel had possessed themselves of means to open a bottle, even several. He may have moved in their direction. I returned to bed.

The main life of the Conference took place in several interconnected lobbies on the ground floor of the hotel, where delegates would sit and talk with each other or their individual interpreters, be interviewed or televised. As with engaged couples, all meals were taken with one's interpreter. The scene would have made a good setting for a play. On one occasion an Italian sent a message by his interpreter to congratulate me on the brilliance of my speech at one of the morning sessions. I never traced with certainty to whom this compliment should rightly have been addressed, British or American.

One of the Soviet delegates was Yevgeny Yevtushenko, mentioned earlier in connexion with our Cambridge visit to the Amises fifteen years or so before. He was big, fairhaired, wearing a blue open shirt covered with white lace embroidery, sometimes crowned with a Tolstoyan peaked cap. The Soviet poet was always surrounded by a group of hangers on of varying nationality, and appeared to entertain them with a few words of almost every language.

I was introduced to Yevtushenko just as we were both about to enter the hall in which sessions took place. Being unprepared for the meeting at that particular moment I suffered one of those mental hiatuses which link a name to an earlier rather than later connexion. In fact my mind went back to Cambridge and Amis's account of showing Yevtushenko round.

'I believe you know Kingsley Amis,' I said.

'Unfortunately I do,' replied Yevtushenko. 'The shit.'

He remarked that quite genially. Almost before the words were out of his mouth I was aware that I had committed a piece of monumental tactlessness, unless I wanted deliberately to provoke a row. Indeed Yevtushenko could hardly be blamed if he supposed that.

There had been plenty of things other than Yevtushenko to think about at the Conference. Some trick of memory had caused me to forget later developments after Yevtushenko's tour of England and well advertized outspoken views. Since then he had been toeing the line obsequiously enough; for instance after Pasternak's former mistress Olga Ivinskaya was sent to a labour camp for four years Yevtushenko later dutifully joined in the general campaign to blacken her reputation and Pasternak's.

Consequently, when in 1968 Yevtushenko stood for the Oxford Professorship of Poetry—though why anyone should have put him up for that post is unguessable—he was given official backing by the Soviet Embassy. Amis and others had vigorously opposed this (unsuccessful) candidature on grounds that poets and writers can keep out of politics—

indeed are often better doing so—but if they dabble with politics, as Yevtushenko had, they must be expected to behave differently from the manner in which he had behaved.

I should have remembered all that in Sofia. Even at that moment I could recall no more than that Yevtushenko's conduct had been regrettable. The whole episode of the Poetry Professorship had gone out of my head. I could do no more than reply with geniality equal to his own that he must not speak like that about my friends. While this exchange was taking place we were all moving forward into the auditorium.

The following day I was waiting for the lift to take me up to my room when a voice beside me said:

'Thinking of your friends?'

It was Yevtushenko. There was nothing to do but laugh. I explained that I had forgotten about subsequent Amis/Yevtushenko developments.

'I don't like professional Westerners,' said Yevtushenko, this time rather sulkily.

No doubt that statement was perfectly true, though far from reassuring. I took it to mean that he had abandoned any pretence of even mild dissent from what was laid down by the régime, and would in future confine himself to those vapid generalities that a satisfied but humorous official poet might be expected to make in public.

Later Yevtushenko asked me to see a film he was showing more or less privately, but I had to refuse on account of an invitation received from the British Embassy.

I was struck with the extent to which Yevtushenko, both in outward appearance and demeanour, exemplified that favourite type in the classical Russian novel, the buffoon; the man always playing the fool, not only for his own amusement and love of exhibitionism, but also with the object of keeping everyone in the dark as to his own inner views and intentions.

One thought of all those clowns in Dostoevski whose mental and physical antics sometimes make the reader laugh aloud; characters with a clear eye to the main chance, who not uncommonly play a momentous if not particularly alluring role in the development of the plot. That was how Yevtushenko was behaving at the Conference. When the American writer John Cheever remarked (in an interview) that Yevtushenko's ego would crack crystal at twenty feet I think he underestimated the potential.

Cheever himself, and his wife, were at the Conference. I had an occasional word with them. They seemed to know quite well a lot of the people there. Another American writer present was William Saroyan, who wore a long Mexican-type moustache, and had an unusually penetrating voice. Saroyan would potter about the lobbies imparting maxims of homespun wisdom in a rasping tone that effortlessly echoed above the buzz and whine of international writers' chatter.

An acceptable touch of light relief was brought by Gore Vidal. I found myself next to him looking at some of the pictures taken of the sessions, which were stuck up on the walls outside the auditorium. In several of these Vidal was shown beside an Indian delegate.

'I always sit next to a man in a turban,' he said.' You get photographed more.'

I was wearing a red shirt, and Vidal was kind enough to add: 'Your shirts at this Conference are the envy and admiration of the American delegation'.

When Violet and I had been in Florence some years before we had dined at La Pietra with Harold Acton.

'Gore Vidal turned up here the other day,' Acton said.' He had a suitcase with him containing the body of his dog which had died in Rome. He wanted to bury it in the garden here.'

'Which you arranged for him?'

'Of course—so like Gore.'

I was struck by the idea of the formal grounds of this Medician villa being turned into a Pets' Cemetery, a kind of animals' Happy Hunting Ground, but one out of Ariosto; and was surprised when not so very long after that a distinctly tart piece written by Vidal about Acton appeared in the *New York Review of Books*.

'I heard from Harold Acton a year or two ago that you arrived on his doorstep with the remains of your dog for burial.'

'The dog had defenestrated itself,' Vidal said. 'I had to find somewhere for its interment.'

'You were rather sharp with Harold afterwards.'

Vidal laughed.

'Harold made me cross,' he said.

There had been some incident about a goodlooking young man in Naples, so far as I can remember from the paper. Vidal had given at length his own version of the story. He readily agreed that he had run the risk of a riposte from Acton:

> 'That corpse you planted last year in my garden
> *Has* begun to sprout. It will bloom this year.
> Oh keep the Man from hence, that's friend to dog
> Or with his nails he'll dig it up again.'

5

The Bulgarian invitation had not been precisely defined in regard to duration, delegates encouraged to stay another week. That was tempting. The Thrace of earlier Greek writings had included not only the Roman province, but Rumania, some of Hungary, northern Greece, southern Russia. New relics of this comparatively unexcavated civilization were being excavated almost daily by the Bulgarians, who, notwithstanding Slav and Turkish invasions, liked to claim, indeed might retain, some strain from the Thracians.

I had seen the Thracian treasures when on loan to the British Museum. The archaeological sites of this people would be worth inspecting. Their mounted deities, warring cults of Orpheus and Dionysus, depicted on Thracian works of art, had reminded me of Parthian sculpture in Iran. The demands of work remained. Besides I feared a surfeit of model blocks of flats and power-stations apt to accompany organized tours in People's Republics.

Throughout the Conference it had not been at all uncommon to find Bulgarians who talked good English, and their passion for books, especially English ones (hard to obtain though a few trickled through the permitted secondhand shop) can only be called phenomenal.

At one of the official parties a young man pouring out a glass of Bulgarian wine for me said: 'When in Rome do as the Romans do.'

He had evidently drunk a glass or two of wine himself.

'When in Sofia do as the sophisticates do,' I suggested.

We had another on the strength of that. There are many varieties of Bulgarian wine, only two previously known to me. I find them very drinkable, Violet, however, complaining of a touch of the Black Sea.

Snow—sometimes addressed as Lord Charles by Bulgarians—had

been very helpful through the Conference, having no doubt attended many such gatherings and knowing *les détours*. On the day of departure I was instructed to be ready at 7.15 a.m., and understood Snow was taking the same flight. I descended about ten minutes before time. No one from the Conference was about in the hall of the hotel.

I waited alone for about half an hour. Then a young man arrived in a car and asked for me. We drove off together at great speed. On reaching the gates of the airport all formalities were ignored, and we dashed straight on to the tarmac among the waiting aircraft. A man appeared. Some sort of altercation with my driver took place. This seemed to be on the question of whether or not sufficient time remained for me to be embarked on a given plane. Finally the official turned to me.

'Do you want to go to London, please?'

'Yes.'

The answer at once caused relief.

'In that case get back into the car, please.'

I wondered where I should have been taken had he not bothered to ask about my preferred destination.

We returned and I was shown into what was evidently the VIP lounge of the airport. There drinking coffee were the Bulgarian Deputy Prime Minister (stated also to be a poet), a Bulgarian writer (who later kindly presented me with a bottle of *mastik*, a drink like *ouzo* or *raki*), Snow, our respective interpreters. Snow, whose train fever must have been even more acute than my own, had risen an hour earlier than instructed, and been whisked off immediately to the airport.

We had a lot of strong black coffee and two double brandies, an admirable *petit déjeuner* in the circumstances. The Deputy Prime Minister said through my interpreter:

'The Bulgarians are sometimes called the English of the Balkans.'

'The English are undoubtedly the Bulgarians of Northern Europe.'

I think it was then that we got on to the subject of drink, and I was given the *mastik* as a souvenir.

In the plane Snow and I once more crowded in with each other. After we had dished up the Conference he remarked on Sholokhov not having turned up at Sofia as billed. I asked about Snow's visits to the Sholokhov stately home in the Don country. Snow said that by Russian standards it was all very luxurious.

'Sholokhov is in Soviet terms a rich man?'

'Sholokhov's son once remarked to me,' said Snow. 'You know when my old man dies I shall be *very* well off.'

'But won't it all be taken away from him.'

'No.'

'What does the son do?'

'He's a meteorologist.'

The idea of a Cossack meteorologist was engaging.

'Could he just live on the income he inherited?'

'That would arouse social disapproval.'

Snow returned to the subject of the Conference.

'You know,' he said. 'you were a great success. They had never seen anybody like you before. There was an argument as to whether you looked like a professor or a soldier.'

He fell into silence, seeming to ponder the strangeness of the personality with which I had lived so long, and was still illusive to Bulgarians. I had often wondered about it myself.

X

Grave Goods

On our first Hellenic cruise in 1960 one of the guest lecturers on board had been Sir Mortimer Wheeler. I had seen him once, before the second war, at a party of Bumble Dawson's (*Messengers*), but we did not meet. He already possessed considerable fame as an archaeologist and director of museums, also moving to some extent in the Augustus John world, where he had a certain reputation as a womanizer. After the war his celebrity on television was so great that, boarding an empty bus late one rainy night when in a white tie with rows of medals, a conductress arranged with the driver to take him to the door of Wheeler's small house off Haymarket.

Mortimer Wheeler—Rik to his friends, one of his names being Eric— had wanted to be a painter in early life, and was capably equipped in several fields. A powerful dramatic sense supported an appropriately histrionic appearance: height well over six foot; sweeping grey hair (worn longish even before the male fashion for flowing locks came in); moustache well-kept and bristling; an air of command. There was a hint of C. Aubrey Smith (*Faces*) playing the Colonel in a film about the North-West Frontier. That did not mean that Wheeler was without ironic humour nor ability to laugh at things.

This military appearance was justified by a dashing career in both wars; in the second, promotion to the rank of brigadier, rare command for a civilian in operations, and in Wheeler's case an important formation, the Eighth Army Anti-Aircraft, then including some Free French. He was withdrawn from the army before the defeat of the Axis Powers in order to take over the top post in the archaeology of India.

187

That was not only quite a dangerous assignment, anyway out on the sites being excavated, where, law and order having to some extent broken down at that moment, archaeologists had been murdered by bandits, but, Independence followed by Partition in the offing, also an extremely delicate one.

Wheeler himself has told the story: how, for instance, at his suggestion India and Pakistan tossed a coin to decide which country should have first choice of the two most valuable museum treasures to be shared out (statuettes of a god king and a dancing girl, rather a poetic touch); how certain necklaces had to be severed in two; how in short the whole process was settled both fairly and amicably.

When it was announced that Wheeler was undertaking a guided tour of Pakistan and Northern India in 1966 Violet and I thought this a chance not to be missed. The trip was to include the Third Millenium BC excavations at Mohenjo-daro (only opened up in the 1920s); Indo-Hellenic influences at Taxila and elsewhere; Skira with its ancient cultures from three sources and the first known appearance of the double-headed eagle; then up to the mountain kingdom of Swat, farthest extent of conquest in those parts of Alexander the Great's armies.

Although in a general way anxious to see the Subcontinent, I was unprepared for the emotional impact. India has a moving tragic quality that creates an unforgettable impression; splendours; squalors; an overwhelming awareness that remains of two centuries of British rule; the last, in one sense, belonging to the past as completely as Roman rule in Britain; in another, leaving behind the sort of atmosphere that can almost be felt, as one looks north towards the hills from Hadrian's Wall. For some reason Ceylon, a beautiful country with extraordinary monuments of the past, imposes none of the Subcontinent's haunting grip on the imagination.

Violet had often spoken of *On the Face of the Waters* (1896) by Flora Annie Steel (1868–1929), a novel with a background of The Mutiny that had much impressed her. This trip renewed her interest, resulting in her writing a biography *Flora Annie Steel: Novelist of India* (1981), which makes plain the immense influence Mrs Steel had on subsequent novelists tackling Indian subjects. *On the Face of Waters*, which is of considerable length, may suffer failings in style and construction, but is in no way behind Kipling in breadth and grasp of the Indian scene.

In what is now India (more I think than in Pakistan) it was not unusual to be stopped in the street and asked one's nationality; the answer always followed by 'Good, good', and perhaps an account of the enquirer's visit to England years before. I was struck by the manner in which army officers in uniform (who would sometimes accompany our expeditions) reproduced with an amazing exactitude the tone of the old pre-1914 British army; both in smartness of turnout and a certain lounging elegance of carriage that might have been thought endemic to its inventers. In many other respects too (old-fashioned breakfast with porridge) the Subcontinent is a kind of living museum of Great Britain in the past.

After the Northern tour we again accompanied Wheeler to Southern India and Ceylon in 1969. I was prepared for an anticlimax. On the contrary the South is no less enthralling, though very different. Travelogues are to be avoided in memoirs. I will say no more than that one spot, where there was little or nothing to see in the way of excavation, seemed at the same time curiously exciting; a Roman trading station near Pondicherry (in the town *képis* persisted and the French had managed to make the local hotel staff look like Arabs), where had been found shards of amphorae still bearing the dark red stain of wine; on their base the mark of a Tuscan wine merchant.

On these two trips I sharply revised my own estimate of Wheeler. I had always enjoyed his company on Greek cruises, his lectures (rightly geared to a fairly popular appeal) were never less than scholarly; at the same time his inordinate love of showing off was not to be denied. To be fair he had on that particular occasion to keep his end up with Maurice Bowra (they met for the first time on that 1960 cruise and got on well), Bowra himself a consummate showman, whose malicious wit was combined with being by profession a classicist, thereby a formidable rival.

The tours with Wheeler in the Subcontinent convinced me that his gifts rose well above being an unusually talented archaeologist with a flair for catching popular attention and cutting a figure in the press or on the media; an amusing talker who liked drink and girls. In short Wheeler was rather a great man. Great men—great artists included, if it comes to that—need a touch of bravura. Self-promotion can seem bogus at the time, but—something that must be faced—self-promotion in certain circumstances may be a positive requirement.

No one without a degree of greatness about them could have satisfied both countries so thoroughly at the moment of Indian Partition, retained the personal popularity that was Wheeler's in both Pakistan and India. For a number of years after the second war he was Director General of Archaeology in India; Archaeological Adviser to the Government of Pakistan.

That was on the official level, where the almost mythological task he had been set, and mastered, caused him to be received everywhere with admiration and friendship. Possibly more impressive was an incident in a garden we visited. The old gardener, suddenly recognizing Wheeler, knelt down and kissed the hem of his garment; the only occasion when I have witnessed that biblical tribute being paid.

Like most persons of strong natural ebullience Wheeler suffered bouts of black melancholy. When assailed by these he would sit alone at a table deep in thought. He was always withering if asked silly questions by the unwary; disapproved of those who drank Coca Cola whatever the heat of the day; could never believe that either sex had a need to urinate however long sustained the journey.

The phrase: 'Nice again this morning', especially if used at 5.30 a.m. on the way to catch a plane for the day's sightseeing, always indicated that small talk was unacceptable. Not every traveller recognized at first sight such storm signals. Equally (though in his eightieth year during the South India itinerary) he was not unknown to exclaim at breakfast: 'Had a marvellous time with some old friends last night. Lots to drink. Didn't get to bed till two.'

Rather unexpectedly Wheeler was by no means opposed to those rambles through bazaars, silk factories, and the like, towards which local guides with an eye to a rake-off love to divert the traveller of otherwise serious intent. This was understandable in Wheeler, for instance, at a fairly sinister smugglers' market visited not far from The Khyber (we traversed the Pass), the wares were often strange items percolated across the Afghan and Soviet frontiers or from even further afield. Wheeler bought a fire-arm (with ammunition) shaped like a large fountain-pen, which could be carried in the breast pocket. On account of his devotion to the opposite sex he was equally entranced by more humdrum emporia, in spite of his professional dedication spending hours trying to decide on just the right individual textile for a string of girlfriends at home.

Wheeler's love of flirtation (no doubt more if available) remains enshrined in an unforgettable vignette when one cruise had ended at Venice.

The ship had not gone alongside and passengers were being taken off in open boats with short rows of seats facing each other.

Wheeler had been making great going during the cruise with a girl who could not possibly have been less than half a century younger than himself and was travelling with her mother. The girl and Wheeler sat side-by-side in the boat holding hands, their locked fingers hidden under a floppy grey hat which rested on his knees; the girl's mother, a little wistful, tight lipped, glassy eyed, sitting opposite them almost knee-to-knee, gazed out over Wheeler's shoulder towards the waters of the lagoon.

Another side (Wheeler by that time deceased) was illustrated by a story told me by a nonagenarian traveller who had served as brother officer in Wheeler's battery on the Italian front in the first war. The veteran had not in fact greatly cared for his battery commander, but acknowledged that he was an undoubted card.

Soon after this officer (as a regular Gunner) had reported for duty in the line Wheeler had arrived in his dugout one night after dinner wearing a tin hat, mackintosh, and carrying a walking stick.

'Get yourself up like me,' he ordered.' We're going hunting. Remember to move very quietly.'

The two of them went out together into the night, taking a course away from the line. After proceeding a short distance Wheeler whispered:

'Don't make a sound. Here's our quarry.'

In the gloom it was just possible to make out the figure of an Italian soldier advancing slowly towards them. The Italian paused, and seemed to be examining the ground round about him. Then, having apparently settled on a suitable spot, he began to make preparations that were evidently prelude to relieving himself.

Wheeler, followed by his subordinate, crept forward. When the Italian's intention had reached an all but critical stage Wheeler advanced swiftly. On coming level with the crouching figure he dealt a sharp whack with the stick he carried. The victim, giving a loud yell, disappeared into the darkness in the direction of his own trenches.

The explanation of this bizarre encounter was that Wheeler's sector of the line had been troubled by the Italian unit on its flank omitting to construct any proper latrines; in consequence Italian military personnel sensing an urge for evacuation merely moved out of range of their comrades' immediate vicinity for that purpose; with the result that Wheeler's battery

area was becoming increasingly encumbered. Wheeler—by that time widely known along that part of the Front as the Mad Major—had taken upon
himself to enforce sanitary discipline. Even the teller of the story had to
admit that his battery commander, like him or not, had achieved that
limited objective with complete success.

2

One of the places visited on both Indian tours was the holy city of Benares,
where stands the red-ochre stained façade of the temple of Durga, sometimes loosely known as the Monkey Temple. Durga, a goddess also designated Kali in myth, like her consort Shiva has terrible moods of destruction. Her more compassionate side, however, is glorified in one of the
bells hanging in the Temple's porch, which was presented by a British
official of the Honourable East India Company. The boat carrying himself
and his family had been caught in a whirlpool of the river. Death seemed
imminent. The boatmen made supplication to Durga, their prayer was
answered, the party at last with much stress reaching the shore in safety.

The monkeys after which the temple is sometimes called reside in the
trees nearby. They loiter for ever in the precinct, listening to the drum
musicians beat three times a day within the walled courtyard, and affecting
the air of bigoted testy worshippers waiting for all human beings to with-
draw, so that pious monkeys can devote themselves in peace to their own
formal and clandestine religious observances.

In spite of this assumed irritation the monkeys pass the time pleasurably
enough, watching the intruders who thus invade their parish church, at
times mimicking the grotesqueness of human behaviour, or accepting it
and trying to join in. On these two visits, separated by about three years,
the demeanour of individual monkeys at the Durga Temple particularly
struck me on both occasions.

A kind of causeway runs round the upper exterior of the pillared building along which visitors can traverse the roof and look down on those
enclosures of the temple more or less open to the sky. In one of these small
chapels or oratories a young woman in a yellow robe was holding in her
arms a new-born baby over whom a priest was pronouncing some benedic-

tion; the ceremony watched by a small group of spectators that included a monkey.

As the ritual appeared to be reaching its climax the monkey could no longer bear the tension of remaining a mere onlooker. Feeling himself unjustly excluded from spiritual benefits being bestowed, he tugged at the woman's dress to show that monkeys too could be moved by religious rites; then, unable to control his fervour, tried to climb on to her arm and substitute his own body for the baby's.

This unrestrained conduct provoked embarrassed resistance. The monkey, expelled from the congregation, hurried off loudly cursing the priest and others ejecting him; no doubt bent on spreading the story of his discourteous treatment in a place of worship, indeed in the monkeys' own meeting house. Here, one felt, was much to ponder.

Another incident also seen from the roof of the Durga Temple on our second visit struck me even more forcibly. A long way below in a less enclosed, perhaps less sanctified, area of the temple a monkey was seated on the floor gazing at the middle opening of a tattered newspaper. He held the pages stretched out before him as if reading the leading article with close attention. This concentration of thought continued for perhaps half a minute.

Then suddenly—as if all at once uncontrollably exasperated with the world as it is today—he jumped up, cast the paper from him, leapt from where he was sitting. Bounding upward he made a steep ascent, flying from buttress to buttress, projecting point, to projecting point, higher and higher, always gaining altitude, until he had reached the topmost ledge where a secluded niche could still be found in which to rest, meditate, regain lost composure.

In that parade of utter dissatisfaction with things I became at once aware of a strong fellow feeling. How often do the papers report some item that seems to demand just such energetic and immediate form of self-release—had one the monkey's agility—as the only practical means of discharging inward discontents, rage, contempt, despair, at what one reads in the papers.

But—especially for those lacking simian flexibility of physique—it is better to remain calm; try to remember that all epochs have had to suffer assaults on commonsense and common decency, art and letters, honour and wit, courage and order, good manners and free speech, privacy and scholarship; even if sworn enemies of these abstractions (quite often wearing the disguise of their friends) seem unduly numerous in contemporary society.

In Webster's *The White Devil* a character is mentioned who 'prepared a deadly vapour in a Spaniard's fart that should have poisoned all Dublin'. Why Dublin I don't know, unless the keenest pungency was in those days deemed necessary in that city to make any noticeable impression. The invention would find a welcome, morally and physically, among many disturbers of the world today. Indeed this ambitious project seems to have been largely realized on an international scale, fumes extruded from uncounted human organs rather than one solely Spanish individual outlet; so much that one's own inward conviction begins to increase that retirement from such an ambience might not be too bad.

Even after reaching one's early sixties letters start to arrive from insurance firms and the like opening with the words: 'You will soon be sixty-five, etc., etc.', causing the recipient to reflect: 'Well, it's been kind to allow me to stay so long.' As the eighth decade gradually consumes itself, shadows lengthen, a masked and muffled figure loiters persistently at the back of every room as if waiting for a word at the most tactful moment; a presence more easily discernible than heretofore that exhales undoubted menace yet also extends persuasive charm of an enigmatic kind.

> Death is the mother of beauty, hence from her,
> Alone, shall come fulfilment of our dreams
> And our desires

Anyway that was what Wallace Stevens thought; others too. Again—as with loudly decrying the world and its ways—a tranquil approach is probably to be preferred, rather than accept too readily either Death's attractions or repulsions (contrasted with each other like Durga's attributes); better that the dual countenances of the ubiquitous visitant should not cause too prolonged musings on either the potential relief or potential afflictions of departure. Better, certainly, not to bore other people with the subject.

All the same the presence in the corner—whose mask and domino never quite manage to keep out of sight the ivory glint of skull and bones beneath—seems to imply, even if silently, something of that once familiar cadence, harsh authoritarian knell of the drinker's passing day, to which Bobby

Roberts used to attach such mystic significance: 'Last orders, please—time, gentlemen, time', in this case the unspoken sanction: 'Last conclusions, please.'

Henry Adams—'Little Adams' as Henry James called him a trifle defensively—remarks that 'only on the edge of the grave can a man conclude anything'. Even when the graveyard, if perhaps not the grave itself, must be admitted to have moved closer into the foreground of one's local landscape I do not find conclusions at all easy to formulate; certainly not rules for life.

By no means everybody takes that view. For many years now acquaintances have been standing conclusions generously in the all too crowded bar of this masquerade; a bar made warm by argument like that warmed by the Blessed Damozel's bosom pictured in the imagination of Rossetti; a bar by now attended so long that to offer a final round of conclusions at one's own expense seems almost superfluous. It would be easy to pass out simply from a surplus of conclusions.

Hesitation in paying one's round is not due to parsimony so much as a sense of my own conclusions seeming to sound too humdrum a note; when not humdrum, pretentious; sometimes both.

For instance there seems a lot to be said for that mystic precept of the 19th-century magician Éliphas Lévi (quoted more than once in *Dance*): 'To know, to will, to dare, to be silent'; but I'm not sure the Mage's words make a very refreshing draught at so late an hour. It can be said for his recommendations, however, that they leave options wide open; are certainly not to be taken as aiming at a mere success story.

Again, one might offer (Bowra would not in principle have refused) a double Kipling's *If* on the rocks without soda. Once more those daunting prerequisites are more likely to be an embarrassment than a restorative; especially if topped up with a dash of Apollinaire's *Marizibill*, the closing lines of which are worth bearing in mind in most human dealings:

> Je connais gens de toutes sortes
> Ils n'égalent pas leurs destins
> Indécis comme feuilles mortes
> Leurs yeux sont des feux mal éteints
> Leurs coeurs bougent comme leurs portes

I'm never quite sure whether this final stanza of the poem is spoken by

the little Cologne tart—'offerte à tous en tout mignonne'—or the poet himself is asserting that her nightly experience parallels his own in life. I suppose the former. It doesn't much matter. In either case such raw sprits are
rough on the palate as a nightcap. In fact, if procurable at the bar, a packet
of literary prejudice however dry might be preferable to general conclusions; possibly even more revealing.

3

How, for example, should I rightly have answered the Japanese professor's question: 'What do you think of Shakespeare?'; bearing in mind
that, even if one manages to remain the right side of sanity, Shakespeare
provides possibly the easiest subject upon earth about which to become a
bore.

In the first place I find inexplicable the difficulty so many eminent persons have found (especially American ones as Cyril Connolly once pointed
out) in believing that the plays and poems were written by the actor-
manager of Stratford.

Allowing for an undoubted sprinkling of aristocratic poets, a distinct
vein of writers of all sorts who began life in submerged conditions, the
overwhelming majority of great artists in any field have emerged from
backgrounds comparable with Shakespeare's. Indeed Shakespeare might
be thought almost ideally situated to encounter most sides of life; especially those experiences trying to the spirit (neatly summarized by Hamlet
and in Sonnet 66) from which the art of writing is so largely woven.

Mighty efforts have been made to depress William Shakespeare's social
standing, but if his father John Shakespeare had not suffered financial disaster, William not been the genius he was but only possessed his undeniable dexterity in handling real estate, no one would have thought twice
about application for a grant of arms.

John Shakespeare and his like were just the sort of people on the upward grade who applied for a coat of arms as a matter of course. The
several Shakespeares listed as archers at Bosworth (an army branch offering
possibilities of social promotion as seen earlier in Sir John Hawkwood the
condottiere) may well have been the forebears referred to in the grant who
did 'valiant service to King Henry VII'.

Grave Goods

As we know the Shakespeare background was darkened by bankruptcy.

My Balliol tutor Kenneth Bell used to say that it was impossible to exaggerate the advantages of having a drunken father in forcing a man to think for himself. Possibly a degree of latent Micawberism in John Shakespeare ought to be taken into account in assessing the formation of his son's powers.

In the circumstances marriage at eighteen to an older woman certainly suggests sexual impetuosity. On the other hand parallels in contrasted age for both contracting parties would be easy to find in parish registers, and a form of 'hand-fasting' (regarded as binding) may explain the early birth of the first child as much as disregard for convention.

Nonetheless impatience for bed does seem indicated in either case; borne out by Sonnet 145, which has no relevance to the rest of the sequence, is rough hewn in style, and seems clearly to include puns on the name Hathaway.

This and much else mark out Shakespeare as heterosexual; then—at what must have been an inconvenient moment in making a career—he fell into the anguished love with a young man that The Sonnets record. That anyone can believe The Sonnets are about other than actual agonized love seems to me, to say the least, strange.

For a writer of supreme insight and sensibility to walk a sexual knife-edge is hardly surprising. What is interesting is that Shakespeare clearly found his condition embarrassing. Had he been congenitally homosexual (like Marlowe), even a practising bisexual (they must have existed then as now) the desperate inner discomfort of The Sonnets would have been differently expressed.

The phrase 'one houre mine' (Sonnet 33) can scarcely mean anything other than that some sort of sexual scuffle took place between Shakespeare and The Friend. The poet-critic William Empson has suggested (I quote from memory) that 'rather grudging masturbation' may have been implied. Empson's surmise accords with a tone of voice not without self-contempt. A physical follow up seems to have ensued, anyway for a short time, and Shakespeare's love, as such, appears to have lasted not much less than four years at least.

It is hard to believe that Shakespeare's tone in The Sonnets—still less the sexual liberties evidently taken—could have been applied to any patron who was not only a 'Great Prince' but himself heterosexual. The Friend

197

was undoubtedly a social superior from what is said, but even apart from sexual aspects could Pembroke or Southampton be spoken of as having a 'budding name' (Sonnet 95)?

The Dark Lady seems to me less interesting. She is a female figure easily imaginable in any society. Mrs Shakespeare too is not hard to conceive, fascinating as it would be to know more of her.

At moments The Friend's name seems Will (Sonnets 135, 136), yet Hew is often punned upon (Sonnets 20, 67, b2, 98, 104), giving rise to Wilde's ingenious short story about an imagined young actor called Willie Hughes. Could it be that Hew was a private joke, a symbol for the male organ? I have never heard this put forward, but Sonnet 104 would not contradict that meaning, nor for that matter the famous Master Mistress Sonnet 20.

In spite of unsolved enigmas I lean towards Leslie Hotson's William Hatcliffe as The Friend: not only for Hotson's cogent reasoning that the recurrent poetic imagery recalls Hatcliffe's ceremonial instalment as Prince of Purpoole, but—more strongly and in fact taking a contrary view to Hotson—from what little is known of Hatcliffe, who seems to me just the kind of figure to fulfil the part The Friend plays.

William Hatcliffe, son of a Lincolnshire squire, was studying Law at Gray's Inn. The Hatcliffes were related (through the Clintons, Earls of Lincoln) to the Dymokes of Scrivelsby (*Infants*). Sir Edward Dymoke was patron to Samuel Daniel, sometimes canvassed as the Rival Poet in The Sonnets. The last fact catches the attention but need not be material.

In 1587 William Hatcliffe, only four years and a few months younger than Shakespeare, was chosen to be Prince of Purpoole, the title given to the elected Lord of Misrule who headed the carnival at the lawyers' Christmas revel held by the Inns of Court. In short Hatcliffe had won a kind of charm-and-beauty competition that made him a male Miss Inns of Court. Most people can recall some such goodlooking popular Steerforth type, possibly with a touch of bisexuality, who filled the bill in university days or the equivalent.

Hotson—showing it seems to me naivety in psychology—expresses surprise that a young man who had been the most hero-worshipped student of his year (not to mention the possibility of having stirred Shakespeare to the depths) should in later life have disappeared into an obscurity that is only less than absolute because documentation survives to show that Hatcliffe frittered away his Lincolnshire inheritance.

Surely (I use the adverb in the British interrogative sense rather than the American usage of 'certainly') what happened to Hatcliffe is the fate of many if not most of the young men who in early life become Princes of Purpoole. That is just how I see The Friend.

What effect did this crisis (whether or not caused by Hatcliffe) have on Shakespeare as a writer? How far are personal experiences in emotion required? The answer seems to be that variety sometimes produces literary results; sometimes that is achieved without participation. I feel pretty sure, incidentally, that Shakespeare would not refer to venereal infection in the terms he does without firsthand knowledge. The Friend could have added a dimension, uncomfortable and painful, on which to draw, simply on account of Shakespeare being temperamentally unhomosexual.

An aspect of Shakespeare's keen appreciation of relationships between the sexes that seems to me often missed is that of *The Taming of the Shrew*, admittedly a lesser play. Shakespeare rises above the artificiality of the plot and conventions of the period by showing how two narcissists might hit it off in marriage. Petruchio was just as neurotic as Katharina; no doubt why he had to go so far afield in the first instance to find a wife. As so often in Shakespeare there is the impression that the couple depicted in *The Shrew* were drawn from individuals known to the dramatist. With necessary re-adjustments the situation could well be a modern one.

When epigrams detonate in *The Importance of Being Earnest* Wilde's voice can be heard. I like to think the same is true of Shakespeare's: that (phrases chosen at random from thousands available) 'a geminy of baboons', 'She is able to freeze the god Priapus', 'Arts-man, perambulate', are what Shakespeare would have said over the dinner-table. Enough conjecturing about The Bard: what are your conclusions? I have remarked earlier in these memoirs that learning what to avoid from reading the works of the ungifted is often an easier method of finding out about writing than trying to pin down the genius of the great. In that last respect Shakespeare is no exception. Again and again one asks oneself how he brings off his effects; sometimes with effortless simplicity; sometimes with masterful elaboration.

Shakespeare was not, however, a perfectionist. If not feeling at the top of his form, or when committed by a particular play to tedious material, he forges ahead, forcing himself to write.

The choice between perfectionism and getting something down at all costs is one that writers have to make. Among the great writers it is not easy to find examples of the former. Flaubert, perhaps; Joyce, perhaps; Balzac and Dickens very much on the other side. Dostoevski was a great artist who took enormous pains to research his material, he was hardly a perfectionist; nor for that matter was Proust. A long list of contrasts could be drawn up.

It seems to me that the choice for or against perfectionism must be decided by personal energy, the crux lying in individual strength of creative vitality. If you have the powers of Balzac or Dickens (Joyce, for instance, didn't) a certain amount of poor stuff mixed up with all the invention, action, poetry, does not greatly matter. Plod on and hope for something better, which always turns up in the case of the giants sooner or later. If that inner energy is lacking a writer cannot afford to take risks, let up on the standard already set. Perfectionism must be the aim.

Naturally Shakespeare had the energy to behave as he liked in that respect. He rarely loses touch with reality of one kind or another, and always refuses to be tied down by theory. In this last respect he has been censured, especially by the French, for disregarding set rules. Accordingly, let the French be refuted by one of themselves, their greatest novelist and greatest rule-breaker:

'Saint-Loup n'était pas assez intelligent pour comprendre que la valeur intellectuelle n'a rien à voir avec l'adhesion à une certaine formule esthétique . . . ne jugeant chaque chose qu'au poids d'intelligence qu'elle contient, ne percevant pas les enchantements d'imagination que me donnaient certaines qu'il juge frivoles.'

Shakespeare would have agreed with Proust on this point, both of them appreciating that 'great' themes are not necessary for great art; while neither would have underrated the sheer difficulty of 'writing well', whatever that may mean. Perhaps chiefly stimulating the reader's imagination in a new way, while at the same keeping the writer's own imagination under control.

As remarked earlier, most if not all the great writers have been well supplied with humour, lack of which (not uncommon in critics) should put the reader on guard where excessive claims are made. At the same time satire and irony are to be employed with care. They are elements that can get out of hand. Lady Mary Wortley Montagu wrote sagely on that point:

Satire should, like a polished razor keen,
Wound with a touch that's scarcely felt or seen:
Thine is an oyster knife, that hacks and hews:
The rage, but not the talent to abuse;
And is to hate, what love is in the stews.

But if the consolation for life is art, what may the artist expect from life?

An incident mentioned quite casually in Vasari's *Lives of the Most Excellent Italian Architects, Painters and Sculptors* always seems to me worth recalling. It teaches several lessons: that if you want something done get the best executant available to do it; that minor jobs are often worth taking on; that duration in time should not necessarily be the criterion in producing a work of art.

Vasari says that on a winter day in Florence, when snow was deep on the ground, one of the Medici sent for Michaelangelo to build a snowman in the courtyard of the Medici palace. Notwithstanding those (like Constant Lambert) who dislike the High Renaissance one can scarcely doubt that the finest snowman on record took shape.

Index

Illustrations in italics